MW01242382

THE WAR JOURNAL (2011-2020) Volume III

THE WAR JOURNAL (2011-2020) VOLUME III

Copyright ©2019 Paula Matthews

Cover: Paula Matthews

Unless otherwise noted, scripture quotations are from
The Holy Bible: Authorized King James Version,
@2003 Thomas Nelson, Inc.

Published by
Spirit & Life Publications^{sm}
Atlanta

Printed in the United States

ISBN: 978-1-7357642-1-4

THE WAR JOURNAL
(2011-2020)
Volume III

The Healing And Restoration Of America

PAULA MATTHEWS

Ş
Spirit & Life
Publications[sm]

To *Two Valiant Warriors* who fought the good fight and won.

My Dad,
"Reverend" David Scott
(January 24, 1932 - December 5, 2019)

• • • •

United States Armed Forces
Korea 1952-1954

My Cousin,
Beatrice Taylor Underwood
(March 24, 1943 - April 25, 2020)

• • • •

United States Navy
1961-1964

• • • •

United States Senate
Executive Assistant to Senator Paul Wellstone (D-MN)
April 1991- November 1997

Thus Saith Our Lord God Almighty,

"This Is MY KINGDOM'S Finest Hour!"

Prophetic Word Received April 2, 2019

CONTENTS

PROPHETIC WARNING!

This book, like previous War Journal books, began as my personal prayer journal. The information revealed comes from my conversations in prayer with Almighty God. They were initially meant for prayer and intercession on behalf of the Church, the nation, the leaders and the people.

In obedience to God, I am releasing these conversations. God said that the information released would cause many in the nation to be delivered.

Due to the sensitivity of what is this book, please be advised to enter these pages prayerfully. Tread lightly when it comes to your personal opinions about the issues therein. The Holy God is speaking His Word for purposes of ministering TRUTH that will heal and deliver us.

Do not, I repeat, do not, take pleasure in the judgments written for others. Whatever you do, or speak over others, God promises to make happen for you (Ephesians 6:8). God has a prophetic agenda that must be fulfilled before Jesus returns. Anyone who attempts to interfere with what God is doing, will be removed, even by force if necessary.

God is a just god. He takes no pleasure in the death of the wicked. His desire is that they repent and live (Ezekiel 33:11), but, He does require obedience.

Finally, God has given the Righteous, the authority over every situation in this earth. I truly believe that although judgments have been executed against specific leaders of this nation, God can still turn things around if the people of God humble themselves and pray.

That is my hope and my prayer as Apostle, Prophet of God's Kingdom and Author of this book.

Paula Matthews

"The king's heart is in the hand of the Lord,
As the rivers of water: he turneth it whithersoever he will."
Proverbs 21:1

AUTHOR'S NOTE
The "Corollary To Matthew 24"

The Holy Spirit called this book, *"The Corollary to Matthew 24."* Normally when people think of a corollary, it refers to something that can be easily deduced from something that has already been proven. At first, I didn't understand what He meant. Then He gave the following explanation, and it made *perfect Kingdom sense.*

Matthew 24 is a chapter in which Jesus describes in detail, the evil atrocities that will occur before the end of the world as we know it. However, the important things of the Kingdom are briefly mentioned, yet these are the keys to understanding the notion of *"corollary."*

- *"Take heed that no man deceive you."* (v4)
- *"All these are the beginning of sorrows."* (v8)
- *"But he that shall endure unto the end, the same shall be saved."* (v13)
- *"And this gospel of the kingdom shall be preached in all the world for a witness unto all nations; and then shall the end come."* (v14)

Don't be deceived! **God is in control**, not the devil. *"His Kingdom rules over all (Psalm 103:19)."* In these last days, it will be **"God's love and power"** shaking the world, not the chaos of the evil one. God's will is *salvation* and *the witness of the gospel. Deception* and *sorrows* are from the evil one. He wants to stop God's Kingdom from advancing. Therefore, the Kingdom is striving in violence (Matthew 11:12). The gospel message brings hope to mankind. It also manifests the Blessing of the Lord without sorrow (Proverbs 10:22). The devil's fear is that people will see it (witness), and run into God's Kingdom for refuge.

Thus the corollary:
"The Beginning of Sorrows for the world is a sign of the Beginning of Blessings for the Kingdom."

The gospel and the Blessing are synonymous. The details of God's glorious plan are **"hid in a mystery, to be revealed by the apostles and prophets in these last days, to bring the Church back into alignment with God's ordained order:"**
The Church of Jesus Christ,
*"Built upon the foundation of the apostles and prophets,
Jesus Christ himself being the Chief corner stone."*
Ephesians 2:20

"Surely,
The Lord God Will Do Nothing,
But He Revealeth His Secret
Unto His Servants
The Prophets."

Amos 3:7 (The Holy Bible KJV)

PREFACE

The Role Of Prophets, Kings & Priests

It was Almighty God who commissioned yet another War Journal book. The format is a bit different from the previous journals in that God is looking at what was prophesied in the earlier books and showing how these things either did, or didn't come to pass and why. As such, this book is both revealing and analytical from God's point of view. Now that I said that, God wanted me to immediately address the authority that He has given me to speak as His *"Mouthpiece."*

My first call to the ministry of Jesus Christ was that of a prophet. Like the Prophet Samuel, I was called as a child and formally appointed to the Office of the Prophet in 1997. Less than a year later, the Lord said that He was *"sending me out like He did the first apostles, to heal and deliver His leaders."* Since that time, the Lord has been sending me to some of the most troubling places in this world; places where His Heart was heavy concerning issues that involve His people. These are citizens of God's Kingdom, saints, members of the household of God, *"built upon the foundation of the apostles and prophets, Jesus Christ himself being the chief corner stone . . . all of the building fitly framed together groweth unto an holy temple in the Lord . . . for an habitation of God through the Spirit* (Ephesians 2:19-22)." These are God's precious children whom He loves dearly. Touching them, is touch *"the apple"* of God's eye (Zechariah 2:8). The Bible expresses God's heart towards His people saying, *"He suffered no man to do them wrong: yea, he reproved kings for their sakes; saying 'Touch not mine anointed, and do my prophets no harm* (Psalm 105:14-15).'"God is about to stretch forth His Hand against His enemies, those who have arisen to harm His people. The Lord will thoroughly perfect all that concerns the people of God (Psalm 138:7-8).

As the Church of Jesus Christ, we are to continue *"the seek and destroy mission of our Lord."* Jesus came to destroy the works of the devil (I John 3:8). He came to seek and save the lost (Luke 19:10), all for the purpose or restoring God's Kingdom in the earth. Jesus' ministry is our ministry. We have a *"two-fold mission"* to seek those lost both in the Church and in the world. This is a more dangerous mission because *the lost* in the Church have been deceived and have very little knowledge of the truth of why Jesus came. It was never about religion, but about building God's Kingdom upon the earth. Religion has taught that the Church is waiting for Jesus to come, in the power of His Kingdom, and change the world. In the meanwhile, Jesus is waiting on the Church to *"Go into all the sectors of the world"* with the gospel, then He will change the world and reveal the Kingdom in our midst. Many have no knowledge. They are quite comfortable warming the bench every Sunday, filling the pews, but doing nothing to change the suffering world around them. One has better chances of reaching the world than reaching the Church in this hour, but God is faithful to His word. *"And this gospel of the kingdom shall be preached in all the world for a witness unto all nations; and then shall the end come (Matthew 24:14)."* God blames Church leadership for the lack of obedience to the mission.

My initial assignment in the Kingdom Mission was to go up against what God called, the ***"real criminals."***[1] These are men and women pretending to be God's chosen leaders. According to the Lord, they are using ***"mafia tactics to kill His people."*** These are leaders, in both the Church and in government; ***"wolves dressed in sheep's clothing for the purpose of deceiving and killing the people of God."*** In this season God will ***"expose and dethrone"*** these leaders and put in their place those who will do all of His will. This book will reveal specific words of judgment God has spoken upon certain leaders who have persisted in their attempts to harm the people of God.

In this season, God will avenge His people in Biblical proportions. God calls this ***"His grand finale"***[2] before Jesus returns. ***"Fire in the Sky and Earth; Fireworks. It's the time of God's justice; good and bad rewarded for their persistence."*** These are not my words. I am speaking only what the Lord told me to speak. I cannot but speak the things which I have seen and heard (Acts 4:20), exactly as they were revealed to me. I aim is to decrease and let Him increase. Like my Master, I desire not to do my will, but the will of Him who sent me (John 5:30). I want to see God's Kingdom come upon the earth. Jesus taught us to pray *"Our Fa-*

1   Matthews, Paula. "Year 2000: Move To Ohio, Word About Taking Up My Cross." *The War Journal (1999-2010) Volume I.* Los Angeles: Spirit & Life Publications, 2010. 121. Print.
2   Matthews, Paula. "Year 2002: The Enemy Exposed And God's Plan Revealed."*The War Journal (1999-2010) Volume I.* Los Angeles: Spirit & Life Publications, 2010. 181. Print.

ther, which art in heaven, Hallowed be thy name. "Thy Kingdom come. Thy Will be done, in earth as it is in heaven (Matthew 6:9-10)." Unfortunately, not everyone wants God's Kingdom to come. They are busy erecting kingdoms of their own. ***"God sends the apostles and prophets to rebuke kings and nations"*** in order to bring them back into alignment with God's purpose for His people and for the earth. It's all about God's Kingdom coming upon the earth; understanding that God is King Eternal (I Timothy 1:17). He alone has the power to remove and set up kings (Daniel 2:21). God made Jesus King over His Kingdom. That Kingdom is coming upon the earth to take over. Don't be deceived! God is taking back the earth for His purpose alone. No other purpose will stand in these last days. This was the word of the Lord to the prophets of old, and this is the message God is releasing through His prophets today. This is, according to the Spirit of God, ***"the end of the last days"*** before Jesus returns. We must be ready. God is busy downloading instructions by His Spirit to the spirits of His people, showing them how to prepare for our Lord's return. Hearing God requires the appropriate connection with his apostles and prophets.

God *will do absolutely nothing* in this earth without first revealing it to His prophets (Amos 3:7). We will never know all the details. God will reveal just enough so that we are prepared, and He alone gets the glory for what is done. The apostles and prophets are those anointed to receive the answers to mysteries for the Church. God reveals His mysteries to us so that we can direct the people. For example, God revealed to Apostle Paul the mystery of the order of the Church. He also revealed the mystery of God's will for the Gentiles (Non-Jewish) believers. *"Whereby, when ye read, ye may understand my knowledge in the mystery of Christ. Which in other ages was not made known unto the sons of men, as it is now revealed unto his holy apostles and prophets by the Spirit; that the Gentiles should be fellowheirs, and of the same body, and partakers of his promise in Christ by the gospel* (Ephesians 3:4-6)."

God's revelation of Kingdom mysteries are "***His vision for the people of the earth.***" Without a vision from God, the people perish (Proverbs 29:18). They would have no hope for the future. Anyone listening to the American news media for sustained periods of time would lose hope of life itself. This is the voice of the *false prophets*, the prophets of doom and disaster. God's prophets speak *life* and give hope. They may have to rebuke people, but only for the purpose of blessing and not cursing

19

them. God never reveals doom. He may reveal unpleasant things coming our way, but He will always provide *a way to escape* (I Corinthians 10:13). God says in His word, *"For I know the thoughts that I think toward you, saith the LORD, thoughts of peace, and not of evil, to give you an expected end (Jeremiah 29:11)."* God has a blessed future and gives us hope. The world has no such hope, and yet it is always forcing its vision upon God's people. Even the word *television* is revealing to us the world's vision in order to influence us to conform.

God has commanded His people, *"And be not conformed to this world, but be ye transformed by the renewing of your mind, that ye may prove what is that good, and acceptable, and perfect, will of God* (Romans 12:2). *"* If we want to see the will of God in our lives, we must put away the old way of living. We must put on the new man, walk as a new creation, living for God. Everything God reveals by His Spirit leads to this end; that His people would walk in the newness of life. Again, not everyone wants to live for God. They want to do what is right in their own sight. They are often offended when apostles and prophets speak this way. Historically, the Church has persecuted and killed the apostles and prophets (Luke 11:49). Jesus said that a prophet is not honored in his house or his country (Mark 6:4).

This was made clear to me, when God called me to the Office of Prophet. *"I send thee to the children of Israel, to a rebellious nation that hath rebelled against me: they and their fathers have transgressed against me, [even] unto this very day. For [they are] impudent children and stiffhearted. I do send thee unto them; and thou shalt say unto them, Thus saith the Lord GOD. And they, whether they will hear, or whether they will forbear, (for they [are] a rebellious house,) yet shall know that there hath been a prophet among them* (Ezekiel 2:3-5). *"* This was one of the scriptures God used to call me into ministry. No one chooses to be a prophet of God. Certainly there are false prophets in the world. They seem to have it easy, but true prophets speak out of fear of God. If God has a warning and we don't speak, calamity will come upon the people and God will required their blood at our hands. If we speak and they don't obey what was spoken, then their blood will be on their own hands. (Ezekiel 3:19-21). The Spirit of God has come down on my head to write this book. There are judgments written that God is commanding that I release. Some are very sensitive and personal to certain individuals. I asked why God wanted me to release such matter. He said, it was

20

"for deliverance of the nation." God is concerned about the nations, beginning with the United States of America. He is about to use this nation to set an example around the world. What happens in America will lead the nations on the path of righteousness for our Lord's sake. Jesus is coming quite soon. His return will be the event of all times. We must get ready.

Jesus is King. He is coming in all the glory of His Father, to set up His throne in the earth. This is no ordinary monarch. God made Jesus *"higher than the kings of the earth* (Psalm 89:27). *"* He is King of kings. What does that mean for earth? The coming of Jesus Christ will not be like any regal procession earth has ever witnessed. His throne and Kingdom are supernatural, and more powerful than all the powers of both heaven and earth. The Prophet Daniel wrote, *"And in the days of these kings shall the God of heaven set up a kingdom, which shall never be destroyed: and the kingdom shall not be left to other people, [but] it shall break in pieces and consume all these kingdoms, and it shall stand for ever* (Daniel 2:44). *"* Jesus is not coming to conform to this world. He is coming to take over. We are about to witness *"the restoration of God's Ancient Kingdom Dynasty in the earth."*

What shall proceed the coming of our King? There will be signs and wonders in the earth and sky. Sure, there will be trouble between nations and kingdoms. There will also be earthquakes and famines and pestilences (pandemics). We said that these are just the beginning of sorrows (Matthew 24:8). *"Everything will be shaken back into God's order."* There will be great tribulation (trouble) that this world has never seen. *"Immediately after the tribulation of those days shall the sun be darkened, and the moon shall not give her light, and the stars shall fall from heaven, and the powers of the heavens shall be shaken: And then shall appear the sign of the Son of man in heaven: and then shall all the tribes of the earth mourn, and they shall see the Son of man coming in the clouds of heaven with power and great glory. And he shall send his angels with a great sound of a trumpet, and they shall gather together his elect from the four winds, from one end of heaven to the other* (Matthew 24:29-31). *"* The Kingdom of God is a kingdom of transformation, changing people from darkness to Light, from the power of satan to the power of God (Acts 26:18). The first thing to be shaken back in order will be the Church of Jesus Christ in America. God is taking us back to His original purpose for ordaining a church. Remember that God said this was *"His Grand Finale,"* which means He is in charge of what happens in these last days. It's God's production, His show, not the devil's. God chose the actors for every part. We just need to follow His script and His direction if we want to live and prosper during these end-times.

Everything God is doing in these last days is in preparation for Jesus' return to the earth. God has made every grace available for the Church to welcome our soon coming king. We must receive both the grace and the wisdom concerning the times and seasons in which we find ourselves today. From what will be revealed on the pages to come, it will become evident that *the world as we know is out of order with God.* Not only the world, but also the Church. According to God, *"the world is in rebellion because the Church of Jesus Christ has forfeited its place of authority"* in the earth. It has become lukewarm concerning the things that matter to God and His Kingdom. Religious pursuits and *"political "cronyism"* have become the order of the day. The Church at large, in all its piety has become arrogant like the Laodicean church in the Book of Revelation. Jesus spoke these words to the church of Laodicea. *"I know thy works, that thou art neither cold nor hot: I would thou wert cold or hot. So then because thou art luke warm, and neither cold nor hot, I will spue thee out of my mouth, because they sayest, I am rich, and increased with goods, and have need of nothing; and knowest not that thou are wretched, and miserable and poor, and blind and naked: . . . be zealous therefore, and repent (Revelation 3:15-19). "*

In Volume II of **The War Journal**, God called the behavior of the Church, *"organized rebellion"* against Him. This is the quote, "The word of the Lord came to me saying, *'This is The American Church.' Then I saw a beautifully formed, powerful physical structure in the form of a man; muscular in form like a champion body builder. Atop the body was a handsome strong head; but what I saw next startled me. As the body moved, it did so without the head. There were no lacerations, no broken skin fragments about the neck. It was then that I realized; that body and head were never connect! The Lord said that 'the Body of Christ in America was in agreement with its members. The Church was built in the similitude of the Tower Of Babel. '"*[3] Like Adam, the Church in America decided to turn from God to do their own thing. Also, like those who God preserved in the flood, they also turned away from obeying God to build a tower in order to make their names

3   Matthews, Paula. "A Kingdom Divided." *The War Journal (1999-2010) Volume II.* Los Angeles: Spirit & Life Publications, 2010. Back cover, 39. Print.

great. According to God, the Church in America was in agreement with all of its members that it needed no head. Yet, the Bible says that *"Christ is the head of the church (Ephesians 5:23)."* It also says that *"the head of Christ is God (I Corinthians 11:3)."* Then the vision of the American Church is that more disconcerting, knowing that the Church is not connected to God. They are doing what is right in their own eyes, but here is the thing. We are *either with God, or against Him* (Matthew 12:20). Here is what people don't seem to understand. Mankind is a spirit being, either being ruled by the Kingdom of God, or the kingdom of darkness. There are no other spiritual choices. There are only two categories of spirits in the earth; those from God the Father and those from the realm of the demonic. ***"To abandon the one, is to join with the other."*** As the Bible says, *"No man can serve two masters (Matthew 6:24)."*

Look at Adam. When he turned away from God, the serpent became his master. ***"That which the man was ordained to dominate*** (Genesis 1:26)***, dominated him."*** We see the same thing happening with the Church of Jesus Christ in America. Instead of dominating the evil that has overtaken the nation, the Church in its silence, has bowed its knee to satan, denying everything that Jesus bought with His Blood. ***"It's time to face the giants,"*** says God. It's time for the Church to be the Church that Jesus founded when He said, *"Upon this rock I will build My Church; and the gates of hell shall not prevail against it* (Matthew 16:18)."* What was *"this rock?"* It's the revelation of the person of Jesus Christ, as revealed by the Father in Heaven. The Church of Jesus Christ was to be based solely on the revelation of the Head of the Church Jesus. Once we get a revelation of Jesus, we will get a revelation of who we are, and how we fit into His Body. This revelation is revealed by the Holy Spirit of God. In the vision of the American Church, God said that the Church is ***"in agreement"*** that it needs no head. So, even if there was revelation from Heaven, the Church decided to go another way. Ergo, their disconnect from God.

Now, if the Church is disconnected from God, how can it speak for the Lord in this hour? They don't know Him or His plan. They have no power to overcome what is in the world. Thank God for the *remnant* of believers. They are aligned with both the wisdom and the revelation of God (Ephesians 1:17). This revelation comes in the form of *prophecy*. The Bible is a book of *prophecy,* but what is revealed by God's Spirit is ***"relevant prophecy"*** for the moment and time in which it is revealed.

It may not manifest immediately, but it is our inheritance (Deuteronomy 29:29). It is revealed by the Holy Spirit, *to show us things to come* (John 16:13). According to the Lord, the Church in America **"tends to outlaw prophecy in deference to scripture."** It operates in a form of godliness, but denies the Spirit of God to release the power to change things in the earth. I also heard Him say, that **"all scripture is profitable, but without the Spirit, it is dead."** No doubt, scripture is profitable, but the Bible says, that it all came from the Spirit of God. *"All scripture is given by inspiration of God* (II Timothy 3:16).*"* The Church needs to wake up and return to the *"former things"* that were experienced on the day of Pentecost. After Jesus' resurrection, it was first established in the earth, what God expects in these last days, a **"resurrection of His Church in all its power . . signs and wonders all kinds of miracles at the Hands of His people."** Somewhere in our history the Church put away the things of the Spirit. They outlawed the work of the Holy Spirit and all His gifts that were given to propel the church into **"its glory."**

Jesus is coming back for a church that is **"glorious in power, demonstrating that the gates of hell cannot prevail in the earth."** These are *the ministers of the New Testament; not of the letter, but of the spirit; for the letter killeth, but the spirit giveth life* (II Corinthians 3:6).*"* We must learn when, and how to use the word of God. Only the Spirit of God can guide us. He reveals it to our spirits. He speaks it through His servants the prophets, revealing His times and seasons with instructions for God's people. The essence of revelation and all prophecy from Heaven, is to reveal Jesus in our world. As the Bible says, *"the testimony of Jesus is the spirit of prophecy* (Revelation 19:10).*"* According to the Lord, **"the Church will not survive what is coming upon the earth. They need the working of the Holy Spirit."** He said to me, **"Jesus could not live without the Holy Spirit. What makes My People think they can survive without Him?"** After His resurrection, Jesus told the first apostles, *"And ye are witnesses of these things. And behold I send the promise of my Father upon you; but tarry ye . . . until ye be endued with power from on high* (Luke 24:48-49).*"*

Jesus knew that the apostles could not be effective witnesses without the power of the Holy Ghost. He didn't want them going out in ministry until they had that power (Acts 1:8), and yet much of the Church today has dismissed the Holy Spirit. Even those who call themselves Pentecostals believers see the Holy Ghost as something that makes them shake and speak in tongues. We will discuss this to a greater degree in the chapter about the glory. In the meantime, the Church needs to repent for making the power of God a *"sideshow and a missing ingredient."* The power of God reveals Jesus in our circumstances, letting the world know that Jesus is alive; that He hears and responds to our needs. It's not just about what the Bible said when it was spoken to holy men thousands of years ago.

Jesus launched His Church with signs, wonders and miracles, in order to cause a perpetual change throughout every generation of the earth. The Church was to continue this ministry from the time of Jesus' resurrection, until He returns. ***"The Church dropped the ball in favor of religion."*** They never realized that every sign, wonder and miracle was proof that Jesus came in the flesh. They never understood that there was a purpose in walking by the spirit; that every prophetic word, every vision and dream that the Holy Spirit reveals has a specific purpose in the redemption of the earth. Much of what the Holy Spirit reveals is for intercession in prayer. The Bible says the Spirit makes intercession for us because *we don't know how to pray as we ought* (Romans 8:26).

The Church is suppose to be a "House of Prayer" in the earth. We have been made *"a royal priesthood* (I Peter 2:9)*."* We have been made *"kings and priests unto God"* to show His glory and His dominion (Revelation 1:6). What does God require of a king? What does He expect from a priest? The Holy Spirit spoke to me while I slept. He said, ***"The power to change the world belongs to God's kids. The devil's kids want power, but true power belongs to the heirs of God."*** Then the Holy Spirit began demonstrating that power by quoting scripture. The Body of Christ has the power from on high to ***"rule in the midst of our enemies*** (Psalm 110:2)***."*** The Body of Christ alone has the authority to decree a thing and it shall be done (Job 22:28). The devil knows this all too well. He was a witness to how Adam and Jesus operated on earth. That is why he tries so hard to influence the Church to speak everything but God's word. That devil wants to use God's kids to bring his wicked words to pass. Why do you think the enemy has been trying to shut the Church up. He knows the power we have speaking God's word. These are words of life that wield much power in the mouth of a *"sanctified saint."* Holiness is the key, obeying God with the whole heart. That is why the Bible says, *"If my people, which are called by my name, shall humble themselves, and pray, and seek my face, and turn* *from their wicked ways; then will I hear from heaven, and will forgive their sin, and will heal their land* (II Chronicles 7:14). *"* The Bible does not say the Republicans or Democrats have the power to heal America. No! Only the *holy* people of God have that power. When we humble ourselves, pray and seek God's will and turn from doing our own thing, then our nation will be healed. God is the only one who can heal the nation, but He can only work ***"if the people of God pray and obey."***

All authority has been given to the people of God. We are kings along with Jesus, the King of kings. We are sons and heirs of God (Romans 8:16-17). ***"Heirs of God's Kingdom like Jesus; joint heirs to God's power."*** We are kings and priest like Jesus. ***"As He is, so are we in this world. We shall reign with Him."*** The Holy Spirit didn't stop there. He began talking about how every member of the Body of Christ can also become a prophet over their own life and destiny. ***"With God's words we can become prophets, kings and priests. God puts His word in our mouths to root out, pull up and plant."*** God spoke the same words to the Prophet Jeremiah. *"See, I have this day set thee over the nations and over the kingdoms, to root out, and to pull down, and to destroy, and to throw down, to build and to plant* (Jeremiah 1:10). *"*

Notice the first thing God told Jeremiah was that he was given authority over the nations and over the kingdoms of this world. This is same authority given under Abraham's Blessing. *"And it shall come to pass, if thou shalt hearken diligently unto the voice of the LORD thy God, to observe and to do all his commandments which I command thee this day, that the LORD thy God will set thee on high above all nations of the earth:* (Deuteronomy 28:1). *"* God given this same authority to all His people. He has raised us up together with Christ, and made us to *"sit together"* with Him in the heavenly places (Ephesians 2:6). Where is Jesus seated? God raised Jesus from the dead and *"set him at His own right hand in the heavenly places* (Ephesians 1:20). *"* God has all power. Jesus is seated at the right hand of the Father, which means the Son is partaker of the Father's power. We are *also seated together with the Son* as ***"joint"*** partakers of the Father's power.

When we think about Jesus seated it may be evidence that He is finished with His work and waiting for something else to occur in the earth. Recently, the Lord gave me a *vision* of the Lord. *He was no longer seated. Jesus stood up, dressed in full regalia with the scepter in His hand.* It was as though He was stepping forth to take His rightful place in this earth. This is the season in which we live. Jesus is coming and He is coming soon. It is more important than ever to take heed of the word of God's apostles and prophets in these last days. As Jesus said in Matthew 24, the devil is going to pull out ever stop before our Lord returns. There will be deception, so great as to sway the very elect. The only thing that can eliminate deception, is the truth. God's word is truth (John 17:17). Jesus said we would know the truth and that truth would make us free (John 8:32).

We need a word from Heaven to survive what is coming upon the earth, but be assured of this one thing. We said it in previous volumes and will say it again. Lord spoke to me saying that *"The Kingdom of Heaven is indeed suffering violence, and that violence will be coming to earth before Jesus returns."*[4] Don't be deceived by the noise of the devil. God said it would be His power that would shake the earth. He is coming with a power that will frighten His people. It's a power never seen before. We need to get ready. The people of the earth need to prepare for this great shaking.

Knowing what God is saying by His Spirit is imperative in this hour. It will be the only way to know truth from deception. There will be many false prophets. We see them even now, persuading people to receive death and violence, viruses, sickness and death. What did God say in His word? What is God speaking to your spirits? What is God speaking through His prophets? There is so much deception in the world, one needs to be able to find the truth, that is, if they want to find it. The Holy Spirit is the Spirit of Truth (John 16:13). He speaks to the hearts of believers (those who want to know the truth). He also speaks through God's prophets. God gives words to the prophets so that the people of God can also *root out* the evil and *build* and *plant* what God desires.

Remember that Jesus came to destroy the works of the devil. This is the Kingdom Mission, but it is also the mission of every believer who is bold enough to speak what God speaks, and do what God says to do by His Spirit. The power of God works to produce whatever God speaks. We saw this at creation. The Spirit of God hovered over the earth (Genesis 1:1-3), waiting patiently to bring to pass whatever God spoke over the earth. This is faith in action. We believe. We speak. The power of

4   Matthews, Paula. "Year 2000: Move To Ohio." *The War Journal (1999-2010) Volume I.* Los Angeles: Spirit & Life Publications, 2010. 113. Print.

God through the Holy Spirit brings the word to pass. Jesus said it this way, *"The words that I speak unto you I speak not of myself: but the Father that dwelleth in me, he doeth the works (John 14:10)."* The power is not in our words, but in the words of the Father. When we speak His words, we give God honor. It is indeed an honor to God, when we seek what He wants to do and say, instead of doing things our own way, or focusing on our own pleasure or speaking our own words (Isaiah 58:13-14). This is what it means to delight oneself in the Lord. Psalm 37:4 says that if we delight ourselves in the Lord, He will give us the desires of our heart. The more we yield to what God desires, then He place those godly desires within our hearts. These are the things He has prepared for those who love and obey Him (I Corinthians 2:9).

We have to hear from God. We must know what God desires in order to use *"the keys of the kingdom (Matthew 16:19)."* Then we bind on earth, whatever Heaven wants us to bind. We loose on earth, whatever Heaven want us to loose. This is the duty of prophets, kings and priest of our Lord. If there is something evil in the earth, it is because the Church of Jesus Christ has permitted it to be so. We are the caretakers of the planet. If things don't line up with what God says, we bind (*root up, pull down, throw down*) it's operation. Then we loose (*plant*) what God desires in the earth. For this process to work, one must allow the Holy Spirit to speak. One must hear from God. As Jesus said, *"Man shall not live by bread alone, but by every word that proceedeth out of the mouth of God* (Matthew 4:4)." Whatever God speaks, we speak. Whatever He says do, we do it (John 2:5). Then the Holy Spirit (the power of God) does the work (John 14:10).

Jesus said to his apostles after His resurrection, *"All power is given unto me in heaven and in earth. Go ye therefore, and teach all nations* (Matthew 28:19)."* Jesus has all power. We are to take His Power, and go in His Name. Beloved, if we believe God, then we will be safe and secure. If we believe His prophets then we will prosper (II Chronicles 20:20). In these last days. We must put God's word in our mouths and develop the faith to bring it to pass. Faith works, if we work it. *We shall have what we say* (Mark 11:23). *Anything we ask according to His will, He will give us* (John 14:14; I John 5:14-15). This is the kind of power we have with our Heavenly Father. When we serve God will all our hearts, He serves us. It is a **"symbiotic relationship."** God needs our bodies presented as a *"living sacrifice"* for His work (Romans 12:1). We need

His Holy Spirit to complete the work, and both sides benefit greatly. It's a partnership between Heaven and earth. That is how I write books. God uses my talent and I write whatever He tells me to write. It's a prophetic operation. God leads and I follow Him into some of the greatest revelations of earth's mysteries. It's a nonstop adventure.

God spoke in times past through the holy prophets of old. In these last days, He has spoken to us by his Son, whom God appointed *heir of all things* (Hebrews 1:1-2). We are joints heirs with Jesus to *all things*. Let this sink into your spirit. If you are a child of God, everything that belongs to God is yours. In 2019, the Lord began ministering this idea of being **"heir of this world."** This sound unbelievable, but consider how God called Abraham the heir of the world, but here is what the Bible says, *"For the promise, that he should be the heir of the world, [was] not to Abraham, or to his seed, through the law, but through the righteousness of faith* (Romans 4:13)." This title, *heir of the world* was to *Abraham and His seed* through faith. Jesus is the seed of Abraham. That means that everyone in Christ, is also heir of the world. Now considering that we are kings and priests and prophets of our God, this had tremendous ramifications. Kings possess physical lands and power. Priests possess spiritual land and power. The prophet us calls forth that which God says belongs to us. We have the right to demand that all of the earth yield its fruit, possessions and resources to us as we do the will of our Father. That is exactly what our Abba Daddy would do if He was walking this earth. That is what Jesus did. Remember when He told his disciple to get the colt that had never been road on? He told them that if the master of the house wanted to know what they were doing, say, "the master has need of it (Mark 11:1-3). Jesus did it again when he saw the fig tree far off. He demanded fruit, and the Bible said that the tree answered Jesus and did not bear fruit (Mark 11:12-14). Jesus cursed that tree.

All things work for our good because we are called according to His purpose. All things in heaven and earth belong to God's kids, we can even command the elements. The nations have borders, but In Christ, there are no more borders. As God's heirs, we need to widen the borders of our mind to see that everything is ours. This is why we need to hear the voice of God. It's how we receive our earthly inheritance. The Holy Spirit is the earnest deposit of our inheritance (Ephesians 1:13-14). He is also *"the executor of the covenant"* with God. The Holy Spirit reveals what is in the covenant. He also instructs and empowers us to receive what rightfully belongs to us as heirs of God. To change the conditions of this world, the people of God must be *"endued with power from on high."* We need the Holy Spirit. Without His guidance, we walk in deception, unable to operate as a prophet, king or priest of our Lord. The people of God need to hear from God. From Genesis to Revelation, God is a speaking Spirit. In the beginning, He formed man from dirt, breathed His breath *"the breath of life"* into man's nostrils; and man became a living (speaking) being like God (Genesis 2:7). Man would have remained an empty shell had God not breathed His life into us. It was the *Breath of God* that gave us life and consciousness. The soul and spirit of man were from God, for the purpose of empowering us to dominate and create what God desired on the earth. It is amazing that the Bible says that God formed the animals and brought them to Adam to name them. *"And whatsoever Adam called every living creatures, that was the name thereof* (Genesis 2:19).*"* There are some things that have come upon the earth, things not of God, but from the pit of hell. God is bringing them before His people and telling us to name them, but without the Breath of God (the Holy Spirit) leading us, we will speak what we hear the world speaking. We need to be imitators of God (Ephesians 5:1), who saw the darkness of the earth, but never called it by what He saw. No! God called forth light and the darkness had to flee. Likewise, we are seeing evil in the world, but the power to change the world begins with the words spoken by the *true believers* who walk by faith and not by sight (II Corinthians 5:7); the *prophets, kings and priests* of God. **Whatever we call it, so shall be the name thereof,** yet to speak something begins by hearing something from Heaven. In this book, I am calling situations as God saw them. It may be shocking to some, but so be it. In order to conquer the darkness of this world you have to know exactly what spirit you are dealing with.

God is still speaking by His Spirit. He never stopped speaking. The Church stopped listening. That is about to change. In these last days, God will speak ever so boldly and He will not be ignored. We are about to see manifestations of His Spirit that will shake the earth. *"For the earth shall be full of the knowledge of the Lord, as the waters cover the sea* (Isaiah 11:9).*"* This will be the proof the world has been waiting for; proof that God is real; that He really did send Jesus (John 17:21). It will be proof once and for all, that Jesus Christ is the same, yesterday, today and forever (Hebrews 13:8)!

The Power Of Ancient Words In A Modern World

As one ages in this life, we realize that we are not as smart as we thought we were in our youth. We can look back and say, "How stupid we were back then." Every generation thinks that it knows more than the previous generations. It was King Solomon who said, *"There is no new thing under the sun (Ecclesiastes 1:9)."* People live and die. The sun will still rise. The wind still blows and rivers continue to run into the sea. This is the pattern of earth. There are great inventions and innovations in the modern world, only to find out that although technology is new to us, there were always ancient forms of the same things in existence in previous generations. We just didn't know about it.

We find that in human nature, all of the times and seasons of man are the same for every people and every generation. The pattern is so distinct that some believe that there is no purpose for this life, no reason for our being here other than to live and then to die. Certainly this was perceived in the heart and mind of Solomon as well. He saw the *"vanity"* of man's efforts in life and sought to find words of wisdom to explain the value in this human existence. Here was the richest king on earth. He had everything any person could imagine. Solomon had more wealth, power and wisdom than any man of his time, or in ages to come. Solomon spoke three thousand proverbs and wrote a thousand and five songs (I Kings 4:32), yet, the king was still searching for meaning in this life.

Since the serpent beguiled Adam and Eve in the garden, man has always been curious about his existence in this earth. He has been in search of God. He has been in rebellion of God. This attraction to and repelling from God has occurred in every generation of mankind on earth. We want protection and provision from God, but we don't want Him meddling in our personal affairs. We know that we need Him, but we don't really want Him in our lives. I don't know who this is for, but I'm hearing that ***"you cannot milk a cow without the cow."*** In other words, you cannot receive the Blessing of God, without the God of the Blessing being in your life. What parent is pleased with a child who asks for money, but refuses to obey the parent's rules? God is the same way. He delights in blessing the child who is attentive to obey Him. *"And all these bless-*

ings shall come on thee, and overtake thee, if thou shalt hearken unto the voice of the LORD thy God (Deuteronomy 28:2)." God is not so pleased to sorely discipline one who does not obey, He said, "But it shall come to pass, if thou wilt not hearken unto the voice of the LORD thy God, to observe to do all his commandments and his statutes which I command thee this day; that all these curses shall come upon thee, and overtake thee (Deuteronomy 28:15)." These are Old Testament scriptures, but the New Covenant says the same. God will render to each man (and woman), "according to his deeds (Roman 2:6)."

The Bible is our instruction book from God. The Holy Spirit says, **"It** [The Bible] **is our manual for living a prosperous life on earth."** According to Joshua 1:8, it also says, "This book of the law shall not depart out of thy mouth; but thou shalt meditate therein day and night, that thou mayest observe to do according to all that is written therein: for then thou shalt make thy way prosperous, and then thou shalt have good success." The Bible is also **"a portal into God's supernatural Kingdom."**[1] It opens up one's spirit to be able to receive everything that God promises in that Book. Sure these are ancient words, but the power of those words have been working in the universe since time began. God, Himself is called the "Ancient of Days (Daniel 7:9)." Why we surprised of the power of His word. God and His word are the same.

Years ago, I got a revelation of just how ancient those words were. God had given me my first book to write. Every time I would begin writing what the Holy Spirit was saying, another book would surface from that original book. Every other sentence that the Holy Spirit gave me to write, spun off another book. These books would literally come out of the sentence and form a new book. It happen so many time that I became frightened. What I was writing came from God. It was His word being spoken by His Spirit, but it had a life of its own. But, it was scary. I took the book and put it in the trunk of my car. That is how much this book shook me up. I don't know how long a time had passed, but God, the Father asked me, **"Paula, where is My baby?"** That was the first time that He called my book, His baby. I said, "It's in my car." I felt so convicted that I went out to my car and got it. When I brought it in, that book manifested in a way that both shocked and puzzled me. It turned into a baby, but a very old, baby with wrinkly old skin. It looked like it was several hundred years old, but it was wearing a diaper. It spoke to

1   Matthews, Paula. "God Gives Us The Desires Of Our Hearts." *Living In The Faith Zone*. Atlanta: Spirit & Life Publications[SM], 2019, 68. Print.

me saying, "Don't you love me?" It had the voice of a rickety old man. I didn't know how to answer. I just received the book as my assignment even if what I saw and heard made no earthly sense. Today, I know it to be confirmation that the words I am hearing and writing are ancient, but are finally being birthed in this earth. This is word power that had yet to be tapped into, reserved for these end of last days. That has to be one of the strangest spiritual experience I have had so far. But this is the power of ancient words in this modern world.

God and His word have not changed. If we believe and obey God's word then we will prosper. If we don't believe and disobey, then we will fail in this life. To prosper is to operate in the Blessing. To fail is the curse. Romans 2:8-9 reads, *"But unto them that are contentious, and do not obey the truth, but obey unrighteousness, indignation and wrath, Tribulation and anguish, upon every soul of man that doeth evil, of the Jew first, and also of the Gentile; But glory, honour, and peace, to every man that worketh good, to the Jew first, and also to the Gentile: For there is no respect of persons with God* (Romans 2:8-11). "

There is much tribulation and anguish in the world today. Jesus said it would be that way, however He left us with a solution. Jesus said, *"In the world ye shall have tribulation: but be of good cheer; I have overcome the world* (John 16:33). " In Christ, we have refuge from the world. Jesus said, *"Come unto me, all [ye] that labour and are heavy laden, and I will give you rest. Take my yoke upon you, and learn of me; for I am meek and lowly in heart: and ye shall find rest unto your souls. For my yoke [is] easy, and my burden is light* (Matthew 11:28-30). "

America and the nations of the world need Jesus. This is not some religious saying. It the reality of the cross and what it provides for all human kind. Jesus said, *"I am the bread of life: he that cometh to me shall never hunger; and he that believeth on me shall never thirst. "* The words Jesus speaks are *"spirit and life* (John 6:35, 63). " They are ancient words, but they are *"words of life"* given for the welfare of the entire world. He is the *"Living Bread"* that came down from Heaven to feed us all. God will not force His way on man. We must come of our own free will. God loves us, but He will also let us live a life of hell if we choose. There is a way that seems right to a man, but it was Solomon who said that the way ended in death (Proverbs 14:12). Part of what God gave me in this book are looking at modern every day news that fits the pattern of ancient demonic spirits that God want eradicated from the earth. Certainly, we wrestle not with flesh and blood, but against principalities and powers and rulers of the darkness of this world. In these last days, God said that *"everything is supernatural."* True power is supernatural. It's a power that belongs only to the people of God. However, the devil wants to take it for himself. It won't happen. God's power manifests only in righteousness. You must be in right standing with God to wield this kind of power. As the Bible says, *"The effectual fervent prayer of a righteous man availeth much* (James 5:16).*"* You must be righteous to tap into the power of God.

Now, the devil and the kingdom of darkness also has power, but it is not real power. What we see in America, and we will discuss later, are specific leaders of the nation who are tapping into demonic power in order to overrule what they believe is a weak, wimpy Church. God has identified these demons by name so that we can execute justice as He designed for theses evil spirits. What is before us is similar to what Moses when through when he went up against Pharaoh. Whatever supernatural feat God told Moses to perform, Pharaoh's magicians figured a way to do something similar. It was a counterfeit, but it looked almost the same. Of the ten plagues, it got to the point where the king's magicians could not figure out what God did. In the end, it wasn't until God sent the plague of death, that Pharaoh let the slaves go free.

In this volume of **The War Journal**, we will see how the ways of our leaders have brought a plague death upon our nation. We will observe some of the national and international events that God highlighted, compare what we saw in the news, with what God said actually happened behind the scenes. There are many voices clamoring for our attention in this world. We will narrow our discussions to three voices, that of God, that of the Church and that of the nation. We will analyze our recent past and where God says we are going in the future, based upon His words of prophecy. The world news agencies are prophesying their future, but every last person will be judged based upon what God has said in His word about the future of America and the nation of the world. No one will escape what God has spoken over our lives. Not even those of us who are messengers of that word. Take for example King Solomon. He spoke words of wisdom that came straight from God. Even he could not even escape the words he spoke to the kings and nations of the world. Solomon's passion for *strange women* (those outside of the covenant) led him to disobey God's command. *"Of the nations [concerning] which the LORD said unto the children of Israel, Ye shall not go in to them, neither shall they come in unto you: [for] surely they will turn away your heart after their gods: Solomon clave unto these in love. And he had seven hundred wives, princesses, and three hundred concubines: and his wives turned away his heart. For it came to pass, when Solomon was old, [that] his wives turned away his heart after other gods: and his heart was not perfect with the LORD his God, as [was] the heart of David his father (I Kings 11:2-4)."*

Solomon let his weakness for women to cause him to lose his place with God. The Kingdom was divided and ten tribes were given to the king's servant. The remaining two tribes remained with Solomon, only because God had to honor his covenant with David. God promise that a king would be from his lineage for all eternity (I Kings 11:26-43). Solomon reigned for forty years, and had to live with the fruit of his own rebellion against the commandments of God. The king who had everything, including great wealth and wisdom, had to be chastened by God. His position did not shield him from the wrath of God. His promise, like most of what God promises, was conditional. What God promised would come to pass, **if we hearkened** (took heed and obeyed) God's word. This is what God said to Adam in the garden. He spoke the same way to every king who was set over His people. God is still speaking in the same manner to us today. If we are *"willing and obedient"* we will eat the good of the land, but if you refuse and rebel, you will be destroyed (Isaiah 1:19-20). In America, we will witness how these ancient words will judge those who continue to rebel against God. It shall be done publicly so that all will learn to fear Almighty God.

By the end of the book of Ecclesiastes, we find King Solomon realizing that there was indeed more to life on earth. It would seem that he had gained wisdom for his own life. He was compelled to write these ancient words for our benefit. *"Remember now thy Creator in the days of thy youth, while the evil days come not, nor the years draw nigh, when thou shalt say, I have no pleasure in them . . . Let us hear the conclusion of the whole matter: Fear God, and keep his commandments: for this [is] the whole [duty] of man. For God shall bring every work into judgment, with every secret thing, whether [it be] good, or whether [it be] evil (Ecclesiastes 12:1, 13-14)."* I pray that these words and revelations from God will lead America to repentance, The wrath of God is against our nation, but like it was with David, God has a covenant to uphold. Therefore He cannot utterly destroy America. But also, like Solomon lost ten tribes, God said that *"the country will lose its world status and power."* Some people have predicted that America would become a third world country. God said, that *"His people will get the wealth and power to sustain the nation under Kingdom authority."* How will this be?

The Lord told me that there would be *"two worlds operating in America."* After writing this chapter, God revealed that the time for this two world manifestation is now. Here is what the Lord told me almost ten years ago. *"There will be two worlds operating in America."*[2] *"One that is obedient to God that will prosper because God will transfer all the wealth to them. They will run God's Kingdom on earth as it is in Heaven. Oh, and they won't care about tax breaks and tax loop holes. They will render to Caesar that which is rightfully Caesar's and under gird the financial health of America."*

God then describes the other world that will be in operation in America. *"They will continue to live like they do, but the money will be scarce. They will not live in prosperity, but in lack and in fear for their future. There will be more violence, and hatred as they fight for the meager resources. Men will become lover's of self, covenant breakers, disobedient . . . Most of those suffering will go to God's Kingdom for relief. The others hate God so much that they will war against God and lose their lives."*

Finally, God prophesied how it all will end in our nation.
"'What's established under God's Kingdom mandate will never be destroyed; even in a country where violence will increase. God's Kingdom will remain. But many will die offended that peace and prosperity will only be in God's Kingdom. The invitation to come to God will be extended, but instead, they will try to tear down the Kingdom and its dwellers. Evil will increase, but so will prosperity' says the Spirit of Grace and Peace."

> "O give thanks unto the LORD; for [he is] good:
> For his mercy [endureth] for ever."
> Psalm 136:1

---

2   Matthews, Paula. "Questions And Answers." *American Heritage 101.* Los Angeles: Spirit & Life Publications, 2012. 77-78. Print.

INTRODUCTION

Only The Truth Of God Can Heal America

It was God who subtitled this book, *"The Healing and Restoration Of America."* At the writing of this book, America would seem to be at her lowest position politically and economically since becoming a prosperous nation over a century ago. God wants to heal us, but the healing process can be quite painful, especially for those who have treated deep wounds like minor scrapes and bruises. Healing for America and for any nation begins with uncovering the deep wounds with truth. The world is in short supply of truth these days. Experts think they know truth, but it's only their opinion of truth. They put their own spin on what they consider to be truth, and it ends up being supposition. Even the Church says it believes in the truth of God's word, but we know what one believes by what they do. If the Bible is true, why aren't God's people following it? All of this search for truth could leave one more confused than ever. So, where does one go to find truth? Jesus said that if we continued in His word that <u>we would know the truth</u>, and *the truth* would make us free (John 8:31-32). The words of Jesus are in red letters in many Bibles. He said, <u>if</u> we continue in His word. That assumes that we have started to read and follow what Jesus said. It sounds like a tall order to fill considering that few people have actually read and understood Jesus' word. Nevertheless, Jesus said that only under these conditions would we know the truth. Notice that Jesus did not say we would know truth, but we would know *"the truth."* The truth Jesus is talking about is set apart from ordinary truth, or from what people perceive to be truth. Jesus is talking about *absolute truth,* that which God says, is *the truth*. This is the truth by which our nation can be healed. *"He sent his word, and healed them, and delivered them from their destructions* (Psalm 107:20). *"* God's word is truth (John 17:17).

In the Bible, Jesus had much to say about truth. He brought up the subject of truth came just moments before His execution on the cross. He made a very powerful statement to Pilate the Roman ruler. He said, *"and for this cause came I into the world, that I should bear witness unto the truth. Everyone that is of the truth heareth my voice (John 18:37). "* Let's pause here. Jesus came to show us *the truth* and everyone who is of *the truth* hears His voice. So, if we have an ear (desire) to know *the truth,* then Jesus says we can hear it through His word. It was Pilate, the officer of the Roman court who responded to Jesus asking, *"What is truth?"* He then walked away. Pilate did not stay around for Jesus to answer that question. Some of you may not stay around for this discussion either. As Jesus said, you must have a desire for truth. Let us continue.

In another conversation with His disciples, Jesus said that He was *"The Truth* (John 14:6).*"* Indeed, He came *"full of grace and truth* (John 1:14).*"* It was a radical thought for someone to claim to be a witness of truth, but then Jesus goes as far as saying that He was The Truth. Let's put it in perspective. This notion of *"truth"* needs to be clarified. Take for example, the discourse between Jesus and Pilate before the crucifixion. The religious leaders were making all sort of accusations against Jesus. He never responded. Pilate said to Him *"Speakest thou not unto me? Knowest thou not that I have the power to crucify thee, and have power to release thee?"* Was this the truth? Well, according to Roman law it was truth, but Jesus made this clarification. *"Jesus answered, Thou couldest have no power at all against me, except it were given thee from above* (John 19:11).*"* Didn't Pilate have power to execute Jesus? Sure he did, but *the truth* of the situation was that God sent Jesus to die on the cross. It is the whole reason He came to earth. *"Him being delivered by the determinate counsel and foreknowledge of God* (Acts 2:23).*"* It was the will of God that Jesus be crucified. As Jesus said, *"Therefore doth my Father love me, because I lay down my life, that I might take it again. No man taketh it from me, but I lay it down of myself. I have power to lay it down, and I have power to take it again. This commandment have I received of my Father* (John 10:17-18).*"*

Even though it was a fact that Pilate had power under the Roman government to either execute or release Jesus, the Bible repeated called Jesus, the lamb slain *before the foundation of the world* (I Peter 1:19-20; Revelation 13:8). Jesus' execution was *foreordained* before the foundation of the world. Which means it was determined before mankind's appearance on earth. So, "what is the truth?" Whose power was at work at the crucifixion, Pilate's or Almighty God's? As Jesus said, it was God who holds the ultimate power in that situation. For mankind to be redeemed, Jesus agreed to lay down His life for the entire world. When one obeys God, even to obedience on the cross, it is the power of God (even the glory) that is in operation. This is something the Lord taught me early on in ministry. He said that whenever I would obey Him that the laws of His Kingdom would supersede all other laws in the universe. *The truth of God and His purpose will always supersede the power and purpose of mankind.* Also, He taught me that *"wherever He sends me and they reject me, they reject the one who sent me."* Obedience to God makes us His emissary. It is as if God Himself is going and doing the work. This is a powerful truth that will override the facts any day. It can also cause healing to flow into one's life.

The pursuit of truth put one on a course of victory over every evil thing in the earth. *Truth is absolute.* Most people, even Christians think they know truth, but what are they actually believing? We are always in search of some authority to give us reliable truth, but it cannot be found outside of God and His word. Human beings have limited capabilities in, and of themselves to perceive truth. Look at where we get most of our information in this world. The media cares little about truth because they go after breaking news stories to increase viewership. Politicians cannot speak truth because it may cost them votes at the ballot box. Our government is not a paragon of virtue but it has laws to substitute for truth. What about preachers? Well, they are supposed to be purveyors of the truth, but it is all according to how much truth they are able to receive from God. So, where in the world can we find truth, *the truth* Jesus spoke about, *the truth* that will make us free?

We can short circuit this whole search by going back to what the Bible says, *God's word is truth* (John 17:17). You can debate scripture all day long, but pause for a moment. Consider God to be true and every other voice a lie (Romans 3:4). Consider how God created us for His purpose. We did not create ourselves. Consider how the same God who keeps the days and nights, and the seasons in their rhythm and timing, is the same God who predestined our times and seasons. We don't understand, nor have we knowledge of God to replica what He has done in the universe. Perhaps, just perhaps Almighty God knows a little bit more than we humans do. This might be a stretch for some of you who believe you are god, but for the rest of us, we are humble enough to know that we don't know everything. But, as Christians, we know the One who knows all and created all. God alone knows the truth about each and every situation that occurs in this life, and get this. God says that if any person lacks wisdom about anything, just ask Him (James 1:5). How simple is that? And yet too few people, even Christians bother to talk to God about what is going on in this earth. Of course, on the other hand, there is no lack of wisdom in the earth. It's just not sound wisdom from God that will transform the lives of mankind from the curse to the Blessing. Later in this book I will share a prophecy in which God declares that He set the stage, and chose the actors in the earth. He called Himself, the *"Director of It All!"* It would seem that Shakespeare had it right in saying

> *"All the world's a stage,*
> *And all the men and women merely players;*
> *They have their exits and their entrances;*
> *And one man in his time plays many parts."[1]*

The issue is, whose script are the people of the world reading? Most of the world, and even the Church seem to be getting their lines from a source other than God. We seem to be producing everything in the earth, except that which God has ordained. That is why there is poverty, sickness, disease and famine. Mankind is operating according to the script entitled, "The Curse," instead of living in The Blessing of the Lord which makes one rich and adds no sorrow with it (Proverbs 10:22). The Bible says in very direct terms, *"Cursed be the man [or woman] that trusts in man, and make flesh his arm, and whose heart departeth from the Lord. For he shall be like the heath in the desert, and shall not see when good cometh; but shall inhabit the parched places in the wilderness, in a salt land and not inhabited* (Jeremiah 17:5-6). *"*

The curse applies to anyone who turns away from God to rely on human effort for provision and protection. They won't even see good when it comes. Why not? Man has no answers. His resources is limited, so any hope of a better life is diminished. Even if good comes, they won't believe it because it didn't come from "the man" that they consider a reliable source. They are not looking for good to come from anyone but man. So be it, but God's goodness remains for those who want to be healed and delivered from the limits of man. We see the curse in operation in America because we have turned away from God, to follow after the limited and sometimes nonexistent wisdom of men. Worse yet, we have kicked God out of the picture of the American Dream. We want the stuff, <u>without</u> the Creator who endued us with power to get the stuff. Is there any wonder why there are cracks in our nation's foundation? Let's explore some of *the truth* about these cracks that the Spirit of God has revealed.

1   Shakespeare, William. "As You Like It." Source:http://shakespeare.mit.edu/. Kindle Edition.

40

For decades, and some would say for the sake of "unity and political correctness" our nation has glossed over the severe cracks in our spiritual foundation. We thought that we could call ourselves *"one nation under God"* and then remove God from the public square, from our classrooms and from our consciousness, and still be blessed. We thought we could declare over our monetary currency *"In God We Trust,"* and turn against His precepts to hijack the "American Dream." Those were not mere words we spoke as a united nation. Those were "covenant" words spoken before God by generations of America. This is *the truth* that God has revealed by His Spirit.

God made it clear in Volume I of **The War Journal**, that He has a covenant[2] with America. This is also *the truth* of our relationship with God, whether people like it or not. Our covenant is a legally binding agreement that was ratified by the Father and His Son, and sealed in the Blood of Jesus. This is serious business with God. The same God who made covenant with the day and night, and the seasons, has a covenant with America and with the people of this earth. It can never be broken (Jeremiah 33:20-21). God's word of covenant is eternally binding. He will never forsake us, but if we forsake Him, we will reap the consequences. In fact, we are seeing those consequences even now. This message is also for the Church of Jesus Christ in America. The healing of our land, and the healing of the nations of the earth, is dependant upon the obedience of God's people. This is again, *the truth* that God has revealed. As God promised, *"If my people, which are called by my name, shall humble themselves, and pray, and seek my face, and turn from their wicked ways; then will I hear from heaven, and will forgive their sin, and will heal their land* (II Chronicles 7:14).*"*

America is in crisis. Where are the people of God? He is asking the Church the same thing He asked Adam after he sinned in the garden, *"Where art thou* (Genesis 3:9)*?"* God knows their physical proximity. He is asking about their spiritual allegiance. "Where are they? Whose side are they on?" How long will vacillate between opinions? *"If the Lord be God, follow him* (I Kings 18:21).*"* If the Church would stand for God, the nation would not falter, but if God's people will not stand for righteousness, the nation will continue to fail. Again, going back to Adam and Eve after they sinned. They were in the garden hiding from

2   Matthews, Paula. "The Judgment Of God Revealed." *The War Journal (1999-2010) Volume I*, Los Angeles: Spirit & Life Publications, 2012. 73. Print.

God because they realized that they were naked. They even sewed to-gether fig leaves to cover themselves and their sin (Genesis 3:7-10). Likewise, the Church in America has clothed itself with the fig leaf of religion, and can be found hiding from the presence of God. As the Body of Christ in this nation, we chose religion and materialism, instead of relationship with the Father. We changed *the truth* of God into a lie and worshipped and served the creation more than the Creator who is blessed forever (Romans 1:25). The Church can complain about the po-litical leaders in America. They can complain about abortions and gay marriage and racism and the like, but the bottom line is this. We said in Volume I of **The War Journal** and we say it again here, God holds His people responsible for what happens in America.[3]

The nations of the earth either prosper or fail based upon whether the people of God obey God or rebel against Him. It's like what happened to Jonah. Instead of going to Nineveh and speaking *the truth* that would cause that city to repent, Jonah got on a boat going to Tarshish to flee *from the presence of the Lord* (Jonah 1:3). Why are God's people fleeing or hiding from His presence? They do so because their deeds are evil, and they don't want to *"fess up"* to God. Unrepentant sin and rebellion will cause one to flee from God in shame and condemnation. I get it. Sin makes you feel real dirty in the presence of a *Holy* God, but there is another side to this sin issue. If you don't confess, you will continue to walk in darkness, outside of the fellowship with the Father. That's not the worse part. If you don't confess, then you won't be forgiven. If you are not forgiven you cannot be cleansed from unrighteousness (I John 1:7-8). If you remain unrighteousness, you become *devil bait*. You are no longer under the protection of God. Let me give you an analogy of what that would be like.

Did you ever see the police shows where a good cop turns bad and he is jailed with the same criminals he put away? What happens to that cop in jail? Those criminals have a long memory and a passionate desire for revenge. In jail, you find yourself on their turf. The same is true of the Christian who walks in unrighteousness. The devil and his imps would enjoy having free reign over your life, your family and everything you own. Be quick to repent. Confess to God. Give that devil no place in your life. Get cleansed and move back under the Blessing.

3   Matthews, Paula. "Year 2009: A Better Understanding Of Things To Come." *The War Journal (1999-2010) Volume*. Los Angeles: Spirit & Life Publications, 2010. 357, 360. Print.

Unfortunately, Adam and Eve didn't repent. They made excuses for their behavior. God expelled them from the Garden of Eden into the cursed world as their reward. Their sin brought forth the curse, forcing them to live outside of the Blessing where the abundance and protection of God flourished. Therefore, man was left to his own devices. He would have to find ways to survive and protect themselves from the evil he unleashed in the world.

Let's pause here a moment. Adam and Eve sinned. *Their sin didn't just affect their family.* It spread like a ***"generational plague"*** upon all the families of the earth. Their sin was rebellion against God and His governance of the earth. Look familiar? The same thing is happening in America. We have rebelled against God. We have turned against the godly foundation that made us a *Blessed* nation. It was Almighty God who gave us the abundance and protection we enjoy. *"But thou shalt remember the Lord thy God: for it is he that giveth thee power to get wealth* (Deuteronomy 8:18). *"* Americans act as though we are the source of our own prosperity. No! It all came from God because of what our founding fathers put in place. It's not perfect. It never was, but it was just enough to make *lasting covenant with the Holy God* for the protection and wellbeing of these ***"united"*** states. The saddest part of what we see in America today, is that we put our trust in men and women who only want power. They want to make their names great. They are more concerned about "their legacy" than about the wellbeing of the American people.

It's a dangerous thing to be in covenant with God and make a man (or woman) your idol. It brings a curse upon the third and fourth generation of those who hate God (Exodus 20:5). Could it be that is what we are seeing in America? God has a Kingdom *precedent* for dealing with leaders who hail themselves as gods. Here is an example. *"And upon a set day Herod, arrayed in royal apparel, sat upon his throne, and made an oration unto them. And the people gave a shout, [saying, It is] the voice of a god, and not of a man. And immediately the angel of the Lord smote him, because he gave not God the glory: and he was eaten of worms, and gave up the ghost. But the word of God grew and multiplied (Acts 12:21-24). "* This is God's penalty for leaders exalting their thrones above His. In these last days, God alone will be glorified. Notice that as the ruler was struck dead, the gospel grew among the people. I bet it did. Watching a political leader drop dead publicly would make anyone a believer in Jesus Christ. Stay tuned. We are about to see that and more in this season. God is determined to get the glory in these last days, and it begins in 2020. Praise God! Anyone who comes against Almighty God may be taken off the earth suddenly and swiftly. God will deal with America and the nations, but He will also judge the Church, if we don't judge ourselves. This may shock some members of the Body of Christ because it is widely held that God does not judge His people. We have been already judged and found righteous.

Sure, during salvation God put our sin on Jesus so that we *"might be made the righteousness of God,"* in Him (II Corinthians 5:21). Our position in God never changes. Whether we stay under the provision and protect of that righteous position is another thing. That's up to us. It is according to whether we choose to obey God or not. We can suffer because of disobedience, but it is better to obey God and endure the suffering thereof. Everyone who lives godly will suffer persecution. That comes with the assignment. If we, as the righteousness of God openly sin against Him, we will be judged. *"For the time [is come] that judgment must begin at the house of God: and if [it] first [begin] at us, what shall the end [be] of them that obey not the gospel of God* (I Peter 4:17)*?"*

The Church at large needs to repent. They have turned away from God to service idols. If the Spirit of God was allowed to enter in that religious setting, the devil would reveal his ugly face. Religious people resist the Holy Spirit of God. They resist the miracles, the signs and wonders Jesus said would follow those who believe (Mark 16:17). Religion talks about Jesus, but they don't practice Jesus. They tend to rise up and rebel against the resurrection power that God sent to heal and deliver the world. That makes religious people the epitome of those who have *"a form of godliness, but denying the power thereof* (II Timothy 3:5)*."* The Bible tells us to turn away from this sort who resist *the truth.*

The world is looking for Jesus, His love, His miracles His redemption. The religious arm of the Church keeps mankind bound to sin and condemnation. They don't believe in Jesus the Healer. They use God and His word as a weapon to bind and hurt people. These are self-righteous ones who have no connection with *the truth* of God. They have made religious practice their god. Religion kills the human spirit. It is not of God, which is why Jesus always spoke against the religious hypocrites

44

of His day. *"Woe unto you, scribes and Pharisees, hypocrites! for ye compass sea and land to make one proselyte, and when he is made, ye make him twofold more the child of hell than yourselves* (Matthew 23:15)."* Take the example of Jonah. He knew what would happen if he went to Nineveh. He didn't want that city to repent. This is the *religious devil* at work. They make the judgement call that some people are not worthy to be saved. There are some preachers who say the same about the United States. Woe unto those hypocrites, the children of hell! Jesus died for the world. He made no distinction. All men need salvation.

Let's continue with *the truth* God is revealing. As a nation, we assumed that prosperity by any means necessary was working for us. We assumed that building a nation upon the backs of various people groups would profit us. Indeed we prospered for a season. Certainly we profited in the short run, but we thought it was all about the ends justifying the means. In reality, another, more certain law was in motion; the Law of Seedtime and Harvest. As the Bible says, *"Be not deceived; God is not mocked: for whatsoever a man soweth, that he shall also reap* (Galatians 6:7)."* This is the truth that we are seeing manifested before the eyes of the world. We have been deceived. We thought we could do anything, anyway we pleased and not experience the negative consequences. We thought that we were far above the Law of God. Yet, as the Lord had me print on the back cover of Volume II, ***"The secret things belong to Me. I will reveal them all."*** God is revealing secrets in order to uncover *the truth* that will bring healing and restoration to our nation.

When a severe injury is left unattended, infection can occur. People have been known to die from infection alone. What we see in America is ***"the festering of a severe wound"*** that has left a people infected; many are sick and dying, not from a virus, but of a lack of hope. This is what happens when our world is separated from God. He wants to restore and prosper the United States once again, but it requires that we be healed from past hurts and ailments. We need healing in ***"the chasm"*** amongst the various people groups whom we have abused in the formulation of our nation. We touched upon this in Volume II. We will deal with it more thoroughly in this book. Then, God has revealed **His Dream** for America. It is not exactly like what we have come to know as the American Dream which is material in nature. God's Dream for our nation is based upon righteousness (right standing with God). Material possession and greatness comes as a result of a right relationship with God. There have been copious prophetic words not only from this prophet but also from others both near and far, concerning God's plan for America. Every word tends to point to a glorious end, but the path the nation must take is a rocky one. This same theme resonates throughout this book. Even while writing, I could not help but reflect on some of those prophetic words I received directly from the Lord, and ask, God Almighty, "What happened to the American dream?" "Where did we go wrong?" "Where do we go from here?"

In Volume I, the Lord identified the failure in America to raise up competent leaders who walk in integrity. It's time out for the **"yes men and atta boys."** America is in desperate need of leadership from those who will lead, and not follow the opinion polls, who will not court the media or anyone who tends to wield their influence in our culture. We need leaders who don't use minorities for their votes and then oppress them with their policies. We deal much with leadership in this book. Change in our nation can only begin with a change in our leaders. When I first began writing Volume I of **The War Journal**, the Lord spoke much about **"change"** coming to America and to the nations in these final days before Jesus returns. This change is required to prepare the way of the Lord. The heart of the Father was turned to the world when He sent Jesus. Now is the final hour in which the hearts of the children (the world) must return to the Father (Malachi 4:5-6). In fact, *"all things"* in this world, its people and their possessions must restored (Acts 3:21) to God, the Father of it all. If they are not willfully returned, they will violently be taken by force. That is why everything in our day is being shaken. The governments, and every structure within the nations are being shaken. The only things that cannot be shaken, are the things that God has ordained for His Kingdom rule. Outside of His Kingdom order, nothing shall remain.

This shaking is actually a blessing from God. Rather than have the entire world destroyed curse when Jesus returns (Malachi 4:6), God shakes us into Kingdom order so that we can be saved. God has declared that **"America shall be saved."** So no matter what befalls us, God will pick us up, dust us off, heal our wounds and put us back onto His path for our lives. Does that mean we have divine protection and can do as we please? No! Definitely not! Much of what is happening and will continue to happen is because we have chosen to do our own thing without God. Which means the curse has been activated on our behalf. Think about it. Something is definitely wrong in a nation when government leaders want to "defund the police" and allow rioters in the streets to loot and pillage the small businesses that uphold the communities. This kind of insanity promotes anarchy. If the people want to protest, it should begin by voting these *"corrupt"* leaders out of office. Here is *the truth* God is speaking about race in our nation. *"America does not have a race problem. She has a sin problem."* We let the devil separate us by race, by political party, and so on. We are no longer acting like *"One nation under God." "We are one nation under siege of demonic oppression and witchcraft."* People are frustrated with the wickedness of government leaders who care more about themselves than the people they have sworn to protect. So the people are given to more wickedness. What does that solve? It only results in more destruction, driving one deeper into the curse. We need Jesus. We need to repent and turn back to God and let the healing begin. This is not a religious saying. It is *the truth* that will set our nation free. Jesus came to give us life and that more abundantly (John 10:10). Jesus said that He was the Truth (John 14:6). Only the truth can make us free, but lies and deception will continue to keep people in bondage. Here is a news flash, most of the world does not want *the truth* to be known. Therefore in this book, we will explore *the truths*, as revealed by God, that will make America and the people of the nations forever free!

This volume is the next progression in our study of America's relationship with God. In the first volume, God demonstrated His covenant protection over this nation just prior to the attacks on 911. God revealed the attacks weeks before, and commanded His people to pray for the safety of their cities. God did this because He wanted us to know that He was watching; that there was nothing that escaped His all seeing eye. AND that God had a plan in place before the foundation of the world. He knew all of this would happen and put together a plan that could only be revealed by His Spirit to our spirits, if we sought Him in prayer. God also revealed the political climate and it's weak leadership that opened the door for America to be invaded. In that book, the Lord also explained the role of the Church in His divine plan for the earth. We continued with the second volume, we had a deeper discussion of the issues in the Church that needed to be corrected in order for the nation to be healed and returned to God. Healing can come to a people, even before they return their hearts to Him. In fact, healing opens the hearts to the goodness of God. It's the goodness of God that causes men to repent

(Romans 2:3-4). In these last days, we will see a whirlwind of healing over the nations. God is about to lavish His goodness upon His people and they will take it to the world! No matter what it looks like now, God's plan for unleashing His goodness upon us. It has not been delayed or overturned. God is not a man. He cannot lie. He hastens to bring His word to pass in our lives (Jeremiah 1:12). Therefore God's word will not return to Him void, but it will accomplish what He intended. It will prosper wherever He sends it (Isaiah 55:11).

As a prophetic writer, I don't claim to be an expert on matters of government or world politics. I don't write about these things from my human intellect or desire. I write only because God has commanded me to write. I write only what He tells me to write. Some have heard me say that I am indeed a *ghost* writer for God. More perfectly said, I am a *Holy Ghost* writer. I write whatever God the Father, the Son and the Holy Ghost give me to speak. It's God's voice and God's message. Period. I have no other agenda.

It is at the prompting and urging of the Holy Spirit, that this latest volume of **The War Journal** was released. Will there be another volume? God only knows. It was never my desire to write about religion and politics in the first place, but this has been the road that the Lord has placed me on for the past twenty plus years. America, the Church, and the nations are of great importance to God, or He would not be exhorting me to keep writing on the subject. This alone should be an encouragement to many people who have the belief that God is not relevant in our generation; that He was only necessary in times of lesser technological advancements and human development. Not so! We all need God, especially in these last days. It's about to get real ugly in the world, but the Kingdom of God is advancing with power. Let *the truth* be known. God has always been relevant to our human lives, because He is the Creator. He is the one who created us. We are very important to God. He created everything and everyone in this earth for His purpose (Revelation 4:11).

It was God who saw the earth in darkness and void of form; and spoke into existence all the beauty that surrounds us. We take for granted the things that science cannot explain. Did mankind orchestrate the sun and moon to operate in their times and seasons? We take for granted, even the breath that flows through these mortal bodies. What keeps everything in this world operating? Surely it is not ourselves. Even our wisest men, have yet to discover how all of this began. Many have fought creationists who believed that God created it all. Others believe it was the Big Bang theory. Was there an explosion that caused all of this? There could have been such an event. Believe it or not, Jesus talked about an event that He witnesses, that would have caused a big bang in the universe. *"And he said unto them, I beheld Satan as lightning fall from heaven (Luke 10:18)."* Could it be possible that both the Bible and Big Bang theorist were talking about the same event? The Book of Revelation mentions a *"great star"* falling to the earth. The Book of Genesis begins talking about how God created the heavens and the earth, but then in verse two of the same chapter, says that *"the earth was without form, and void; and darkness was upon the face of the deep."* Something happened in the universe that caused the earth that God created, to become *without form and void*.

This is not a discussion about the differences between science and the Bible, but to show how closely they are linked in timing and events. Both would agree that something happened to cause the earth to be created. The Bible says that is was God who created it all, including every human being. No matter how mankind attempts to deny the existence of God in our lives, no scientist has yet been able to explain how we got here. They cannot explain why it is that every thing remains to this day. We tend to glorify that which was created instead of glorifying the Creator. Some have denied that it was God, but there are others who are now beginning to have glimpses of the Father at work in the universe. In these last days, more and more science will begin to confirm that the word of God is true. Yet, one does not have to be a science enthusiast to know that God is true. The Bible says that we are without excuse. *"Nevertheless he left not himself without witness, in that he did good, and gave us rain from heaven, and fruitful seasons, filing our hearts with food and gladness (Acts 14:17)."* God has been good to us all, yet we tend to ascribe to God the evil that happens in life. We simply don't recognize the goodness of God. Think about it.

Why do we call horrendous earthly disasters, "acts of God?" Good deeds we ascribe to men. Doing a good deed, does not make you good, especially in the sight of God. Some people do good, in order to feel better about themselves. They find someone who is lesser than themselves, and throw them a bone, and it makes them feel superior. Others do good out of a legitimate heart to help others. That makes them feel good, but that still does not make them good. There are "do good-ers" in life. There are also politicians who appear to do good in order to get your vote. Obviously *"doing good does not equate to being good."* The Bible repeatedly talks about *"there is none that doeth good."* Then there are *the fools*; those who reject the wisdom and knowledge of God. King Solomon wrote, *"The way of a fool is right in his own eyes* (Proverbs 12:15)." *"A wise man feareth, and departeth from evil: but the fool rageth and is confident (Proverbs 14:16)." "A fool despiseth his father's instruction* (Proverbs 15:5)." This is *the truth* about fools. To reject instruction and wisdom is a fool's way of living. That is why defunding the police is foolish idea being *"promoted by wicked men."*

Most people operate like fools in the world, rejecting wisdom and instruction and doing whatever they desire to do. Being good is not in their hearts. Left to our own discretion, most people would rather do their own thing, even if it hurts others. This is the nature of the "fallen" or cursed man. We are all born into the curse. That is why is it necessary to be born again. Jesus who said, *"There is none good but one, that is God* (Matthew 19:17)." If *the truth* is that God is the only one who is good, then our definition of what is good must come from Him. Think about this. We think of all the good that Jesus represented, but even Jesus didn't want anyone calling Him good. *"Goodness and being good is a holy attribute of God. Good is who He is."* Now, God can place this holy attribute upon man and He does. The Bible says that God anointed Jesus *with the Holy Ghost and with power.* This anointing enabled Jesus to go about doing good and healing all who were oppressed by the devil (Acts 10:38). The Bible says specifically why this enabled Jesus to do good. *" . . . for God was with Him."* Goodness (God) was with Jesus. God, through this anointing was empowering Jesus with His goodness.

It takes the anointing (power) of God for anyone to go about doing good, and yet mankind refuses to recognize this power deficiency in his life. He knows that he is deficient in power against the evils of this world, yet he does realize that the power he needs comes from Almighty God. Everyone wants power. That is why we strive with one another. But that is not God's way. When we strive one with another, we tear each other down rather than build one another up. We are one people under God's great earth, whether as a family, a community, a church, or a nation. We breathe the same air. We occupy the same space. Like it or not, we are all members of one another. We, in a sense are married, or covenanted together. To live in harmony with one another. Therefore, we must honor one another, in light of the Blessing of God that we desire for our lives. Don't get this twisted, if it is God's Blessing we desire to retain in our nation, then we must adhere to God's word and His ways to receive it. Before many of you offended any further, let me take a moment to explain something.

"Christianity is not a religion." It never was. It never will be in the eyes of God. He told me so Himself. Christianity was designed to be a way of living on earth with our fellowman. Somehow the Church, got it twisted. It is not a way of separating from the world, but a way of showing the world how to live the best life possible on this earth. We, the Church are to show mankind how to live days of Heaven upon the earth. We are supposed to lead mankind back to the Garden of Eden. Many of you have never heard this before. Few people are preaching it. The reason why only a few are preaching and teaching this, is because only few leaders are spending quality time with God. They are those who have a personal relationship with Jesus Christ. They know how to get into the presence of God. In that secret place (Psalm 91:1) is where God reveals His secrets. This is a serious deficiency in the Church. Moses spent forty days and forty nights with God came down the mountain with the Ten Commandments (Exodus 34:28). Jesus prayed and fasted forty days in the wilderness and *"returned in the power of the Spirit (Luke 4:1-12)."* You cannot spend quality time with God without coming out with His greatness seen on you. God has mysteries He wants to reveal to the world, through His people, concerning their lives, that of their families, their businesses, their communities and cities, even that of their nation and its leaders. God has great inventions and innovations He wants us to bring into the earth, but we must be in His presence to hear His voice.

Imagine going before God in earnest prayer, and coming out with the vaccine for dreaded viruses, even before they occur in the earth. God can and will do it, in Jesus Name. Imagine going before God again and coming out with wealth secrets that would prosper our nation to its greatest heights. We are about to see such things before Jesus comes. Beloved, the Church was never meant to conformed to this world and its way of living. We have been called to be the "salt and light," which is a better way of living through Christ. This is the role of the Church in this world, but according to the Spirit of God, *"the American Church at large, has no connection with Him."* They go to church. They pray.

51

They read the Bible, but it is all ritual, no relationship with the God they claim to serve. Therefore it is difficult for them to receive *The Spirit of Truth*, who is the Holy Spirit of God (John 16:13). He alone is assigned to lead us into all *the truth*. Sure, you can read about *the truth*, but in order for truth to manifest in your life, one must be led by the Spirit to operate in *the truth*. We will talk later in this book about the ***"Winds of God"*** that come when His Spirit breathes upon us and upon the words of the Bible. One needs the supply of the Spirit to go where God has destined us to go. He truly is the wind beneath our feet!

This absence from the Spirit of God brings us to one very important question. If the Church has disconnected itself from the Truth, how can it lead the world into *the truth*? In the absence of *the truth*, the Church has perverted the gospel of God's Kingdom and brought it down to the level of a religion. This is ***"the lowest common denominator of human understanding of God."*** The Church has devalued God and His Kingdom in the eyes of the world. For this sin alone, God will make ***"a powerful correction"*** in this season. The true gospel will be preached. Understand that God's idea of preaching includes signs and wonders following the word that is preached. That means God will magnificently demonstrate His word in the eyes of the world. This has to happen before Jesus returns to set up His throne. The world needs to be prepared for the Kingdom transition. Both the Church and the world must be able to distinguish the works of God from the works of mankind, and those of the devil. This must demonstrated before the world, and then Jesus will return.

Is God surprised that the world does not recognize Him? Not at all. If those called by His Name don't know Him, how can they present Him to the world, truthfully? If the Church is not searching for the truth about God, why should the world? Our most brilliant minds don't venture to search out who masterminded it all. Scientist call it an *"unknown."* This reminds me of when the Apostle Paul addressed the people of Athens, who made altars to various gods. They even created an altar to a god whom they did not know. Here is briefly what Paul said, when He revealed the identity of this so called "unknown" god (Acts 17:23-28). *"For as I passed by, and beheld your devotions, I found an altar with this inscription, TO THE UNKNOWN GOD. Whom therefore ye ignorantly worship, him declare I unto you. God that made the world and all things therein, seeing that he is lord of heaven and earth, dwelleth not in temples made with hands; . . . he giveth to al life, and breath, and all things; and hath made of one blood all nations of men for to dwell on all the face of the earth, and hath determined the times before appointed, and the bounds of their habitation; that they should seek the Lord, if haply they might feel after him, and find him, though he be not far from every one of us: for in him we live, and move and have our being."*

This is the reason, Almighty God commissioned me to write **The War Journal** series. God wants the world to know Him. The devil has been lying about God and His intentions since creation. God loves us. He sent Jesus to the cross to prove His love for us. God has been trying to prove His love since He created man and put him the garden of Eden. This was the Father's habitation for His earthly family. Every *good thing* God created was in the garden. Then He created man and put him in that garden to cultivate *all that goodness* (Genesis 2:15). God had only good intentions towards mankind since the very beginning. *"For I know the thoughts that I think toward you, saith the Lord, thoughts of peace, and not of evil, to give you an expected end (Jeremiah 29:11)."* This was God thoughts towards His people Israel, but they apply to every human being on earth. God created us in love for His purpose of doing good towards us. God also sent Jesus for the purpose of doing us good all the days of our lives. At His birth, a multitude of angels began praising God and saying, *"Glory to God in the highest, and on earth peace, good will toward men (Luke 2:14)."* This is God's heart towards us. Mankind has willfully turned away from God, but the Heavenly Father has never left us. He has been patiently standing by, waiting for us to return to Him. God is ever ready, continually reaching out to us in His love.

This is why Jesus commanded us to preach the gospel. The word gospel means *"good news."* Listen to this. When Jesus began His earthly ministry He came saying, *"The Spirit of the Lord is upon me, because he hath anointed me to preach the gospel to the poor; He hath sent me to heal the brokenhearted, to preach deliverance to the captives, and recovery of sight to the blind, to set at liberty them that are bruised, to preach the acceptable year of the Lord (Luke 4:18-19)."* God never intended for the gospel to be preached alone. Signs and wonders always follow the word that is preached. Anyone hearing (and believing) the anointed word of God can expect to be healed from poverty, from a broken heart, from all types of captivity, from blindness, from pain and suffering. This is good news indeed, which is why the devil fights against the preaching of the gospel. Imagine what would happen if mankind heard the gospel and everything that ailed them began to heal. They would see that God is good with only good plans for their lives. This is the intent of God through the gospel. Therefore Jesus commissioned the Church to preach the goodness of the love and grace of God. Unfortunately, many in the Church have yet to hear the gospel themselves. They may read the Bible, but have not clearly understand that those good things written, are for their lives too.

It is time to turn back to God and His original purpose for our lives. Jesus came to turn the hearts of the Jews back to their Father God. Before Jesus left the earth, He commissioned the Church to go into all the world and do the same. In Paul's speech to the Athenians, he did not identify the *Unknown God* as the God of the Jews, or the God of the Church. No. He was returning the hearts of the people back to the God who created all men and Blessed them in this earth. The Lord commissioned Paul to go preach the gospel to the Gentiles of the earth, *"To open their eyes, and turn them from darkness to light, and from the power of Satan unto God, that they may receive forgiveness of sins, and inheritance among them which are sanctified* (Acts 26:18). *"* Paul knew the amazing grace of God that transformed his life, and anointed him to preach the gospel to the Gentiles (non Jewish) of the world. He received the revelation that God has made believers *"ambassadors of Christ* (II Corinthians 5:20). *"* We have been given the ministry of reconciling our families, our friends and even people we don't know, back to God.

According to God, it is **"time out"** for political agendas. We must seek *the truth* of God for all Americans. Jesus is coming very soon, but before that happens, we will see increased dimensions of both the good and the evil. God loves America. He wants to prosper us, but we must walk in His ways. To walk any other way will only bring more destruction. There is a way that seems right to a man, but the end of that way is death (Proverbs 14:12). Jesus came to give us the abundant life (John 10:10). God is **"obligated"** to make it happen now because of the fervent prayers of the righteous. Therefore, God has **"taken over the helm of America for righteousness."** Learned and accomplished men and women will not be able to stand against Almighty God. He is taking back the United States of America for His Glory! Amen!

"Blessed is the nation whose God is the Lord."
Psalm 33:12

A Missed Opportunity Leaves An Ace In The Hole

Before we can continue in this book, one point must be made perfectly clear. According to God, *"America is not a Christian nation."* This may be a shock to many Christians who have been told otherwise, but this word came directly from the Lord Himself. He sent me on a quest to investigate the founding of this nation. In the national archives alone, there exists a wealth of information to suggest that this country was based upon Christian ideology. Our nation's history also reflects the fact that as Americans, we are a conflicted people There is evidence throughout history that we wanted God, but we also wanted our liberty to live any way we choose, under God's heaven. Take for example Francis Scott Key who wrote these powerful words in the last stanza of *The Star Spangled Banner* in 1816 during the War of 1812.[1]

O thus be it ever when free man shall stand

Between their loved homes and the war's desolation.

Blest with vict'ry and peace, may the heav'n rescued land.

Praise the Power that hath made and preserved us a nation!

Then conquer we must when our cause it is just.

And this be our motto, "In God is our Trust!"

And the star spangled banner in triumph shall wave.

O'er the land of the free and the home of the brave.

Francis Scott Key was a Maryland lawyer who owned slaves and yet he could write *"when free men shall stand."* Was Key referring to the freedom of his slaves as well? Many of our founding fathers owned slaves. Still Key and others could boldly sing calling America the *"land of the free."* What we call America's National Anthem was written during a brutal war when in that moment we realized that without God this nation would not be freed from the tyranny of England. Here is the conflict. How could they ask God to set them free, while holding others captive? The law of God's Kingdom says that whatever we sow, that is what we reap. So, if we truly wanted freedom, we should have set the slaves free. To win the war, the issue of slavery would be swept under

---

1   History.com Editors. "The Star-Spangled Banner." History.com, A&E Television Networks, 28 Sept. 2017, www.history.com/topics/19th-century/the-star-spangled-banner?li_source=LI.

the carpet until the Civil War. Key also "coined" the term *"In God is our Trust,"* it too would inspire our nation's motto *In God We Trust* [2] that was imprinted on the two cent coins during the Civil War. What's also interesting are the reasons behind our the institution of this motto. Again, we are talking about a time of brutal warfare in our nation. In 1861 Treasury Secretary Salmon P. Chase received a letter from a minister who suggested that the nation's money should have some mention that honors God. *"One fact touching our currency has hitherto been seriously overlooked. I mean the recognition of the Almighty God in some form on our coins. You are probably a Christian. What if our Republic were not shattered beyond reconstruction? Would not the antiquaries of succeeding centuries rightly reason from our past that we were a heathen nation?"* [3] Secretary Chase responded by instructing James Pollock Director of the Mint of Philadelphia to create the motto. *"Dear Sir: No nation can be strong except in the strength of God, or safe except in His defense. The trust of our people in God should be declared on our national coins."* That was then, what about now?

Francis Scott Key called America, *"the land of the free, and the home of the brave."* Today, America could be called **"the land of the bold and brazen."** It's bad enough that we have tried to take God out of our American Dream, but it's even worse to believe that we as a people have no need of God, that we have all the answers to our own issues. God has had enough of our arrogance and rebellion. We think that we are free to do as we please. Lawlessness does not make a man free. It places us in more bondage to fear. We not as free as we think we are, and we're not very brave. Americans want to stand out in the world as free and brave, but at home, we want clones of ourselves. This is the essence of fear. We have become *intolerant* of those who hold true to our Christian roots. America has a habit of calling good evil, and evil good. It's twisted (Isaiah 5:20), but it's called the norm. Our world is so corrupted that the masses think evil is an acceptable norm. Therefore, there is an intolerance for those who do not believe in their wickedness.

For example, while writing the first Volume I of **The War Journal**, I was fired from a job. I was told that it was because I was a Christian. According to the company attorney, although a male employee harassed me sexually and threatened my life, they believed that as a Christian, I

2   "U.S. Department of the Treasury." History of 'In God We Trust', 14 Aug. 2020, www.treasury.gov/about/education/pages/in-god-we-trust.aspx.
3   "U.S. Department of the Treasury." History of 'In God We Trust', 14 Aug. 2020, www.treasury.gov/about/education/pages/in-god-we-trust.aspx.

just didn't understand how men operated in the real world. Why would someone, especially an attorney say such a thing? In California there is a strong anti-Christian sentiment. Back then, it was a way to inflict harm on a Christian and get away with it politically. They didn't care that the man brought a weapon to the office to use against me. They dismissed me, escorted me out of the building like a common criminal. All I did was report the multiple instances of sexual harassment on the job. Their response indicated that as a Christian my voice did not matter in the scheme of things. The Lord told me to file my case in Federal Court. Later it was revealed that witnesses were threatened, and the security officers involved were fired, in an attempt to cover their criminal negligence. I remember the Holy Spirit asked me *"Paula, why do you think they did this?"* The only answer that came was, "Because they thought they could get away with it."

God had to remove me from California in what He called *"Sodom and Gomorrah."* I cannot tell you how many times I was called names and laughed at for being a Christian. It wasn't as if I was preaching or wearing a sign that said I was a believer. It was spiritual. Los Angeles is the only place that I have ever lived where people asked if you were Christian and if you said yes, they would rip into you with why they hate Jesus and believers. They could express their opinions openly, but they didn't care to hear what I believed. I soon learned to listen and let them ask questions. More often than not, these same people had issues with something that happened in their past. One bad experience, and they develop hatred for all things God. More than hatred, it is fear. The same thing can be seen in racism. People develop hatred based upon something that occurred in their past. Rather than finding out the truth and resolving the matter, they develop hatred towards people, things or ideas.

Again, it is hatred that stems from fear; the fear of the unknown, fear from not knowing the truth about what happened in previous situations. Wickedness is both fear and ignorance based. People think they know something that they really don't know. They really don't know because they reject even the idea of seeking out the truth. As a result *"many Americans have made intolerance of the truth a norm."* They want to make truth a matter of relevance, but according to God, *"truth is absolute."* More than that, Truth is the person of Jesus Christ (John 14:6). Without Jesus, we will never know real freedom.

Our founders to fled England to conquer this brave new land. They wanted freedom from a tyrannical government telling them how to worship. Here we are four hundred years after the Mayflower, and we find ourselves with the government restricting how Christians worship God. This is a sad state of affairs. And we expect God of the Christians to continue to bless America? This is yet another conflict of interest. Our nation was destined to be *"One nation, under God."* We were supposed to be *"indivisible."* Generations of citizens have pledged their allegiance to these ideals. Today, we, the people of the United States of America, have removed God from our destiny to forge a path of our own. Therefore we find ourselves divided into warring factions. Many of our citizens are *not free*. They are in bondage to a government run by many leaders who are *no longer brave*; leaders who caved in to popular opinion in order to get elected to office. These are weak leaders both in the Church and in government who cannot protect the people from our enemies because they are in liege with those same enemies. God calls them **"saboteurs and fools who are willing to risk the lives of Americans and the health of the American economy in order to prevent their opponent from taking office."** The issue is that they think they are going against a person, but they are actually going against God, and many of these leaders don't care. They have belittled Christianity and the power of Jesus largely because the Church has not been a good witness of our Lord. Therefore the nation's leaders are pushing to separate from God and move towards their own way of governing. As a result, the people are suffering.

The Bible says that when the righteous are in authority the people rejoice (Proverbs 29:2). Why is that? Righteous leaders promote godly justice. Wicked rulers legislate so that men can sin. For instance, abortion may be legal, but God's justice requires blood to be shed for the payment of shedding *innocent blood*. The unborn are innocent. Our land is *polluted with the blood of the innocent*. As the Bible says, *"Therefore the wrath of the Lord is kindled"* against us (Psalm 106:37-40). Thus says the Lord, **"America needs to repent."** That means changing our position and direction concerning abortion, if not, there were will be much blood shed in our land. Consider the words of the Declaration of Independence. *"We hold these truths to be self-evident, that all men are created equal, that they are endowed by their Creator with certain unalienable Rights, that among these are Life, Liberty and the pursuit* *of Happiness."*[4] Notice how the founders began by establishing what they call *truths, self-evident truths,* in other words, obvious truths. First of all, that all men are created equal. We already said that God is no respecter of persons. Even those who choose Christ are told that there is no longer *"Jew nor Greek* [Non-Jew]*, there is neither bond* [slave] *nor free, there is neither male or female* (Galatians 3:28).*"* In Christ, we are all one, no barriers, no schisms. We are One Body of Christ, all members being equal in rights and endowment, but each having its own function; *"fitly joined together"* and knitted together so that we can live one to another by that which every joint supplies (Ephesians 4:16).

Listen up America. God teaches that we need one another, whether young or old, rich or poor, Black or White, male or female. We were created by our Creator to live together in earth, and in this very nation. Our forefathers knew that someday there would be people of different nations coming to these shores. They established everyone would have *unalienable rights* to among other things, *life, liberty and the pursuit of happiness.* Again, the founders of the Declaration of Independence believed that only the Creator could give us rights to life, liberty and the pursuit of happiness, and that these rights could not be taken away from us. This is a strong statement. These rights come from God for the benefit of every human being, regardless of stature. These rights are obvious and understood to be in perpetuity. Abortion takes way the rights of the unborn. Where is their defense for the right to life, liberty and the pursuit of happiness? We are a nation full of hypocrisy. What God gives, no man can take away without incurring the wrath of God. According to the Lord, ***"Payday has come. Repent America Repent."***

God wants to heal this nation. How can God heal a nation that removes itself from its very foundations to sacrifice their young? The nation's only direction is to fall. We are a conflicted nation. How could we have fallen so far that we have allowed our courts and law makers to create unjust laws that divide our nation and pit brother against brother. If America were to be presented before a court of public opinion, we, as a nation could be convicted of fraudulent claims and breach of contract. We claim to be *united*, yet we operate in *division*. We claim to be the *home of the brave*, and yet our courts and leadership wimp out at every group that claims to be disenfranchised in this nation. Rather than mak-

4   "Declaration of Independence: A Transcription." National Archives and Records Administration, National Archives and Records Administration, www.archives. gov/founding-docs/declaration-transcript.

ing them strong, we weaken them by labeling them not as American, but as a *subcategory* of American, not even a subcategory, but more like a *substandard* form of an American. People are not simply American, but our government has required us to label ourselves as Black American, or Hispanic American, Asian American, even LGTBQ American, These labels do not denote privileges, but *substandard* labels that signify that somehow these people are not quite up to the *full* American label. Therefore, they are called something more palatable for the masses to consume. We have even allowed our courts to change laws to cater to special interest groups, giving them special privileges under the law, while sorely restricting the liberty of others, and nullifying the power of their voting privileges. Any time the courts of a nation can overturn what the people have voted, something is seriously wrong with the system. No longer is this a government by the people. Instead it becomes a government ruled by the courts. No longer do we recognized *all men,* as being *equal.* The power seems to rest in the hands of those who rule the courts. In our attempts to accommodate the special interest groups, the government has alienated the masses.

That is the government, but where is the Church of Jesus Christ? The government has attempted to silence the Church citing offences stemming from the teachings of Jesus Christ. There has been a gross misinterpretation of scripture. Jesus is only offensive to religion and evil doers (John 3:19). Obviously not all sinners want to know the truth. They will continue to sin. BUT, in the Church religion is a sin against God. Religion is offensive even to Jesus Christ Himself. Jesus called religious rulers, hypocrites (Matthew 23:15) and children of the devil (John 8:44). The Holy Spirit said, ***"Religion is the number one reason Christianity is rejected in America. Religion alone is sending people to hell."*** Religion is a ***"two-headed devil. It repels the unbeliever while luring the believer away from the sacrifice of Jesus Christ, into their own self-righteousness."***

When people think about Jesus Christ, they automatically think religion. Christianity was never meant to be a religion. It is a way of living. That is how Jesus taught the Kingdom. It is also how the apostles taught. They called it, *"that [the] way* (Acts 19:23, 24:14)*,"* signifying the way of God to walk in this earth. The Blessing of the Lord comes upon those who walk in His ways (Deuteronomy 28:9). Jesus is our example to follow. He obediently walked in the ways of His Father, and is Blessed forever (Romans 9:5). Many have been offended by Jesus saying that He was *the Way, the Truth and the Life* (John 14:6). It is important to understand that Jesus never said that He was the Way to the Church, or the Way to religion, and yet that is what we predominately see in Christianity in America. Jesus came and demonstrated that He was the only way to God.

Some people are very offended by that saying, and yet no one has been able to prove Him wrong. Even those who have had death experiences, come back describing Jesus as the Way. Those who are offended, will have to remain offended, until they are willing to prove the Lord wrong. Now, if they decide to go after Christians to persecute and discredit them, then God may just step in and make Himself known to you directly. The Bible tells on a man named Saul who went around persecuting Christians and having them put to death. One day God knocked Saul off of his high horse, blinded and converted him (Acts 9). God not only transformed the man's life. He changed his name Saul to Paul, and he became one of the most prolific apostles of our Lord Jesus Christ. On that note, God welcomes anyone to step forward and search the Truth. You will find Him if you seriously seek Him with all our heart (Jeremiah 29:13).

The hope for America can only be found in Jesus Christ. It won't be found in a politician nor in a political party. It cannot be found in our media, nor the market place. Our hope comes from the *Holy* God who sees all and knows all, even things this earth has not yet seen. Here is what God says about where America is headed, if the people don't repent. It begins with *vision* the Lord gave me. In this *vision, it seemed like two video tracks were playing, maybe even a double vision in which I saw two scenarios playing at the same time. In each scenario there was a single train running on a track. Each train was carrying a specific group of people. Each track represented a way of being and living in this life. On one track, I saw a train carrying people operating as the world does, everyone doing their own thing. They were following the ways of what they heard in the media or what they had seen their families do, or what the culture was telling them. They were on the train the track of everyday life. On the other track, I saw a train carrying people who were hearing the voice of God operating based upon what God was saying. These people did what God told them to do. They spoke what God spoke.* I heard God speaking things, and things happened. I heard

God telling things to move, and things moved. He said, *"Let there be . . ." And, whatever He called by name, came forth. It happened. I heard God speak abundance. Abundant came forth. I heard God speak health and deliverance. Health and deliverance came forth in the earth. All of this happened on this one train track which God called "Life And Abundance." God called the other track, "Everyday Life In America." People were shooting. They were killing. They were deceiving. The Word of God was being preached, but no one on that train was listening. They were just going on with life as usual in America. Then the Lord showed that down the track was something that looked like a stone wall. This same stone wall appeared to be on both tracks on which either train ran. It was not only on both tracks, but also at the same location and position on each track. However something was different about how that stone wall appeared. On the track called, "Everyday Life In America" no one seemed to notice that the stone wall had no opening. The train was moving at a fast pace and was about to hit this wall. On the other track called, "Life And Abundance," the train was moving rapidly to the same spot on its track, but there was an opening in the stone wall. There appeared a tunnel that allowed the train to pass straight-through in safety.* Here is how the Lord explained this vision. He said that the *stone wall*, is Jesus Christ. To those who believe, He is precious, but to those who choose disobedience, Jesus is *"a stone of stumbling and a rock of offence* (I Peter 2:7-8). *"* There are people in America, even in the Church, who are offended by Jesus because they don't want to change how they live. Regardless of what they wanted, the train of *"Everyday Life In America"* was headed for destruction. These are the people who live according to what they see, how they feel or how they think. In their minds, they believe their way is right, but again, that there is a way that seems right to a man, but the end of which is death. This train has no choice but to crash into the very thing that offends them. In this vision, the train on the track of *"Everyday Life In America"* hit the *stonewall* and derailed sharply. Everyone on this train died. The other train on the track of *"Life And Abundance,"* passed thru the *stonewall* because there was an opening. All of its passengers were safe.

The *two train tracks* in this vision are the paths we travel in live because of the different words we choose to believe. Notice that God only sees two paths in this life. We are either with Him, or against Him. There is no such thing as "doing our own thing" with God. There is no middle ground. Even Christians grapple at this saying. They want to go to Heaven, but only if they can live anyway these choose in this world.

Therefore, even those who say they are Christians, are not really part of God's family at all. They mentally agreed with God, but their hearts were never convert. Jesus refers to them, as the *"unbelieving* (Revelation 21:8)*,"* or *"the tare among the wheat* (Matthew 13:25)*."* Not everyone who claims to be Christian is a Christian. According to God, the Church in America is just another ***"Tower of Babel."*** In other words, the Church is not even Christian. It is man-made, not Christ *like*. Jesus said that His Church is built upon the Rock, which is revelation knowledge from the Father in Heaven, not that of flesh and blood (Matthew 16:17-18). Most churches in America are built on religion.

There are so many religious people in the Church. These are those who perform the rituals and go through the motions, but they have no relationship with God. They prefer the praises of men over the praises of God. They take heed to the words of men rather than the words of God. Jesus would label them as those who praise Him with their mouths, *"but their hearts are far from Him* (Matthew 15:8)*."* Unfortunately, these are the ones who use the Bible to offend nonbelievers. They do so because the love of God is not in them. Jesus said that Christians are to be identified by their love. If someone claims to be a believer in Jesus Christ and does not express the love of God towards others, especially towards unbelievers, something is wrong. The love of God is either blocked, or He is not in them at all! In either case, these people are also on the track that leads to death, if they have never received Jesus in their hearts. Since those who are on track of ***"Life And Abundance,"*** have received Jesus and obey Him, they will go thru this life with God's Grace. They will prosper and flourish in this life, even in times of trouble.

The Lord said, He sent His Word ***"to save the world from destruction."*** In America, most people are not trying to get on the track that leads to life, because they don't see the value in it. Neither do they see the *stone wall* set before them that will alter the course of their lives and destinies for all eternity. Unfortunately, no one can see the truth of God's plan for their lives, unless they come to Him. Jesus said one must be *"born again* (John 3:3)*,"* to be able to see the things of the Kingdom. No one can come to God and be born again, unless the Spirit of God draws them (John 6:44). This is why the prayers of the saints are vital. We are commanded to pray *for all men*, and especially for those in authority (I Timothy 2:1-2). If the people of God don't pray as commanded, God cannot do His part to save the nations and change the world.

So, what is God saying will happen in America? The Lord says, *"it is time for the crash."* There is no way of stopping the trains. It will crash and very soon. The only option is for people to hear the truth and de-board the train of *"Everyday Life In America."* Mind you that what God is saying can be avoided to a great degree if the people of America would repent or as God says, *"If my people, which are called by my name, shall humble themselves, and pray, and seek my face, and turn from their wicked ways; then will I hear from heaven, and will forgive their sin, and will heal their land* (II Chronicles 7:14).*"*

If the Church would repent, then they could demonstrate the love of God to the nation. What gets their attention, is the love of God expressed through God's people. What gets people's attention are the signs, wonders and miracles that accompany those who speak the word of God. What gets their attention is speaking an encouraging word when the Holy Spirit speaks through God's people. These are the supernatural characteristics of God that help us and others in this life. It is the job of the Holy Spirit to reveal truth to our lives. He is after all the Spirit of Truth, and yet many Christians in America have been taught to deny His existence in the world today. Jesus could not live in this world without the Holy Spirit. What makes Christians think they can? They are deceived. God's people are being destroyed because of a lack of knowledge (Hosea 4:6), not because it isn't available to them. His people often reject knowledge. Unless they return to God, He will reject them too. They may still go to Heaven, but they won't be able to receive the full inheritance that Jesus died and resurrected to give them.

Jesus came to give us life, but we have a choice to make. *"I have set before you life and death, blessing and cursing: therefore choose life, that both thou and thy seed may live* (Deuteronomy 30:19).*"* Since people have rejected life, the only thing that's left is death. The Church is much to blame. They have been teaching about going to Heaven. Little is being said about how to live the abundant life in God's Kingdom here on earth. Jesus spoke about ruling and reigning upon the earth. God's plan was always about bringing Heaven to earth (Revelation 21:2). The job of the Church is to prepare the world for Jesus' return, by preaching, teaching and demonstrating the power of the gospel of the Kingdom. We are to show the world how the Kingdom works. For decades, the Church has taught about getting out of this evil world before the "great tribulation." They are looking for Jesus to return and rapture them to safety in Heaven. It will not happen as soon as they would like. There is much work to be done before Jesus can return. We still have to rescue many from destruction. God is giving them a chance to get into the Kingdom before the end comes. <u>Then</u> Jesus is going to come back. *"For the Lord himself shall descend from heaven with a shout, with the voice of the archangel, and with the trump of God: and the dead in Christ shall rise first: Then we which are alive and remain shall be caught up together with them in the clouds, to meet the Lord in the air: and so shall we ever be with the Lord* (I Thessalonians 4:16-17). *"* The Church is suppose to prepare the world for this transition. The vision of *The Two Trains* is a sign of things to come. As Heaven approaches the earth, there will be more destruction for those who rebel, and more *grace and abundance* for those who obey God's word. The Lord further explained that when America crashes, the Church will think that Jesus is about to break through the clouds in the glory of His Father. It will not happen like that. Not yet. For Jesus to return, the gospel has to be preached and demonstrated to every creature.

America has yet to hear the true gospel message. There are some leaders in the Church who believe that America will be destroyed. Like the prophet Jonah, they refuse to preach the truth to our nation. It is as if they believe America is too wicked to be saved, yet they know the mercy of God towards sinners. Some leaders have preached that America would be destroyed. *"Not so,"* says God. *"I have a covenant to fulfill with the remnant of believers who stand in faith for the deliverance of the United States. It is for them alone, that I spare this nation until the Gospel, the True Gospel is preached in America, with signs and wonders to follow. America must be saved. It shall not be utterly destroyed,"* says God. *"I will spare a remnant who will demonstrate my power to the world . . . and then the end shall come and my son will return to reclaim His earthly throne."*

We are at the end of the final season on earth before Jesus returns. This is a *"kairos"* moment in time. This is God's appointed season for all prophecy to come to pass. God has set all things in motion to bring about His will, no matter what mankind chooses to do on its own. Certainly, *"America must be saved,"* because God has a remnant of believers who say and do whatever God requires. They will walk in the ways of their God and do great exploits to demonstrate His love in America

65

and in the nations of the earth. According to God, America has what He called *"an ace in the hole."* He said that America has a *"covenant with Him."* As the Bible says, God keeps His covenant forever, even for a thousand generations (Psalm 105:8). You might ask, "What is a covenant?" A covenant is a contractual agreement between two parties. God's covenant was initially made between the Father and His Son Jesus Christ, for the restoration of mankind. This covenant was made before the foundation of the world. That means, that God had a solution for sin, even before Adam was created. That covenant was sealed in the Blood of Jesus. When one receives Jesus as Lord, he or she comes under the provision and protection of God's covenant. The Bible says that God's covenant cannot be broken. It will serve God's purpose and greatly benefit the nations in these last days.

America's covenant with God was made even before we were established as a nation. There one historical document that indicates that America's founders made covenant with God on behalf of this nation. The Pilgrims who arrived on our shores in 1620, made covenant with Almighty God. A translation of **The Mayflower Compact** reads as follows:

"In The Name of God, Amen. We whose names are underwritten, the loyal subjects of our Dread Sovereign Lord King James, by the Grace of God of Great Britain, France, and Ireland, King Defender of the Faith, etc. Having Undertaken, For the Glory of God And Advancement of the Christian Faith And Honor of our King and Country, A Voyage to Plant the First Colony in the Northern Parts of Virginia, Do by These Presents Solemnly and Mutually In the Presence of God and One of Another, Covenant and Combine ourselves together into a Civil Body Politic . . ." [5] These Pilgrims came here to advance the Christian faith for the glory of God on this soil. There were also others who came to the New World for other reasons, but *once the compact was made, God's purpose became this nation's purpose.*

America cannot continually defy the laws of God and not suffer the consequences under the covenant. God will uphold His covenant with His people, no matter who's in the White House. I don't think you heard me. God's covenant promises are not dependent upon who holds political office in a nation. It is according to what we do that we receive. We

5   "Mayflower Compact." *MayflowerHistory.com,* N.p., n.d. Web

must stand on our covenant. If you are depending more on the news reports and on what the politicians say more than what God is offering, then you have stepped outside of the covenant. If you want what God has, you must cast down all arguments and conversations that exalt themselves against what God is saying. In other words, measure every word you hear by the word of God. I don't care who is speaking. If their words do not line up with what God is saying, ignore them. Our words are covenant. We are in the days, in which *we shall have whatsoever we say*. America, like all covenant nations, must honor God. Fearing (honoring) God and working righteousness (His ways) is what's required for a people to be accepted with God (Acts 10:35). Righteousness is not according to our standards, but according to what God prescribes in the Bible. We will be judged both individually and as a nation, not by what we think, nor by what the opinion polls or the media says, but by what God says in His word. Jesus is King of kings. Jesus is Lord of lords, now and forever. I decree and declare, that no matter what happens in the nation, *"that at the name of Jesus every knee shall bow, of things in heaven, and things in earth, and things under the earth; and that every tongue should confess that Jesus Christ is Lord, to the glory of God the Father (Philippians 2:10-11)."* Every knee will eventually bow to Jesus Christ. Listen. God won't send you to hell because you are gay. He won't send you to hell because you had an abortion. God understands that people that people sin. That is why He sent Jesus to the earth. Mankind is dying in a sea of sin. Jesus is like a *"life preserver."* If you don't take the *"life preserver"* you will die in your sin. Period. The only thing that will send you to hell, is the rejection of what Jesus is offering. Reject Him or receive Him, we all will bow before Him either in this life, or in that which is to come. God is real. Heaven is real, but so is hell. I've walked through hell, and believe me, it is no place for human beings. Therefore, I decree and declare what God says about the United States, *"America shall be saved!"* God has a remnant of believers in this and every nation, who will not bow their knee to any other but the Lord Almighty. We, who humble ourselves before our God will see His Hand move mightily upon our nation, in Jesus' Name!

Surely, America missed the opportunity to become a Christian nation, but God is implementing the covenant sealed in the Blood of Jesus. The wrath of God will be poured out upon the nations before Jesus sets up His throne on the earth. There's coming a *"new sheriff in town."* The people must be made aware, for their salvation's sake. God is shaking up things in the world in preparation for the return of His Son. America cannot be caught bowing the knee to other gods, when the God of gods is arriving to judge the nations. It's also not the time for the Church to placate the world and its twisted views that oppose God.

People are dying, needlessly, in ignorance of who God is, and the power He has to change their lives for the better. We must stand on our covenant for their sake. God will uphold His covenant for the sake of the few saints that still believe. Again, this is, as the Spirit of God said, our *"ace in the hole."* The covenant must be executed by God's people in prayer and in declaration of His word. Instead of speaking the words of politicians and the media, they must take God's word and put them in their mouths. That is what our forefathers did when they chose, *"In God We Trust"* as our nation's motto. That is what happened when our nation instituted the *Pledge of Allegiance*, in which we declared America to be *"One Nation Under God."* For decades, school children recited the *Pledge* daily. It was a reminder of who we are as a people. We decreed that we were, *"Under God,"* His Blessing, His grace and His protection. *"Land of the Free?"* It is only under God can any man, woman, or child truly be free.

In America we say we are free, but many abuse our freedoms, especially the freedom of speech. We have yet to understand why God gave us a mouth. Many Americans use their mouths to hurt and slander, hate others. We may have a right of free speech, but we don't have the right to intentionally harm others. As Christians, we are taught to speak the truth in love (Ephesians 4:15), not to use our speech to hurt and destroy, but to edify and build up one another. The greatest command is love. It is the royal law of God's Kingdom (James 2:8). Jesus taught us the benefit of laying down our lives for our friends. It doesn't always mean dying physically like He did for us, but it does mean dying to ourselves, and to our desires, in order to help someone else meet their needs.

Does America have a chance at becoming the *"One Nation Under God?"* Absolutely! The nation, and the world at large is looking for something real to believe in. They are about to see the love of God in action. They will hear words of hope in these dark days and run into the Kingdom for refuge. This is the will of God for this and all nations, for all the people of the earth in these end of the last days.

God's Chosen Leaders versus The Cyrus Theory

Throughout the Bible, God has always revealed His choice for king to the prophets. God would also send the prophets to anoint kings before the people. It should be no surprise that God's prophets are still revealing His chosen leaders in our day. In fact, God revealed my assignment to the White House early in 2008 while I was working on a project in Europe. The Lord said to me, *"Your country needs you."* As soon as I heard these words, a burden for America fell upon me. The Lord began showing me that something horrendous was coming upon the nation. I also knew by what God said, that He had supernaturally equipped me to handle what was coming, otherwise He would not be sending me back to America. *My country needs me.* Hearing those words from the Lord pierced my heart with compassion for the people of America. I knew how much God loves this country and this assignment was of utmost importance to the Lord.

There was also a brief moment of sadness in my heart knowing that I had to temporarily abandon my plans overseas. God said to me several months earlier, *"There is so much work in Europe, you don't ever have to come back to America,"*[1] and yet I was being called to return. Today, I know without a doubt, that God sent me back to America *for such a time as this* (Esther 4:14). It's funny that I used those words from the story of Queen Esther. God would later show in a vision, my being dressed in Kingdom royal garments going before the President of the United States. Esther had favor and was able to turn about the annihilation of her people. I was not as fortunate. My message to the king only brought a barrage of witchcraft, death threats and even a sniper on my trail. Hey, it's all in a day's work being a prophet of Almighty God. It is a dangerous, but necessary assignment for the Kingdom. If the Lord is to move on behalf of the people, the word of God must be spoken, even if no one wants to hear it. The word is God's *"power activator"* in the earth. He is the Eternal King. Where there word of the King is, there is, and will be power (Ecclesiastes 8:4). This also presents a problem for the kings of the earth. They are not accustom to someone speak-

---

1   Matthews, Paula. "Year 2007: A Day Of Rest." *The War Journal (1999-2010) Volume I.* Los Angeles: Spirit & Life Publications, 2010. 329. Print.

ing words with power, especially when spoken with more authority and power than their own. Consequently, their pride won't always let them receive. Instead, they may strike back in retaliation. Now, if the king knows God, he will surely back down. Those who don't, will proceed in intimidation and threats to kill the messenger. Don't be surprised. The leaders of the ancient Jewish Church plotted to have Jesus killed too. They could not handle the fact that Jesus carried more weight and authority than they did, and the people knew it. *"Then gathered the chief priests and the Pharisees a council, and said, What do we? for this man doeth many miracles. If we let him thus alone, all [men] will believe on him: and the Romans shall come and take away both our place and nation* (John 11:47-48)."* Dealing with leaders, whether in government, business or the Church can sometimes be like playing the childhood game of *King of the Hill*. Receiving a prophetic word from a servant of God sometimes enrages leaders. Prophets speak God's word with His authority. It's an authority greater than any thing in the earth. Leaders may feel like they are no longer on the top of the hill. Then the object of the game becomes to knock off the one who has spoken for God. The power of God's word gives one the perception that the prophet is the *King of the Hill*. It does not matter that the prophet is only the messenger for God. They cannot see God. They only see the messenger. So, it is the messenger (the prophet) who takes the heat. This is one of the hazards of the prophet's assignment. It's not a position for wimps. When I speak for God, I take the heat for what I have spoken and written. One can speak and then walk away, but as a writer, it's like a constant wave of criticism and attacks every time someone reads what God told me to write. Sometimes attacks come from around the world, even through technology. Years ago, the Lord showed in the spirit what happens when I publish a book. It is like throwing a pass with a football, straight into the heavens high above the earth, then watching it explode and reverberate like powerful firecracker streaming down over the entire planet.

God chose me for this assignment. It was never my desire to write about politics and religion, but God had another plan. As **His Mouthpiece**, I have a duty to speak what God tells me to speak. Back in 2008, it was all about God's then choice for leadership over America, Barack Obama. Understand that I am neither pro Democrat or Republican. I am **God's Mouthpiece**. That is what God said when He called me to the Office of the Prophet in 1997. I refuse to take sides with any man or party against God. Now, I will share some things that are specific to certain leaders.

It is not to expose them, as much as it is to show the grace of God at work in our leaders. No one is perfect. Every leader has weaknesses and strengths. When they obey God, His grace makes up for what they lack. The question becomes, will they obey God for the sake of their constituents? Here is the point. Not everyone chosen for leadership over the nation wants to commit to God. Sure, they take an oath with their hand on the Bible, but their loyalties tend to be with their handlers, not even with the voters. They tend to rely on the support of those who they believe put them in office. It's not so much about the votes. It's actually about the machinery (the people and the money) that fund the campaigns to get the votes. It's all about money and power. This is why it is not wise for Christians to get involved with politics without consulting God first. None of it is without deceit, but it is the best that men can do with human wisdom.

God's wisdom is greater than human wisdom, but it can only be imparted by yielding to God. Leaders are only human. They cannot do their jobs without the support of the believer. It is the job of the Christian to be *"salt and light."* We have the added *"God-factor"* that must be injected into this world system for it to survive. During times of turmoil, we are to *seek the peace of the city*, for in doing so we will have peace (Jeremiah 29:7). We are to *pray for those in authority* so that we may live a quiet and peaceable life in all godliness and honestly (I Timothy 2:1-2). This is the will of God for the people of the earth. We are to speak what God desires for the earth. We are commanded to cast down all conversations and arguments that are opposed to what God speaks (II Corinthians 10:5). And, we don't make idols from politicians.

For example, concerning Mr. Obama, I can only speak what the Lord revealed to me. The Church at large abandoned the man once he got elected. Black folks celebrated, but forgot to keep the man in prayer. White folks were ready to secede from the union. There was also a *"racial divide"* in the Church regarding the Obama presidency. Some Church leaders were very vocal about their disapproval of Mr. Obama. Comments were veiled as a difference between Democrats and Republicans, but it soon became evident that they just didn't want a Black man in the White House. Some found it hard to believe that God would have chosen a Democrat, let alone a person of color. Unfortunately, under the presidency of Donald Trump, the Church has gone too far in the opposite direction. Many are worshipping the man because of the prophecies about his life. They praise the Christian heritage of his mother. These say nothing about President Trump's beliefs. Some have prophesied that President Trump is a modern day Cyrus. We will discuss who Cyrus was in the Bible and if it indeed symbolized the presidency of Mr. Trump. Now, there were just as many prophecies, if not more about the presidency of Barack Obama. No one mentions those prophecies, and those of us who did were not very popular with Church leaders. Mr. Obama was also prophesied to be a modern day Cyrus, but some leaders in the Church threatened the prophets not to speak. It was reported that some of these same leaders created their own prophecies about whom they wanted in the oval office.

Let me clarify one point before moving on with our discussion. God has a plan for ever person on planet Earth. *"For I know the thoughts that I think toward you, saith the LORD, thoughts of peace, and not of evil, to give you an expected end (Jeremiah 29:11)."* God has a good plan, a good future for every human being. That divine plan is revealed to us by God's Spirit (I Corinthians 2:10). For those who are not connected to God, He will send His prophetic word by messenger. God sends His word for only one purpose, to edify and Bless us. God's word may be a word of correct, but only to exhort us to obey Him. The Bible is clear about why God sends the prophets. *"He sent his word, and healed them, and delivered them from their destructions (Psalm 107:20)."* God wants to heal and restore America. How can they receive what they have not heard? How can they hear without a preacher? How can they preach except they be sent (Romans 10:14-15)? This is how the word of God is activated in the earth. It has to be revealed first to the prophets. Then it is spoken into the earth so that it may be brought to pass. It matters not whether people receive it. God's word will come to pass. It will not return to Him void. It will accomplish what He pleases (Isaiah 55:11). If we align ourselves with God's word we will also receive the benefits thereof. That was a brief note. Now, let's move on.

As American citizens, we vote. As citizens of God's Kingdom we pray and ask God how to vote. It is God who chooses leaders. Remember that God's ways and thoughts are much higher than ours (Isaiah 55:8-9). To understand what God is saying and doing in the earth, you have to come up higher. You must step into the realm of the spirit where God lives. For example. The original **War Journal** book was written and dedicated to President George W. Bush. When it came time to meet the president and give him the word from God, leaders in the Church prevented me. Several attempted to take my life. According to God, *"this is about the book"*[2] God gave me to write. Several men of God did not believe that I was qualified to write the book, nor speak to the White House as God's messenger. The message I had to deliver was about events that we see unfolding in our nation today. They had no foreknowledge of these events. It was not their call or purpose. It was mine, and yet they decided it was best to eliminate me rather than let me do my assignment.

After the 2008 Election, God had me send same message for then President Barack Obama. The message of the book was scrutinized by government leaders and dismissed as *"Christian mumbo jumbo"* that was what the Lord let me hear in the spirit. They came out of the mouth of then Secretary of State, Hillary Clinton. I also recall the Lord showing then Chief of Staff Rahm Emanuel also laughing and making light of the messages from God. This was evidence that the Obama administration had no interest in hearing from God. The Holy Spirit said that Mr. Obama *"did not take God seriously. He played the 'church game,' but that is not God. God is holy. God is not a man. He does not lie."* Still, the messages from God continued. Mr. Obama took God's word and His messengers like commoners not realizing that these were holy men and women sent to speak *the truth*. They were sent to help the president succeed in that office. He refused divine wisdom. *"A wise man feareth, and departeth from evil: but the fool rageth, and is confident* (Proverbs 14:16). *"*

According to God, America has been slowly drifting from God over the past fifty years or more. Although most leaders of the United States have called themselves Christian, few have openly confessed Jesus as Lord and espoused Christians values. I recall two presidents in my lifetime who openly professed Christ, Ronald Reagan and Jimmy Carter. Both presidents were publicly ridiculed in the media. Then there were those who claimed to be Christian, but their actions proved otherwise. Corruption has been a trend in American leadership. Here is something most people don't know. Because of our covenant with God, every leader of this nation became part of His divine plan. Surely, they come into office with their own political agenda, but *they are ministers of God for our good* (Romans 13:4). Now, if they choose not to do us good, that is

2   Matthews, Paula. "Year 2007: A Day Of Rest For The People Of God."*The War Journal (1999-2010) Volume I.* Los Angeles: Spirit & Life Publications, 2010. 317. Print.

when the judgment of God would come upon them. When we are obedient to the Lord we will do as the Bible says, *"Honour all men, love the brotherhood. Fear God, honour the king* (I Peter 2:17).*"* America is a covenant nation under God. We have a mandate from Heaven, for the benefit of the people. God has also given us freewill. Not every leader who claimed to believe in Jesus Christ, chose to follow what they heard from God. Many began with God and turned their hearts away when situations became difficult, and temptations too great. No matter who they were, and God gave me the specific names of Abraham Lincoln, Richard Nixon, Bill Clinton, George Bush, and George W. Bush, Barrack Obama or Donald Trump to name a few. They all had a human weakness that they allowed to overshadow what God desired in them. Every last one, was flawed in their own way. They were each called to the position of leadership of the United States of America, chosen by God to uphold this nation in *all godliness and honesty*, in spite of their human flaws. A look at history will prove that **"men are not chosen because they are perfect, but because they were called to duty, with all their imperfections."** Human interpretation would call it politics, but God considers **"anyone in service of our country as a minister to Almighty God."** That means they must answer to God for how they have ruled over His people. This is how God sees every political leader in any nation in which His covenant has been made.

If every political leader is a minister unto God, then how are they chosen? What is God's criteria for a leader? The Bible talks about how many are called, but few are chosen (Matthew 22:14). In other words, there is an assignment and *call* for every leader, but God does not force one to obey. It is more of an invitation to be part of His team. Those who are *chosen* are those who say *yes* to God and His way of doing things. It is a high honor to be called, but to be chosen requires walking the *"narrow"* path (Matthew 7:14). A *chosen* leader stays the course because He fears God. He also knows that he or she cannot accomplish their job without God. King Solomon was such a king. *"And now, O LORD my God, thou hast made thy servant king instead of David my father: and I [am but] a little child: I know not [how] to go out or come in. And thy servant [is] in the midst of thy people which thou hast chosen, a great people, that cannot be numbered nor counted for multitude. Give therefore thy servant an understanding heart to judge thy people, that I may discern between good and bad: for who is able to judge this thy so great a people* (I Kings 3:7-9)?*"* God was so pleased at Solomon's request that He gave the king *"a wise and understanding heart* (I Kings 3:12). " God was honored that Solomon did not ask for long life. He did not ask for riches, nor did Solomon ask for the lives of his enemies. But, because the king asked for himself *"understanding to discern judgment* (I King 3:11), " God honored him with both what the king asked for, and also both riches and honor so that *"there shall not be any among the king like unto thee all thy days* (I Kings 3:12-13). " God honors those who honor Him. *"For them that honour me I will honour, and they that despise me shall be lightly esteemed* (I Samuel 2:30). "

I want to stress what God said about Solomon not asking for the lives of his enemies. No one who gains the favor of God by wishing to defeat his opponent. It is not about "stopping Trump" or "stopping the Democrats." The Bible says that if a man's ways please the Lord, then God will make even his enemies to be at peace with him (Proverbs 16:7). Solomon had enemies. There was a fight for the throne even before the death of his father David. God chose Solomon, but David's son Adonijah declared himself to be king. The ailing King David let it be known that Solomon was to inherit the throne. Then Zadok the priest and Nathan the prophet anointed him king over Israel (I Kings 1:34). Adonijah heard that Solomon had been anointed king, he feared for his life. The king set Adonijah free. *"And Solomon said, If he will shew himself a worthy man, there shall not an hair of him fall to the earth: but if wickedness shall be found in him, he shall die. So king Solomon sent, and they brought him down from the altar. And he came and bowed himself to king Solomon: and Solomon said unto him, Go to thine house* (I Kings 1:52-53). "

The lesson of this message is to seek peace with your enemies. If the nation's political leaders would stop fighting one another and seek peace, God would honor them. If they would seek God's wisdom and purpose in the political office, God would also honor them. Take a lesson from King Solomon who wrote, *"[It is] the glory of God to conceal a thing: but the honour of kings [is] to search out a matter* (Proverbs 25:2). " God's hides solutions to the world's issues in mysteries. They are revealed to those who diligently seek Him (Hebrews 11:6). This is what Solomon did and God honored him. The king also understood that it is the honor of kings to search these mysteries out. Seek God. Don't seek to destroy your opponent, and God will honor your leadership. This is a good word for politicians and for leaders in the Church. Seek first the

Kingdom of God and His way of doing things and all things will be added to you (Matthew 6:33). It's time for the people of God to take what rightfully belongs to them. Jesus said that the kingdom of Heaven is suffering violence and the violent take it by force (Matthew 11:12). To take what is ours, all we must do is obey God. The Holy Spirit will lead us to what is truly ours. After all, it is God who promised, *"And I will make of thee a great nation, and I will bless thee, and make thy name great; and thou shalt be a blessing: And I will bless them that bless thee, and curse him that curseth thee: and in thee shall all families of the earth be blessed* (Genesis 12:2-3)."

God's people are called to bless all the families of the earth. Christianity is not about Church. Christianity is about Kingdom living. It is about a loving relationship with God and with people. We speak God's word of truth because it heals and delivers people. It blesses and prospers them. We speak God's truth in love. What we see today, is a Church steeped in politics instead of being rooted and grounded the love of God. We see a divisive Church that is pulling for one party, when God is not for either party. Hear this. God is neither a Republican nor Democrat. Both parties are working for their own interests, and that which is against God's Kingdom agenda. We don't follow men. We follow God. He will guide the hearts of men in righteousness. But, when the Church disobeys the commands of God to get someone elected, we spiritually tie the Hand of God from helping us. It does not matter to God who is in office, as long as the Church remains loyal to their God to obey Him. Then, as scripture says, *"The king's heart is in the hand of the Lord, as the rivers of water: he turneth it whithersoever he will* (Proverbs 21:1)."

The Hand of the Lord can only operate when God's people are led by His Spirit. We have to obey His voice instead of our own. We have to hear the voice of God. There is a word the Lord gave me about believers in America. It was a stern reminder of something He spoke to the ancient Jews when they demanded to have a king. God chose Israel. It was His desire to rule over them, but they demanded to have a king like all other nations. This angered God who had delivered the people out of bondage and blessed them greatly. Their desire for a king was a slap in God's face. They wanted a man, and rejected God's rulership over their lives. Nevertheless, God gave them a king. The Prophet Samuel said to them. *"If ye will fear the Lord, and serve Him, and obey His voice, and not rebel against the commandment of the Lord then shall both ye and also the king that reigneth over you continue following the Lord your God: But if ye will not obey the voice of the Lord, but rebel against the commandment of the Lord, then shall the Hand of the Lord be against you, as it was against your fathers* (I Samuel 12:14-15).*"*

Surely the people had remembered what happened when their fathers, forgot God and were turned over to their enemies as slaves. They provoked the Lord to jealousy and He removed His protection and provision from their lives. God called them *"A nation void of counsel, neither is there any understanding in them* (Deuteronomy 32:28).*"* This, after the people sacrificed and bowed to strange gods. They turned from being a holy people of God, to becoming the purveyors of idolatry and wickedness. They forgot what God had done for them, and bowed the knee to powerless gods who could not deliver them. This is what happened to their fathers. The same was about to happened to God's people because they want to bow to a man instead of bowing to Almighty God.

This passage of scripture is so fitting for America right now. ***"The people want a king."*** They don't want God telling them what to do. Samuel spoke these words to God's people and let them know how God perceived their desire for a king. *"I will call unto the Lord, and he shall send thunder and rain: that ye may see that your wickedness is great, which ye have done in the sight of the Lord, in asking you a king* (I Samuel 12:17).*"* What then? Should we not vote for a president over our nation? Oh, we vote because that is our right as citizens, but we vote accord to how God tells us to vote. Period. Now, let me clarify something. With God, it is not always about the issues on the ballot or the platform. With God, it has to do with leadership, but not what we think or see. God looks at the hearts of men and women (I Samuel 16:7). This is how He taught me to vote for a candidate for office. The Lord told me to ask, ***"Which of these candidates is Your Hand on?"*** I never vote for a party. I vote according to which person God has chosen for His purpose. Only God can give you that level of wisdom, but once that person is elected, the real work begins.

Too often Christians will vote for a person and once they are elected that is all they do concerning that official. Hear this. If your prayer and vote got them elected, then it will take even more prayer to keep them operating in that office according to the will of God. When left to their own devices, men have come into the White House one way, and soon after turn yet another. They want the office, but they are not spiritually prepared to handle the invisible forces (unseen spirits of darkness) that oppose them in that office. Remember that they are *ministers of God* for righteousness. Therefore, the enemy will oppose them on every front, enticing them into unrighteousness and compromise. Political figures need much prayer. That is why the Bible tells us to pray for those who are in authority, so that we can lead *a quiet and peaceable life in all godliness and honesty*. This is a real need in the world.

We are at the end of the last days. Jesus warned, *"Take heed that no man deceive you (Matthew 24:4)."* This warning is real. Deception is all around us. No one and nothing is as it seems. One must have discernment to be able to know the false from the true. Even when people and things look good, you better ask God if it's the real deal. In our Bible story, the people wanted a king, someone who looked like them, having an appearance of everything they desired. God commanded the Prophet Samuel, *"Fill thine horn with oil, and go, and I will send thee to Jesse the Bethlehemite: for I have provided me a king among his sons* (I Samuel 16:1)."* The Prophet Samuel went to the house of Jesse, as God commanded, to anoint the new king. When the sons of Jesse appeared, Samuel saw Eliab and said, *"Surely the Lord's anointed is before him."* The Lord interrupted the prophet saying, *"Look not on his countenance, or on the height of his stature; because I have refused him: for the Lord seeth not at man seeth; for man looketh on the outward appearance, but the Lord looketh on the heart* (I Samuel 16:6-7)."* Get this, there are people who look like leaders, but God has refused them. In this story, Jesse presented seven sons. Samuel said, *"The Lord hath not chosen these* (I Samuel 16:10)."* Then Samuel asks if there was yet another son. They called in David and God said, *"Arise, anoint him: for this is he* (I Samuel 16:12)."*

David was not the epitome of a strong leader. He did not look like a king, and yet God chose him. People of God, know that in these last days, God is about to raise up leaders both in the Church, in government and in the industries of the world that don't look like leaders. They may not even talk or act like what we think a leaders should talk or act like, and yet God is will anoint them for His service. As the word says, *"God hath chosen the foolish things of the world to confound the wise; and God hath chosen the weak things of the world to confound the things which are mighty* (I Corinthians 1:27)."* Whatever God does in this earth, He does so for His glory. God wants the glory. What better way to get the glory than to choose someone to lead that does not look like a leader? David was a shepherd boy who spent much of his day tending to his father's sheep and singing praises to God. This was God's choice for a king. David didn't have a law degree from Harvard, nor Yale. He was not groomed to be head of state. David had no mentor to train him in governing God's people. He was a shepherd who knew God intimately, and whom God could trust with His people. David had a heart for God, and therefore could be trusted to rule over the people according to righteousness. Here is God's testimony concerning David. *"I have found David the son of Jesse, a man after mine own heart, which shall fulfil all my will* (Acts 13:22). *"*

Men often desire to rule over nations to glorify themselves, but no man will glory in God's presence. If they want to glory, let them glory in the Lord and in His magnificence. This is how David ruled over Israel. God honored him by raising up Jesus as Savior from this man's seed (Acts 13:23). God's Hand was upon David to make His king. This is why the Lord told me to ask before voting, **"Which of these candidates is Your Hand on?"** I always vote for the one God had chosen for that particular season. We are in this world as ambassadors of Christ. We don't live like this world. If we want what God wants, then we, the people of God must see the world as God's see it, and act accordingly. God has blessed us to be a blessing to the world. However, if we decide to go against God, we don't bring the blessing, but the curse to the world.

God allows us to have rulers in this world, but here is a warning. God spoke this over His covenant people. It still resonates for the Church today. *"Only fear the Lord, and serve Him in truth with all your heart: for consider how great things he hath done for you. But if ye shall still do wickedly, ye shall be consumed, both ye and your king* (I Samuel 12:24-25). *"* America has many idols, including rulers and leaders, but hear this! God is a jealous god (Exodus 20:5). We are to put no man before Him. How can we be *salt and light* in this world if we put a man on the throne above God? Salt is something that is added to season and preserve. How can we as Christians preserve life by following the same path as this world? How can we enlighten the world to God's way if we don't know the *Way* nor how to lead them to Him? We are called to illuminate the path of life for the world to follow. I am reminded of something that King Solomon said. *"There is an evil [which] I have seen under the sun, as an error [which] proceedeth from the ruler: Folly is set in great dignity, and the rich sit in low place. I have seen servants upon horses, and princes walking as servants upon the earth* (Ecclesiastes 10:5-7)." Christians are called to reign in this life by Christ Jesus (Romans 5:17). We have been made kings and priest of our God (Revelation 5:10). It is time to stop looking at man on the horse to rule over you. He is your servant. He does not have the answers this world needs. God alone has the answers. He wants to reveal it to His people. Beloved, it's time to look **only** to Jesus, the Author and Finisher of your faith (Hebrews 12:2). Granted, America has missed its opportunity to become a Christian nation. That time is over, yet all things are not over for this nation. God has America just where He needs them to be in order to show His glory in the earth. It may not be pretty, but it will be glorious when the God of Heaven puts His foot down in this nation. As the Lord told me recently, ***"The masses are coming, even in one day!"*** Something is about to happen in America and all the world will see it. Something so horrendous is coming that will cause the *"masses"* to run into the Kingdom for refuge. Everyone and everything that can be shaken will be shaken for God's purpose alone. Healing and deliverance will be released to the nations.

The world is suffering a "pandemic," at least that is what the world is calling it, but for God it is a ***"cleansing or purging of rebellion in this earth."*** Don't get it twisted. God did not send this virus. It was an enemy weapon sent to overthrow the United States and the 2020 Presidential Election. That is what God said months before this virus materialized. It was ***"weapon"*** deliberately created and launched to target at President Donald Trump and his administration. It was never God's plan for the Church to lift up a man. We needed to lift up Almighty God and His plan of destroying this weapon. This was not done. Instead, the Church bowed to the medical community and allowed them to determine the outcome of this virus. God spoke His word concerning this virus. Those who were praying heard God clearly, but some other word diverted the attention of many. God's people began speaking, not what God was speaking, but what the media was speaking. In the meanwhile, God's angels stood idle, awaiting for God's people to *"speak the word only,"* and the nations would be healed (Matthew 8:8). It's as though the Church of Jesus Christ at large, had forgotten God. They forgot that their place is to be the *light of the world* (Matthew 5:14). Light illuminates the darkness of mankind's understanding of what is happening in this earth. We have the Bible that tells us what is going to happen. We have the Spirit of God within us who gives us details of how to navigate through what is happening in the earth. What happened to the Church during the worldwide crisis? They panicked. Fear set in and they fled from God in fear. The Church rebelled against God and clung to the words of either the media, the medical experts, or the words of the president. None of these other words had the solution. They were reasonable suggestions coming from man's wisdom, but they proved not to be inef-fective. God alone spoke the solution, but the masses did not, nor could they hear above the fear, panic and disorder all around them. The enemy orchestrated an outright rebellion against God, against law and order, and against all authority. That devil could not have done such a thing without the permission of the Church.

Herein lies another issue God has with the Church leadership. Although many heard God's voice, some did not appropriate what they heard. Others used the word inappropriately. In particular, there were some prophetic ministers surrounding President Trump. They heard from God, but instead of standing in prayer as a Body before the Lord, they shared what God said and the president repeated it to the media. What God spoke was only for the Body to speak in prayer. When it was spoken by the president, it had no power. It was only ridiculed by the unrighteous masses. The president looked like a fool, and God was mocked world-wide. Fortunately, no one but those who could hear the voice of God knew the words of President Trump had been spoken by God. It was inappropriate for God's people to advise the White House on matters that applied only to the Kingdom.

President Trump spoke words of which he had no clear understanding, and no the power to bring them to pass. It was the job of the Church to speak the word of God and then the Lord would bring it to pass. It was a lack of understanding on all sides. It grieved the Father to hear His word being ridiculed by the media. Instead of bringing the virus to an imme-diate end, the ridicule actually perpetuated an increase in sickness and death. If Jesus is the Healer, why didn't the virus stop immediately as the Lord said? The Church did not have understanding. The Bible says to get wisdom, but in all their getting, to get understanding (Proverbs 4:7). In this case, the Church had no clear understanding, therefore the presi-dent would have gained no understanding from those spiritual advisors. Rather than standing by the president to make Him look good in public, these advisors should have stood by God and His word and reveal His goodness towards mankind. This was a missed opportunity, but this was just a rehearsal for what is to come. Perhaps the greatest oddity we have experienced in this season has been something that has been promoted by the evangelicals in the Church. There had been people close to me witnessing that many evangelical Christians were claiming that Donald Trump was God's King Cyrus from Isaiah 45, who is anointed to lead His people to rebuild the Church. As a consequence of this belief, many of these same people believe every word that comes out of the mouth of President Trump. This indeed is contrary to the scripture which reads, *"Man shall not live by bread alone, but by every word that proceeds out of the mouth of God* (Matthew 4:4).*"* President Donald Trump is not God, nor do I believe he is an oracle (speaker) for God. Mr. Trump is the head of state in this country. Since I have not personally known anyone in ministry who had a revelation from Heaven concerning the Trump, Cyrus comparison, I went to God for my own clarification.

My main concern about this analogy is that it is being promoted by only one segment of the Church. In contrast, we look at the previous administration in the White House. There was at least one prophetic voice who proclaimed that Barack Obama was God's Cyrus to lead the Church, and we know how that turned out. The only difference, in the case of Mr. Obama, the evangelicals refused to acknowledge him as a Cyrus. They refused to even acknowledge him as head of state over their own country. So, this leads us to ask two questions, 1. Who was Cyrus, and what was his role in God's Kingdom? 2. If both Obama and Trump were Cyrus types of kings, why hasn't God's Kingdom been restored in America or in the earth?

Now, if any of you had read any of **The War Journal** books, you know how God gave me a prophetic word for George W. Bush, Barack Obama, and finally for Donald Trump. I wrote what God said He had destined for their lives concerning America. This was nothing that I conjured up. I didn't care one way or another about politics or these men, other than what God said. As a prophet of God, one has to stay out of the realm of public opinion. You have to get use to being a vessel, a mouthpiece for God and for no one else. That means staying clear of media and the opinions of so called experts. I take pride in God's word above even my own thoughts and opinions. Which, when you follow God, one learns that you have no right to an opinion, if you did not purpose nor create the earth and all that dwells therein. What do I know, really? God knows everything. He knows the end of things as well as the beginnings. He created everything and everyone for His purpose. God does not need me to add my two cents worth of nothing to His glorious word. My orders are to deliver the message exactly as God spoke it to me. I don't change a thing, but try to deliver it when spoken, in the same tone in which God delivered it to me.

Here is a portion of the *prophecy* God had me deliver to President Obama on May 15, 2015. *"Are you willing to be my Cyrus in this hour, my champion of the poor and destitute; the man of the people whom I love? Or are you satisfied being a political pawn to mobilize a political party in position for the next election? Have you forgotten that it was I who placed you in office, for not one, but two terms? You have heard my voice, but have yet to follow my instructions. Don't fear what men will say or do, for the lives of millions are at stake. Step forth, for this is your call to lead the people back to their safe place in me; to bring America back to what made her great. That is why I chose you, that is why you still stand in office this day. Heed my voice. Know that I don't want anyone to experience harm, but as a holy God, I do require obedience. Obey my voice, Seek my guidance in everything and don't be afraid to obey. Be Bold. Be Brave, and I will exalt you in ways you could never imagine."* That was what God wanted Mr. Obama to know and do while in office. If he had obeyed, God would have exalted him. Now, we will learn that although Mr. Obama was called to be a Cyrus for God, he chose to go the political route instead.

Cyrus was a ruler in Persia at the time that the ancient Jews were in captivity. We know nothing about the personal life of King Cyrus. We also don't know why God chose Cyrus other than the timing of his reign. It was prophesied that the Jews would be carried away in Babylon and remain captive for seventy years. The reign of King Cyrus was at the end of the seventieth year when Persia overtook Babylon. *"And them that escaped from the sword carried he away to Babylon; where they were servants to him and his sons until the reign of the kingdom of Persia: to fulfill the word of the Lord by the mouth of Jeremiah, until the land had enjoyed her sabbaths: for as long as she lay desolate she kept sabbath, to fulfil threescore and ten years* (II Chronicles 36:17-21). *"* It would appear that God had the Persians under Cyrus' rule, to take captive those who captured the Jews. In that manner did Cyrus set God's people free from Babylonian captivity.

The question remains concerning the role of Cyrus in God's Kingdom. He was not a Jew. Cyrus was an unbeliever, a Persian. We know nothing about his beliefs except for what is written. *"Now, in the first year of Cyrus king of Persia, that the world of the Lord spoken by the mouth of Jeremiah might be accomplished, the Lord stirred up the spirit of Cyrus king of Persian, that he made a proclamation throughout all his kingdom, and put it also in writing saying, 'Thus saith Cyrus king of Persia, all the kingdoms of the earth hath the Lord God of heaven given me; and he hath charged me to build him an house in Jerusalem, which is in Judah. Who is there among you of all his people? The Lord his God be with him, and let him go up (II Chronicles 36: 22-23)."* From this passage of scripture we learn more about the purpose of God using Cyrus. It is also something to note how God works through rulers in this earth. The Bible says that *"the Lord stirred up the spirit of Cyrus."* It was God moving upon the king that caused him to be stirred up to speak the word of God to the people. The Lord did, or revealed something that arouse the heart of Cyrus to make a decree. Let's look at what Cyrus said to the people. *"All the kingdoms of the earth hath the Lord God of heaven given me; and he hath charged me to build him an house in Jerusalem (II Chronicles 36:23)."* If the Lord God of heaven charged Cyrus to build him a house, then it follows that the king either heard directly from God, or he obtained a sense of duty from God concerning building the temple. No matter what happened, God somehow got to the heart of the king and it became his mission to rebuild the house of God. Indeed the heart of King Cyrus was firmly in the Hand of the Lord and He was able to turn it as He pleased (Proverbs 21:1). This would so please God He spoke through the prophet saying, *"I am the Lord that maketh all things; that stretcheth forth the heavens alone; that spreadeth abroad the earth by myself . . . that saith of Cyrus, He is my shepherd, and shall perform all my pleasure: even saying to Jerusalem, thou shalt be built; and to the temple, the foundation shall be laid* (Isaiah 44:24-28)."

Consider that the Prophet Isaiah wrote these words about Cyrus over a hundred years before the king's birth. According to Jewish historian Flavius Josephus, Cyrus read the book of the prophecies of Isaiah, *"For this prophet said that God had spoken thus to him in a secret vision . . . This was foretold by Isaiah one hundred and forty years before the temple was demolished . . . when Cyrus read this, and admired the Divine power, an earnest desire and ambition seized upon him to ful-*

fill what was so written."[3] This is a historian's account of how God "stirred" Cyrus to rebuild the city. Josephus further records that not only did Cyrus let the people go back to rebuild Jerusalem and the temple, but He also that paid for the work to be done. This is all that we have gathered about Cyrus the king of Persia. We will discuss more about how God deals with leaders of nations, but for now, let's compare what we know about Cyrus to what we have learned about President Donald Trump so far.

It is my understanding that before He announced his candidacy for the presidency, Donald Trump called in leaders of the Church to discuss what he felt was a "call" to run for that office. This was out of the ordinary for any one running for office. It caused quite a stir with Christian leaders. It is my understanding that Mr. Trump was considering a run for the White House and requested prayer and support from the Christian community. I do recall the media reporting the droves of people entering Trump Tower in New York to meet with the prospective candidate. To the best of my knowledge those who spoke about these meetings were curious as to what Mr. Trump had to say. Some of the leaders made public comments about the meeting and seemed to believe that Mr. Trump was sincere about his candidacy and his desire to do so pleasing to God. I was not privy to what was said, or of Mr. Trump's true intent. What has been seen is the president's boldness to stand firmly for Christians and Jews. The fact that Mr. Trump as been vehemently against abortion is the heart of God. The man is not perfect, but he seems to be hearing something from, or about what God honors.

According to God, He chose Mr. Trump for a specific purpose. Here is a portion of the message God had me print in **The War Journal (1999-2010) Volume I** as an Exhortation For President Donald Trump. *"On the night of the 2016 Presidential Elections, I received a vision of the Lord placing a crown upon your head. It was then that I knew that God had chosen you for such a time as this. After the election, the Lord explained why He had chosen you to lead these United States. He said that you, Sir, were "the only candidate that would fight for the nation" against our enemies; that you would "stand for righteousness." The*

---

3   Josephus, Flavius. BOOK XI. Containing The Interval Of Two Hundred And Fifty-Three Years And Five Months.-From The First Of Cyrus To The Death Of Alexander The Great. "Chapter 1. How Cyrus, King of The Persians, Delivered The Jews Out Of Babylon To Their Country And To Build Their Temple, For Which Work He Gave Them Money". *The Complete Works Of Flavius Josephus (Illustrated) Translated By William Whiston.* Kindle ed.

Lord also said that for both you and Vice President Pence, these were more than political positions, "this is ministry," unto God."[4] From what we gathered from the actions of Mr. Trump, his tenure in office is aligning with a Cyrus. Mr. Trump does not speak, as of yet, with the power of a Cyrus, but his obedience is remarkable.

I also heard something after Mr. Obama won the 2008 Election. Here is my recollection of what I saw and heard on that day. *"As President Obama gave his acceptance speech. I heard God speaking to my heart. The first thing out of Obama's mouth was a declaration that ALL THINGS ARE POSSIBLE in America. This is what God had me stand in faith for America in the tough days and years to come. This the entire premise of this book. The President talked about healing, restoring, and reclaiming the American Dream: about all of us working together to achieve this goal. It echoed God's Kingdom message coming out of mouth of a prophet. Then Obama declared that CHANGE HAD COME TO AMERICA, and I saw in the spirit, the Hand of God realign the leadership for the country and for the church. I saw a path in the spirit, opening up what looked like a transition from Moses to Joshua; a change from people waiting for God to drop food from heaven, even murmuring and complaining about their leaders; to a mighty army eager to unite the people, equip them to slay the giants and possess what God promised."*[5]

In a Message For President Obama, the Lord explained why change was essential in America. **"The Lord promised that He was changing both religious and political leadership in America. The old guard was about power and greed at the expense of others. God promised to place in power those who had a heart of compassion to aid those who are suffering; and place in leadership, those who would use their wealth and resources to help their brothers fulfill their dreams. We need that in America now more than ever. Some would say that this is the American Dream, but God would say, that this is the core message of the Gospel of His Kingdom."**[6] People don't like change, but it is a natural part of life. The Kingdom of God is all about transforming the

4   Matthews, Paula. "Exhortation For President Trump." *The War Journal (1999-2010) Volume I.* Los Angeles: Spirit & Life Publications, 2010. 7. Print.
5   Matthews, Paula. "2008: The European Connection Defined." *The War Journal (1999-2010) Volume I.* Los Angeles: Spirit & Life Publications, 2010. 339. Print.
6   Matthews, Paula. "A Message For President Obama." *The War Journal (1999-2010) Volume I.* Los Angeles: Spirit & Life Publications, 2010. 8. Print.

lives of mankind from the curse to the Blessing. This is why Jesus came, to destroy the works of the devil and empower mankind to prosper, and do the works of God. It begins when men are born again, changed from ordinary cursed man to a Blessed man who is born of God. The purpose for this change is to glorify God, to fulfill His purpose not ours. It is for the purpose of providing proof that the gospel is true, that God did send Jesus and He is still alive today. Change also builds faith in God's word, proving that it is true. Jesus Christ was changed from God in Heaven into a man living on the earth. Then He transformed from death on earth, alive in hell to life again on earth, and ascension to Heaven. If a person is in Christ, he too is transformed into a new creature! Change!

Jesus came preaching the gospel (good news) of the Kingdom. He began His earthly ministry saying, *"The Spirit of the Lord [is] upon me, because he hath anointed me to preach the gospel to the poor; he hath sent me to heal the brokenhearted, to preach deliverance to the captives, and recovering of sight to the blind, to set at liberty them that are bruised, To preach the acceptable year of the Lord* (Luke 4:18-19). *"* This was a announcement that God was changing the lives of His people in this earth. The poor don't have to be poor any more. Change! The brokenhearted can now be healed. Change! The captives are being set free. Change! Blind eyes are opening. Change! Those who have been hurt and bruised are finally free! Change is the message of the gospel. It is the Blessing activated in the lives of human beings. The Blessing of the Lord, it makes one rich, and God adds no sorrow with it (Proverbs 10:22). The Blessing of the Lord was sent to America in order to bless all the nations of the earth.

God requires change! Therefore, God chooses men and women in leadership for the purpose of producing significant change that glorifies Him. This book covers the presidency of two men called by God for a specific time and season. Both were prophesied to be a type of Cyrus ruler, ordained by the Lord to bring change to America, to rebuild the Kingdom of God in the nation, and change lives many lives from the curse to the Blessing.

In 2008, Mr. Obama, eloquently announced God's message of change before the world. In 2016, Mr. Trump brutishly and abruptly **"maneuvered"** God's plan for change in Jerusalem and for Christianity in the world. Two types of Cyrus rulers and two different results. On the pages that follow, we will examine these and other prophetic words against what actually happened in America. These discussions will demonstrate how God deals with rulers and nations in these end-times. One thing is for sure, the kingdoms of this world are becoming the kingdoms of our Lord and of His Christ; and He shall reign for ever and ever (Revelation 11:15).

Don't get this thing twisted. What happens in America is not about political parties. Nor is it about the plots and schemes of wicked men. What happens in the United States of America, is about God's covenant with a nation and God's agenda for this season. Even while writing this book, the Lord woke me up in the wee hours of the morning saying, *"Pray for change over America."* In obedience to God, I sat up in bed and prayed for God's will to be done in America, and on earth, as it has been ordained by Heaven (Matthew 6:10). Alas, the Kingdom of God has come upon the earth. Let God be true and every man a liar (Romans 3:4).

YEAR 2011-2015:
THE BEGINNING OF TURBULENCE
Birth Pains Of The Sons Of God

Somewhere around 2010-2011, began a trend of unusual number earthquakes, hurricanes, typhoons and tsunamis, massacres and terrorist attacks worldwide. Wars increased in the Middle East, tyrannical leaders were killed. In America there were also domestic acts of terror in schools and public places like the Empire State Building and even at the Boston Marathon. Famous people got married. Other famous people died. We learned knew terms like Ebola, ISIS, Benghazi and gay marriage. Political leaders were elected, others killed. There were international hacks and national security leaks. We labeled these years *The Beginning of Turbulence*, but Jesus calls it *"the beginning of sorrows* (Matthew 24:8).*"*

These times are clearly identified in the Bible. *"Take heed that no man deceive you. For many shall come in my name, saying, I am Christ; and shall deceive many. And ye shall hear of wars and rumours of wars: see that ye be not troubled: for all [these things] must come to pass, but the end is not yet. For nation shall rise against nation, and kingdom against kingdom: and there shall be famines, and pestilences, and earthquakes, in divers places. All these are the beginning of sorrows* (Matthew 24:4-8).*"* Jesus said these were the beginning of sorrows in this earth. So it stands to reason that turbulence will increase in the years to come, but when will it end? When the Democrats take office? When Republicans take office? No! Jesus described all these sorrows in response to the question His disciples asked. *"Tell us, when shall these things be? And what shall be the sign of thy coming, and of the end of the world* (Matthew 24:3)*?"*

These happenings in the earth (turbulence), the wars and famines and earthquakes are serving their god ordained purpose. They all point to one major event. That is *the coming of Jesus Christ*, which signifies the end of the world. Jesus is coming and the powers of darkness are angry. Their hands are being forced to give up the earth, its inhabitants and all its possessions for the purposes of God. It is time out for the ways of man. We have come to the end of ourselves. God is taking it all back, and no one, no devil, can stop Him. Almighty God is ***"Unstoppable."***

Every living thing in this earth is experiencing *"birth pains"* for **the return of Jesus Christ to set up His throne on earth, to the end of the world and it's sin.** Why the turbulence? The birthing process requires a tearing, ripping, a shaking, *"a breaking forth from a place of bondage into freedom."* Adam's sin placed the entire world under bondage to the curse. The man was commanded to *"maintain and sustain"* every living thing *under the Blessing*. Remember that at creation, God blessed man saying, *"And God blessed them, and God said unto them, Be fruitful, and multiply, and replenish the earth, and subdue it: and have dominion over the fish of the sea, and over the fowl of the air, and over every living thing that moveth upon the earth (Genesis 1:28)."* When Adam sinned, the Blessing left and the curse began. It's Adam's curse that plagues mankind today. However, God sent Jesus to restore the Blessing. Fortunate for us, the work that Jesus did on that cross still holds the same power it did after the resurrection. Jesus is the same Christ now as He was then (Hebrews 13:8). Jesus is *the lamb that was slain before the foundation of the world* (Revelation 13:8). It is the amazing grace of God that Jesus died to save us, even before earth was formed.

Take note of this one thing. *God knows all things.* Almighty God created all things, and all things that exist are being upheld by the word of His power (Hebrews 1:3). Don't be deceived. It's God's game plan in operation in this earth. He created this game we call life. We can't cheat Him. We can't cheat life. We can't even win without knowing God, who is the *Master Mind* behind the plan. Listen. If life was a chess match, then God would be the consummate Chess Master, *"The Eternal Grandmaster."* He knows the end from the beginning (Isaiah 46:10). He knows our next move before we make it. God knows every thought of our hearts (Jeremiah 17:10). It's God's game. He chose the players. He created the game. We can't win unless we are on His side. The inhabitants of the earth have approached the *"endgame."* Jesus is returning soon. He is about to call *"Checkmate"* on every person on this earth. We are either with Him or against Him. So why the turbulence?

Jesus made *"His Final Move on earth"* when He resurrected from the grave with *"all power."* What can His enemies do, but kick up dust, squirm and scream, and cry foul while struggling to take back power? The devil cannot win and he knows it. So, he throws a temper tantrum. Hence, the turbulence. Often times the news headlines report the facts as they see it, but it's not the truth of what is really going on. Observing human behavior only tells you what they are doing. God reveals the motives of their hearts. He also reveals the next steps the enemy is plotting. God reveals to His people the *"News before the news,"* and when His prophets and intercessors get a hint of what's about to happen, God will prompt them to intercept the devil before he gets to execute his diabolical plan. This is the power of the sons of God in the earth. This is why Jesus came. Realize this one thing. If Adam had not sinned, this earth would have been filled with righteous men and women who lived only for God. These would have been the original sons of God in this earth.

This earth was created for the pleasure of God and His sons. Adam was to birth generations of righteous people who would rule the earth as their Father ruled in Heaven. That is why Jesus told us to pray, *"Thy kingdom come. Thy will be done in earth as it is in heaven* (Matthew 6:10). *"* Every evil thing that we see happening in the earth is about God's will coming from Heaven into the earth. We cannot escape the reality that God's will is coming to pass whether people like it or not. That is why we should not place all of our hope in what the media says, or what politicians, or even what uninformed pastors and leaders are saying. If they are not hearing from Heaven, they have no clue what is about to happen in this world.

Again, God knew that Adam would sin, even before Adam was created. Therefore, God prepared a solution for mankind before the foundation of the world. Likewise, God knew about the turbulence of our time, before the foundation of the world. He also has a solution that is coming forth, even before Jesus returns. God's plan for man is *"breaking forth"* even now. What we are witnessing in the earth is because all of creation is groaning and travailing together *"for the manifestation of the sons of God* (Romans 8:18-19). *"* God called it a *"Shaking"* that He was doing in the earth. The Lord said, *"The foundations are shaken. Be forewarned. All has been shaken!! Take refuge in My Kingdom! All has been shaken, says the Spirit of Grace."*

Everything that we knew about the world has change. This is a warning for God's people to put aside anything that would distract us. We have a race to endure and the enemy was putting things in our way to cause us to stumble. This is no ordinary shaking. This was the Hand of God picking up the entire world and shaking loose anything that was not of Him. God was moving upon the earth, especially in the Middle East. The turbulence resulted from the enemy resisting change. The sons of God are striving against unbelievers in nations around the world. *"Now is the time," says God, "To answer the cries of the righteous, the martyrs who are suffering at the hands of the enemies of God." "All is not in vain," says God. "For these cries are the travails of the birthing pains as I bring forth my Sons into the earth; the power of such will cause the heavens and the earth to be shaken. The end of which will be the fullness of my glory manifested in this earth . . . full of grace and power. So be patient and endure suffering for my sake . . . the end of which will be birthed inside of your spirit, the fullness of my power."* The sons of God were arising in the earth.

In the meanwhile, God was *"shaking"* America when He put Barack Obama back in the White House for a second term. Don't be deceived. This had very little to do with the voters. It had nothing to do with Mr. Obama's performance or lack there of. It had everything to do with God's plan for the nation. Mitt Romney challenged Obama for the candidacy, but God would not let him win for one main reason. The Lord revealed that the Romney campaign was fueled by witchcraft. In the spirit, I saw witches stand up like a mighty army surrounding Mr. Romney. God called the man *"cursed and so are those who follow him."* According to God, *"Romney thought that obtaining the White House would rid him of his 'inadequacies.' Wealth and power can't rid a person of a curse, only the power of God can do that. He needs serious deliverance. God loves him, but will not allow him to ruin America with his curse."*

At the same time, there were many evangelical leaders who were also determined to elect Romney. According to God, they were not only in agreement with witches, but also they were leading the people of God to hell.[1] America has a covenant with God. For the sake of the remnant believers in the land, He will not let a witch, or witchcraft to determine what happens at the polls. No matter what anyone tries to do to wield undue influence with the voters, God is watching. He will judge. We are a nation in covenant with God. His supernatural power is operating in our favor. Therefore, no matter what people plot do to take over this nation, or the White House, it won't prosper. God will see to it. He alone has the power to remove kings and set up kings (Daniel 2:21).

1   Matthews, Paula. "Election 2012 God Announces An Obama Win." SCRIBD, 3 Nov. 2012, www.scribd.com/document/112012864/Election-2012-God-Announces-An-Obama-Win.

In fact, I recall the Lord saying that He was *taking over the helm of America*. Which means that the nation has been on set a course to its divine destiny and man cannot stop it. Promotion comes from the Lord (Psalm 75:6-7). He puts one leader down and sets another up. Some of you are probably asking, "What about the voters?" Americans still need to vote, but God can put it on the heart of any man to vote the way He desires. In the next section, we will explore just how God toppled the enemy's plans for the 2016 Presidential Election. People were following the pollsters, but God was speaking loud and clear about His plans for the nation. As it ended up, God won.

This is not as human beings think. God's ways and His thoughts are higher than ours (Isaiah 55:8). *God is able to use anyone, at any time for any purpose He chooses.* When God decides to make a certain person a leader over His people, no one can stop it. By the same token, if God determines that someone **will not** be leader, no matter what the polls say, it won't happen. We mentioned how Solomon and Adonijah were in a battle for the throne of their father David. There was a similar battle with Saul when God anointed David as king.

Again, it was never God's plan that His people be governed by earthly kings. Earthly thrones promote servitude, adversity, and wars between kingdoms and brothers. God wanted to be King over His people, but no, they wanted a man to rule over them. So God gave them Saul. He was the people's choice. The people wanted a king they could see, someone who was good looking, with eloquent speech. God gave them Saul. It was great for a short time, but then King Saul forgot about God and **began doing his own thing**. The king violated God's commandments and he was removed from the throne. God chose David to replace Saul as king. God called David, *"a man after mine own heart, which shall fulfil all my will* (Acts 13:22).*"*

David was God's choice, but he didn't immediately ascend to the throne. The Prophet Samuel anointed David king at his father's house. It would be several years before he would reign as king. David had to flee for his life because Saul in his jealous rages plotted to kill him. After Saul's death, another one of his sons was made king over Israel. David was king over Judah. It took awhile, but David was finally made king over both Israel and Judah. The battle for the throne was hotly contested until God was satisfied (II Samuel 5:1-5). That was ancient Israel. Today is yet another story. God gave Mr. Obama four more years in the White House, but according to the Lord, President Obama *"did not fulfill the high calling of God in his assignment."* The prophecies for his White House assignment did not come to pass. Like Saul, Mr. Obama chose **to do his own thing**. Although it was his prerogative to do so, it was not the best decision for the nation. Mr. Obama turned away from God to rely on his own ideas.

Please understand that we are considered "free moral agents." True, but I cringe when I hear Christians claiming to be "free moral agents" because it nullifies the fact that they made Jesus the Lord over their lives. You can't have it both ways. Either you are your own master or Jesus is your master. Both statements cannot be true. In Christ, we are new creatures. Old things have passed away. This means that the old ways of living and being are no longer part of the equation for a life in Christ. The scripture says it best. *"For the love of Christ constraineth us; because we thus judge, that if one died for all, then were all dead: And [that] he died for all, that they which live should not henceforth live unto themselves, but unto him which died for them, and rose again* (II Corinthians 5:14-15). *"* If we are truly saved and love Christ, then we will choose not to live for ourselves, but for the One who died and resurrected for us.

The ultimate goal of Christianity is to live like Jesus. We can do as we please, but God cannot stop the consequences of our actions. The Bible true in saying, that we will reap what we sow (Galatians 6:7). It's a law that is embedded within this earth. No one can escape the harvest of bad seeds, **unless perhaps**, he or she repents and gives everything over to God. Again, the Bible says that a curse comes upon the one who relies on the strength of men, who turns away from God (Jeremiah 17:5). This is how Adam brought the curse upon the earth. God commanded Adam to do one thing and he decided to ignore what God said to do his own thing.

Throughout the Bible, there are examples of how evil came upon the people because *"every man did that which was right in his own eyes* (Judges 17:6). *"* You don't even have to go to the Bible. Look at planet Earth. What would happen if every person in every nation decided to overthrow all authority and do what was right in their own eyes? Chaos, anarchy and all manner of evil. Again, the Bible says that there is a way that seems right to a man, but the end of that way is death.

The Apostle John wrote of Jesus, *"He was in the world, and the world was made by Him, and the world knew Him not. He came unto His own, and His own received Him not* (John 1:10-11)."* These are powerful words of truth, especially for those whom God sends into the world. God could give us the most magnificent vision for our lives and bring it to pass for the benefit of the world, yet the world won't often recognize it. I was sent from Europe to work with the White House as a "David." Here was the original prophecy. ***"The Spirit of the Lord said, "The current administration has inherited a Goliath (economic) that no previous administration has ever wanted to slay. God is sending his "David(s)" onto the field for the purpose of taking this giant's head . . . President Obama's appointment was a deliberate effort by God to place within our nation a spiritual structure to usher in the new leaders God has appointed for this hour."***

This was the plan of God for our nation, but Mr. Obama's heart changed. There is something about power that changes people, and not always for the better. The same thing happened to both King Saul and King David. They changed while seated on the throne, and the change was not good. Power and prominence brought about arrogance and pride that made these leaders change. King Saul loved David *"greatly* (I Samuel 16:21),"* but when the people began singing, *"Saul hath slain his thousands, and David his ten thousands* (I Samuel 18:7-9),"* from that day on the king *"eyed David."* Saul would have jealous rages, a demonic spirit would come upon the king and he would seek to take David's life (I Samuel 18:10-11; 19:9-10; 20:1-3).

After the death of Saul, David took the throne. When some time has pasted King David began shirking his responsibilities (II Samuel 11:1-27). When all the other kings went to battle, David stayed home. In his idleness, he finds a woman bathing and begins to lust after her. He took Bathsheba, who was the wife of Uriah, one of the king's most faithful warriors. King David conceived a child with Bathsheba. To cover up his sin, the king tried to get Uriah to sleep with his wife, but he was too loyal to David to find pleasure in a time of war. Then David sent Uriah into the heat of battle, where he was killed, and the king took Bathsheba for his wife. God was not pleased with the king, so He sent Nathan the prophet to confront David with his sin (II Samuel 12:1-24). *"And David said unto Nathan, I have sinned against the LORD. And Nathan said unto David, The LORD also hath put away thy sin; thou shalt not die."*

Here is what the Lord brought to my attention. David repented. Saul did not. He lost his life battling against God. So what about Mr. Obama? Only God knows for sure, but we remain vigilant in prayer for him and his family. Like David, we continue ahead in obedience. God will avenge us mightily. *"Vengeance is mine; I will repay, saith the Lord* (Romans 12:19)."* Like the Prophet David, we praise Almighty God who delivers us from the hands of King Saul. This is turbulence that God said was *"shaking"* the world. The people of God were stepping out in obedience. The enemy was threatening them and God stepped in. It was God who shook the foundations of the earth because he was angry at the enemy was doing to his righteous sons (Psalm 18:6-7), and rightly so.

I recall what the Bible said happened when that enemy crucified Jesus on the cross. *"Jesus, when he had cried again with a loud voice, yielded up the ghost. And, behold, the veil of the temple was rent in twain from the top to the bottom; and the earth did quake, and the rocks rent; And the graves were opened; and many bodies of the saints which slept arose, And came out of the graves after his resurrection, and went into the holy city, and appeared unto many* (Matthew 27:50-53)."*

Again, we're not hating on people. They were mere puppets for the enemy. Besides, as the Bible says we don't wrestle with flesh and blood. People are not our enemies. The devil is the enemy. We war against principalities and powers, against the spiritual rulers of the darkness of this age (Ephesians 6:12). These are the angels and demons that satan has set over the regions of the earth. Ours is a spiritual battle. It is the plan of the devil to get people to fight one another. If he can divide us. He can conquer us, or at least the devil hopes he can. God loves people, and so do believers in Christ. We understand that the battle is spiritual. People are just being used by the devil that is why they need to get saved. Then God can use them for the good of the world.

"Leadership is spiritual." The spirit of the leader will always flow down to those in that organization. We saw this in the Bible with Moses. God told him to chose seventy men to help him to minister over the people.*"I will take of the spirit which is upon thee, and will put it upon them; and they shall bear the burden of the people with thee, that thou bear it not thyself alone* (Numbers 11:17)."* This spiritual connection can also be seen in corporations and businesses. Years ago I worked for

the local phone company when the Bell System was all one corporation under AT&T. We use to identify company people as those having a "Bell shaped head." It begins with indoctrination and later it becomes habit and then spirit. In every organization, especially those that have been established for a long time, there is a spirit of that company that rests on every employee. We see this in the Church as well. It is easy to identify people by the spirit of their pastor or leaders. Some time ago, I attended a funeral service. The spirit of the apostle in charge seemed so familiar to me. It was close enough to be like family. Later on I found out that his pastor and mentor of that apostle was a close family friend I've known all my life. It is best to know people by the spirit. It is the only way to truly know who is for, or against God. It's important to be under the right leadership, if you want to prosper. Listen to God and go where He says go and you will indeed prosper. Don't just take a job. Don't just move to a new city. In fact, don't many any moves without serious prayer to God. This is for your own protection. Being the wrong place at the wrong time could be very detrimental in these last days.

Evil spirits are transferrable. Demons are always looking for a host body. All that is required is someone out of order with God. That is one of the reasons why leaders are exhorted to not be quick to lay hands on just anyone for ministry (I Timothy 5:22). Neither should you be so eager to have people lay hands on you. You don't want to be in covenant with someone else's sin. Don't let an evil-hearted person touch you without guarding you heart, or their evil could transfer to you. In choosing whom to anoint for leadership, don't choose a thief to be in charge of your finances, nor an adulterer over your couple's ministry. Some leaders are desperate for help and will choose any able-bodied person. Other leaders choose only those whom they can control. You have to hear from God and know with whom you are covenanting for service. Remember that the sons of God are those who are led by the Spirit of God (Romans 8:14). These are those who want to be in right standing with God. They can be trusted to rule over the people of God.

We also see many times in which the Bible speaks of rulers who did *"what which was evil in the sight of the LORD,"* and their actions made God's people to sin (I Kings 14:14; 22:52; II Kings 10:20; 14:24; 15:9,18,24,28; II Kings 23:15). This is also why we vote according to what God says, and not according to what men are saying. You want to be in liege with the right spirit, for the Blessing of the Lord to be upon us and our nation. Unfortunately, America has intentionally groomed leaders who allow people to sin. It's not about doing what is right. It is more of a popularity contest among who can give the people the most leverage to sin against God. Where are the grown-ups? It's as though the immature children are running the nation? This is why the role of the prophets and apostles are necessary. They exhort leadership to align with what God has ordered for quiet and peaceable living. This leads us to the most significant event, a disruption in the norm of things in the nation.

In June of 2015 Billionaire Donald Trump announced his candidacy for the White House. Almost immediately, the Lord began letting me know that Mr. Trump was His choice for the White House. My initial response was cautious, to tread lightly after God spoke to me about Mr. Trump. Experience had shown me that if God chooses to use someone who is totally out of the ordinary to do His will, that means God is begging for a showdown with the devil. It means that God has something to prove and He is about to do it *"in your face!"* He almost has to do such a thing in America because we *"obstinate"* when it comes to the things of God. This is so very much like God. As the Bible says, *"The foolishness of God is wiser than men* (I Corinthians 1:25).*"* As I said before, **"God is able to use anyone, at any time for any purpose He chooses."** When He selects a bold choice of who He uses, that usually means that God is about take down those who think they have it all in the bag. It intrigued me to learn more about what God was planning.

Mr. Trump's name came up in a conversation with another apostle who said that the Lord told him that **"Donald Trump was the leader we deserved."** Wow! Really God? Then I thought about it. Mr. Trump is the **"quintessential American."** God could not get our attention any other way than to place Mr. Trump center stage. He represents the American Dream. His brash, bold, "over the top" persona is typical of what the world would say is "American." For generations, Europeans branded us "the ugly Americans." So, why do we have a problem with President Trump? He is America and all it stands for. Now that he is president, we want him to be meek, mild and humble? Why? It's not who we are as Americans, why demand it from him? God is using the man to reveal the ugly truth about ourselves.

"Those who accuse him are doing the same, even far worse says," God. *"Those who want to expose him, will themselves be exposed. Repent now for my judgment is at hand. And I will expose every secret thing."*

To reiterate this point, the Lord reminded me in the middle of the night, of a similar prophecy in Volume I of **The War Journal**. *"The Secrets Things Belong To Me. I will expose that which is hidden in the earth; every unknown resource and bounty AND every lying scheme and plot against man in the earth: lies and plots against My People." "What was done in the dark will be brought into the Light. That which was spoken in secret closets will be shouted on rooftops. Likewise every secret plan, I will reveal to My People to make clear their inheritance. I will manifest my secret wish to bless and prosper you this day! Yes, The Secret Things Belong to Me, says God and I will reveal them all: both bad and good."*[2]

For you religious Christians who have judged Donald Trump, the man whom God called for the season. Repent! God will judge you. As the word of God says, *"For the time [is come] that judgment must begin at the house of God: and if [it] first [begin] at us, what shall the end [be] of them that obey not the gospel of God? And if the righteous scarcely be saved, where shall the ungodly and the sinner appear* (I Peter 4:17-18)?*"* I remind you that Mr. Trump gave his life to God, which means he is your brother in the Lord. Watch how you talk about him. It will come back upon you. Keep talking about the splinter in his eye, and watch what happens. You won't see it coming straight at you because of that giant sequoia in your own eye (Matthew 7:1-5). Repent!

Now, for you Black folks who are so steeped in your own culture that you cannot see the Blessing of God that is before you. The Kingdom has something for you that this world could never give you. Your divine destiny is something culture could never produce. So we had a Black President, what did you gain? Nothing! In this book, we will explore what God says about why nothing happened. He gave you the *"people's choice"* for president. God gave you a *"the smooth talking"* Black man with *"swag."* You've heard the comments. The old folks loved him because it meant that *"we have arrived."* They were so proud to have a

2   Matthews, Paula. "Year 2009: A Better Understanding Of Things To Come." *The War Journal (1999-2010) Volume I.* Los Angeles: Spirit & Life Publications, 2010. 360-361. Print.

Black president. They made the man and his family into idols, wearing the Obama family pictured on T-shirts and purses and all kinds of idol worshipping paraphernalia. These people went from worshipping God to worshipping a family. God was not pleased with you Black Christians, nor with what the Obama did in the White House.

Other people were happy to have Obama because in one person's words, *"at least we still have our government cheese."* These are the words of Black people on the streets of our cities. A Black President in the White House did not symbolize a change of conditions for Black folk. It meant, the security of keeping the party line, maintaining the "status quo," more of the "same old, same old," more poverty, fewer jobs and more welfare checks. Mr. Obama looked like you, but he **was not** for you.

Christians in general expected Mr. Obama to uplift the cause of the poor and uneducated; to break people out of poverty and into their wealthy place. Well, that was the purpose of God for the White House at that time, but Mr. Obama was opposed to doing things God's way. The man started with the right plan to prosper the nation, including raising up Black people. Mr. Obama chose to follow Mrs. Clinton and other party leaders, in order to establish his own legacy.

This was a poor decision amid all the warnings Mr. Obama received from God's servants. Our nation was heading into tragedy. God sent His David(s) to the White House with a plan to avoid disaster, but the president would not heed the warnings. He chose instead to compromise in order to help Mrs. Clinton take the White House. In fact, Mr. Obama was so sure that they had the 2016 Election in the bag, that he openly stated that he was ready to hand over the keys to Mrs. Clinton. Really, Mr. President? What about the voters? Was the Democrat's plan so well planned out that Obama felt that what happened at the ballot box was negligible? God refused to be mocked. What actually happened and why it happened, will be covered in the next section of this book, but know this, *"Pride goeth before destruction, and an haughty spirit before a fall* (Proverbs 16:18).*"* We all need to humble ourselves before God and let Him exalt us. This is God's **"Grand Finale,"** His time and His season for judgment. All of our times and seasons are in God's Hand, but a "kairos" moment is unchangeable and unstoppable. It's God's appointed season to do whatever He has predetermined for the earth. Once

God tells His prophets to declare the appointed season, the people are being warned. God has an agenda that must be fulfilled no matter what is going on in the earth, and no man can stop Him. If we fight God, we could get hurt. It is best to step aside and let God do what He desires. You can't stop Him. You cannot win going against Him.

Now, people of God, when President Obama turned against God, many of you turned with him. According to God many of you *"Christians were down right rebellious"* under the Obama administration. Some of you continued to rebel, even more under President Trump. When God gave you the king you wanted, you rebelled. Jesus is coming soon. Until then, there will be a whole lot of **shaking** going on. In fact, the **shaking** will increase the closer we get to His return. God does not want you to get hurt, but if you won't listen. So, what's the Father to do?

In a bold, *"unorthodox"* move, God chose Mr. Trump to be a *"disruptive force to shake up the status quo."* Jesus is coming. We don't have time to play around. God will be making many bold moves in these end of the last days. He chose Donald Trump on purpose. This is a sign of the times in which we live. God had said to me, years ago that He was raising up a *"New Breed"* of leadership in America. These are leaders that don't look, nor do they act or speak like traditional leaders. They are **"Bold and Radical,"** like myself. These are Kingdom leaders, *"the elect"* of God who will turn this nation and the world, upside down (Acts 17:6).

These are the sons of God who are led by the Spirit of God (Romans 8:14). God calls them *"His Trojan Horse."* They are awaiting the command of God to move out *"to over take evil territories and end the satanic war of oppression."* God has people positioned in government, in industry, in the Church, and in every sector (kosmos) of the earth. They are positioned to carry out the "great commission" of Jesus Christ when He said, *"Go ye into all the world, and preach the gospel to every creature (Mark 16:15)."*

These are the "true" sons of God whom the world is birthing through all the turbulence. These are the birth pains, the travails, and groans to bring forth God's divine plan for mankind on earth. All of creation is pushing in labor to manifest the Blessing of the Lord in this earth cursed system. The Father is hastening their appearance.

101

Here is the word of the Lord in prophecy:

"I am God. I change not. I set the stage. I choose the actors.

Those who didn't like the part, I have changed.

The performance date has been set, the venue chosen.

It's time to take center stage in this,

My Grand Finale before My Son returns."

"This is it! Take your places now!"

Says, The Faithful God,
Director of it all!

Kingdom Battle Lines Are Drawn

God has revealed His purpose to re-establish His earthly Kingdom. Some Christians expect that this would happen when Jesus returned. The Lord did His part on the cross, where it was finished. Like a mighty army, the Body of Christ is to take up where Jesus left off and occupy til He comes (Luke 19:13). God has moved upon those who are ready to become the sons of God. These are those who are led by the Spirit of God (Romans 8:14). Everyone in the Body of Christ is a child of God, but like most children, there will be a time that we must grow up in the things of God. We are expected to mature and take on the responsibilities of the Kingdom.

God's people are also heirs of the Kingdom, but the Bible says that as long as they are a children, they are no different than slaves, though they be masters of it all (Galatians 4:1). Remaining children is not God's plan for His people. It is time to grow up and become the sons of God, manifesting the signs, wonders and miracles of their Father in the earth. These are the good works that men are looking to see. These are the works in which the world will glorify our Father which is in Heaven. We mentioned in an earlier discussion about *princes walking as slaves while slave are riding upon royal horses*. Solomon called it an evil under the sun, yet, there are some who refuse to step up to the high calling in Christ. They have taken their stand against the Father. It's like Joshua said to the Children of Israel who had not received their inheritance. *"How long are ye slack to go to possess the land, which the LORD God of your fathers hath given you (Joshua 18:3)?"* It's time for the people of God to possess their inheritances in this season, even if it means facing off with the giants in the land. In the meanwhile, the devil's kids are jockeying for the power and the possessions of this world. According to God, ***"they are not even entitled to receive,"*** but that does not stop them from going after it all. They will stop at nothing, including occult powers to get what they want. The battle lines have been drawn and none draws back. God is determined to release Kingdom inheritances. The devil's kids are positioned to intercept what they see coming to the people of God. The people of God have been slow in believing that their Father has an earthly inheritance, and even slower to receive. What the

Father to do? All the inheritances must be allotted before Jesus returns. Now, many years ago, the Lord gave me a word about our inheritances. God told me how He created this earth was for His righteous children. When Adam sinned, satan took possession of what belonged to God's kids, but Jesus had bought it all back! Hallelujah! The Lord showed me the legal document that proved that Jesus has taken it all back from satan. The Lord said that the goods are being held in *"receivership,"* until the people of God claim what is rightfully theirs. When the Lord revealed the things that had my name attached to, I was determined right then, that I will not be denied what rightfully belongs to me through Jesus Christ! Paula is taking a stand against the devil to receive it all, in Jesus' Name!

God has proclaimed the word about His Kingdom **"shaking"** up the earth. Believe me, when the sons of God begin taking back what is theirs, things will definitely be shaken up! God has opened doors that no man can shut and shut other doors no man can open (Revelation 3:8). The Lord has announced that *"the sons of God are arising in the earth. They will take back the earth, its people and possessions for the Kingdom."* As the word is received by more of God's people, they will earnestly begin to pray and to walk in obedience to their Father; walking like giants upon the earth shaking everything in sight. Jesus is coming back soon. The devil knows that his time is short (Revelation 12:12). He cannot stop what God is doing. The sons of God are increasing in strength with each victory. They are taking up the power of the Blessing and rule in the midst of their enemies (Psalm 110:2). The saints continue to pray, to no avail, that the enemy relents for the sake of those who are destined for the Kingdom.

The enemy is determined to break up God's Beloved family by stirring up division. He likes to sow discord among the brethren, but that devil doesn't know everything. You see, there is something special about God being a Creator. Since He created us, He alone knows all things. Remember that God is the Master Chess player. He knows every move of every person, even that of the devil, before we make them. This gives God the advantage over the devil every time. Face it! The Father's Kingdom has come. His Will shall be done in earth as it is in Heaven, and no one can stop Him! Now, there are some Christians who signed up for the army, but they didn't really expect to fight. There were even some who heard prophecies about an *"end-time wealth transfer"* and thought

God was going to drop the loot into their hands (We will discuss more on the wealth transfer in the chapters to follow). What were they thinking? God was talking about *spoils* of a war. People don't just hand over their goods without being provoked. Anyone who becomes a Christian expecting a wonderful fairy tale experience is sadly mistaken. There is a war going on in the realm of the spirit. Jesus said that the Kingdom is suffering violence (Matthew 11:12), but God's militant army is taking it by force.

Sure the battle is the Lords, but we at least have to show up to the battle field. ***"Turncoats!"*** I heard the Lord say. God did not give us the spirit of fear, *"but of power, love and a sound mind* (II Timothy 1:7). *"* We have the power of the Holy Ghost. He gives us the boldness to do what we otherwise could not do. Some of you act as though you are more afraid of the devil than you are of God. Let me give you a scripture to open up your eyes. This is Jesus speaking to the Church. *"He that overcometh shall inherit all things; and I will be his God, and he shall be my Son. But the fearful, and unbelieving, and the abominable, and murderers, and whoremongers, and sorcerers, and idolaters, and all liars, shall have their part in the lake which burneth with fire and brimstone, which is the second death* (Revelation 21:7-8). *"* The lake of fire is not your portion as a son or daughter of God, but you can make the choice of either life or death. God will not force you to obey, but you will sorely miss out on all the goodness He has in store for you and your family.

Please understand that God always prepares a table for us in the presence of our enemies. Consider the condition of the earth. The curse is in operation all around us. The only refuge is in the Blessing of the Lord, in God's Kingdom. God is our refuge (Psalm 91). He prepares a table for us during conflict. Let me share my personal experience of a terrible battle with the enemy that wanted to end my life. Then I will share what the Lord showed me about what was going on in the spirit. [What I am about to share would ordinarily be considered ***"Kingdom classified"*** information, but the Lord for whatever reason, has told me to release this and other prophetic examples. This is grown up material, not intended for novices in spiritual warfare. Woe to the person who would use this information to launch their personal attacks on any individual(s) mentioned.] It all began with the Lord telling me to fast and pray in order to hear His voice concerning my next move. While praying, the Lord had me tearing down strongholds around me and the enemy was exposed. I don't recall the exact words I prayed, but whatever the Lord gave me, confused the enemy and they started turning on one another. It was then that the Lord showed that there was an assassin with a weapon pointed at me. This was a *"government ordered hit"* according to the Lord. It came from the office of President Obama. I mentioned that I was one of the *"David (s)"* sent to help the government according to what the Lord ordered. Mr. Obama wanted the plan, but he didn't want God to have any say in the matter. He became a type of Saul who became jealous and plotted to take my life. God initially revealed this death plot in a dream. This is a portion of that dream as it was delivered to Mr. Obama in a letter. *"It wasn't until I was awaken in the middle of the night hearing Bishop Jakes' voice, that my eyes were opened. Then in the spirit, I saw the Bishop in the Oval Room of the White House asking if you had lost your mind. I don't remember the exact words, but the Bishop told you that my death would not keep your family from being killed. It was then that I realized that I heard similar words a couple of times, some months ago. The Lord spoke directly to you saying, "If Paula dies, they all die." He was referring to your family. I didn't understand what was going on, but since I had no plans on dying anytime soon, I ignored it. Then the Lord gave me a vision of what was going on. In this vision, you were seated at your desk with chains wrapped around your hands and wrists. You were laughing, which confused me until I saw the other end of the chains. You had bound the other end of those chains to my wrists, and you were dangling my body around these deranged killers who wanted my blood and that of my girls. I asked the Lord why you would do such evil, especial being a father of two beautiful daughters. The Lord took me to the parable about a certain man who planted a vineyard. He let it out to husbandmen and went into a far country. When it became harvest season, the man sent servants to receive the fruit of the vineyard and the husbandmen beat them and sent them away with nothing. The man kept sending servants and they beat some and killed some. Then the man said, "They will reverence my son." But the husbandman said, "This is the heir; come let us kill him and the inheritance shall be ours (Mark 12:7)." Sir, I was the "son" God sent to the White House. When you saw my inheritance, you desired it for yourself."*

This was the dream as I shared with the president. I also sent copies to Bishop Jakes and several other men and women of God, urging them to pray for the president's deliverance, and for the safety of me and my family. This was a real life Saul versus David murder that was being planned in the realm of the spirit. Now, there were people around me who saw the death plots in the realm of the spirit. They were afraid that

Obama would take my life and cover it up like he did with Miriam Carey.[1] They talked about how she was shot and killed in front of her child. There were to my knowledge no news stories about this incident. I don't recall that there was any investigation. Someone passed me a link on the Internet about the woman's pastor claiming that she wasassassinated" by Mr. Obama after an alleged affair and pregnancy. Supposedly the child in the car with her at the time of the murder was Mr. Obama's child. Was there any truth to the story? Well, a few years later, the Lord called me into prayer. I saw a man in a trench coat lurking over the bed of a young child with a gun. The Lord commanded me to stop the man and cover the child in prayer. Afterwards, the Lord said it was Miriam Carey's child who was allegedly fathered by Mr. Obama. God also declared justice in this case for a Black woman whose life didn't matter enough for the authorities to seek justice. Those around me heard about this story after I shared the dream. They were fearful for my life. My situation was different. I am a woman of God on a mission from God. Whoever comes against me is coming against The One who sent me. I fear for their lives.

I don't fear for my life. I fear more for those who come against me. I have seen what God will do to those who come against *"His anointed."* As the Bible says, *"He suffered no man to do them wrong; yea, he reproved kings for their sakes; saying, Touch not mine anointed, and do my prophets no harm* (Psalm 105:14-15). *"* I've seen people plot against me one day, and end up with dying the next. I've seen people threaten my life and end up attempting to take their own life. God is not playing with people. He wants them delivered, even if it means putting His anointed out there and dangling them before the devil like bait. And, God will dare the devil to touch you. God did that to Job.

The Bible talks about how the devil was walking up and down the earth looking for someone to devour. God offered Job. *"Hast thou considered my servant Job, that there is none like him in the earth, a perfect and an upright man, one that feareth God, and escheweth evil* (Job 1:6-8)? *"* Notice that God offered up Job to the devil. Obviously God knew something about Job that the devil did not know. He didn't just hand Job over to satan. God put restrictions on what satan could do to Job. *"Behold, all that he hath is in thy power; only upon himself put not forth thine hand*

1   Matthews, Paula. "Sexual Deviance Marks The Obama Administration." Scribd, Scribd, 10 Oct. 2016, www.scribd.com/document/327117713/Sexual-Deviance-Marks-The-Obama-Administration.

(Job 1:9-12). *"* The enemy took his cattle and slew Job's servants. Then fire came down and burned up the sheep and the servants, consuming them all but one. A band of thieves stole his camels and slew his servants, again, all but one. Then a "great wins" came and destroyed the house killing his sons. All of these tragedies fell upon the life of Job. Before this story was over, Job's friends got in the mix and attempted to explain why all the tragedy was happening to him. Their conversations angered God. In the end, Job had to pray for them that God's wrath would be turned away from them. And so it was in my case. God told me to pray for the president's deliverance. The powers of darkness had taken over his heart and mind. God wanted the man freed.

Did my warfare with the president end? Not a chance. It is not just about Mr. Obama, it is about the principalities and powers of darkness that have held the White House and this nation for decades. I can tell you that the more we prayed, the more those demons raged. They began to overtake the president and his wife commencing with demonic stalking and terrorism. They both would get in the spirit and threatened me with guns. As they pointed the gun at me, that same gun would turn and shoot them. I recall the Lord telling the president that *"if he continued plotting to take my life, that the life of his wife and children will also be taken."* If he still didn't stop, God was *"going to take the lives of Joe Biden and his family."* If the president still didn't stop, God was *"going to take the lives of his staff and everyone connected to Mr. Obama."* Did he stop? No. The curse of death fell upon them all, and remains even to this day. The threats did not stop, but increased for the next several years, even encompassing the nation.

In May 2015, God had me send a strong word to the White House. It was a message of correction for the president. It came from God with a warning. If President Obama did not obey, God promised that the lives of Americans would be at stake. *"President Obama, it's time," says God. "The National Day Of Prayer Is A Political Farce, While America's Darkest Hour Is Before Her." I have humbled great rulers and mighty kings. I can and will humble you with plagues greater than those that took down Pharaoh. It is not my desire that any one is harmed, but you hold their fate in your hands. You see, I have ordained you as leader over my people of this nation. All power inherent in your office comes from me, Almighty God. I once had both your heart and your ear, but you allowed political pressures and compromises to turn your heart away from me and from my will for the people. America's greatness came from me. Don't be fooled. It is by my power that a nation stands. I love America more than you could ever know. I have a great and mighty plan for both her deliverance and for her ascension in the world, but it all depends upon you Sir."* This was the most difficult message to hear and even more difficult to deliver to any leader. Although at least one prophecy called Mr. Obama a Cyrus, God used the example of another king who did not do as God commanded. In one such message God referred to Obama by using a scripture that was spoken the King Saul, whom God dethroned. *"When thou wast little in thine own sight, wast thou not made the head* (I Samuel 15:17)*"* over *America?* What happened to President Obama?

He went from speaking "change" in his first term, to speaking "status quo" in the final term in office. When first elected Obama spoke what God spoke and the world cheered. By 2015, something drastically changed. My specific assignment was the White House. Many of us were assigned to pray for the president and speak God's will over his life. Then Mr. Obama seemed indifferent towards the increased number of police shootings. Crime in his home base of Chicago had reportedly been worse than it had been in over ten years. It was in the wake of the Trayvon Martin killing that Black Lives Matter came on the scene. Mr. Obama kept silent. When the southeast was repeatedly flooded and people lost hope. People began asking, "Where is President Obama?" He came out of hiding to reveal that he was on a family vacation. This was the end of the Obama years in the White House. Something that begin with such promise with God's support, became an utter disappointment to those of us who hoped in those glorious prophecies.

What happened that Mr. Obama caved in to political pressures? God kept showing how the president had allowed darkness to take over his soul. Many of us saw his pain and we prayed for his healing and deliverance, to no avail. There was something inside of his heart that caused him to resist the relief God was offering. Then arrogance and pride took over and Mr. Obama began acting as though God and His people were his enemies, yet we remained vigilant in prayer for the president. We never gave up that God could do a mighty work in this man's life whether in politics or not. In the realm of the spirit, President Obama changed from being a Cyrus to becoming a Saul. God had promised to send **"David(s)"** to the White House to assist President Obama. Nothing happened. The president agreed to obey God, but yet he did nothing. The more I pressed in prayer, the more that spiritual violence arose against me from the White House. It came in the form of witchcraft. The very person whom I was sent to help, the one whose life was in my hands, was plotting to take my life. This is what Jesus went through when His own people, *the lost sheep of Israel*, wanted to have Him crucified. *"Pilate saith unto them, What shall I do then with Jesus which is called Christ? They all say unto him, Let him be crucified . . . When Pilate saw that he could prevail nothing, but that rather a tumult was made, he took water, and washed his hands before the multitude, saying, I am innocent of the blood of this just person: see ye to it. Then answered all the people, and said, His blood be on us, and on our children* (Matthew 27:22-25) *."*

Jesus' assignment was to die on the cross. The enemy could not touch me. I was protected by God for my assignment. I never broke rank, even after the death threats came. This was a battle for America. It was the battle for the soul and life of a seated president and his family The stakes were too high for me to be offended. This was my duty to God, to my nation and to all of humanity. Then in November of 2015, the Lord had me send a message to President Obama urging him to repent so that the nation could be blessed once again. *"a dark spirit over took your heart, and the prophetic words from God were being received with hostility. I didn't know how far that hostility had gone until last week. I know that you have me under heavy surveillance. Nothing I do or say is private. You even have access to at least one of my bank accounts. I know that as well. None of that moves me. I work for Almighty God. Not only is he all powerful, but he is all knowing. So I am not impressed with what power you perceive to have over my life. It pales in comparison to what God has given me over you and over this nation. You Sir, are my assignment, as are the people of this nation. I am a watchful and obedient soldier of the Lord. Nothing can happen on my watch without my knowledge or my approval. Wherever God calls me, he also gives me dominion, Kingdom Dominion to Bless the land and the inhabitants thereof. That is why God sent me from Europe back to this nation. But, you Sir, have caused a curse to come upon yourself, your family and the nation. Let me remind you of what the Bible says in Jeremiah 17:5, "Cursed is the man who trusts in man and makes flesh his strength, whose heart departs from the Lord." In the prophecy the Lord gave you (May 10, 2015), he said that your heart departed because you submitted to political pressures and compromise. When you departed, you allowed the curse to operate upon yourself and upon this nation. God's plan was always to prosper you and this nation. God never left you. It was you that left God and his plan through compromise. God is calling you back into his Blessing, but you will have to repent and do things his way, despite the political pressure. Don't worry about your legacy, God has that too. Just repent and obey. God will make your name great."* There was nothing that God could say through His prophets or the angels that could get through to Mr. Obama. His stubbornness seemed to be refueled by the candidacy of Donald Trump for the White House. The president began the "Stop Trump" campaign that remains today. Now, God had already warned the president to stay out of the campaign. God further warned that if the president refused to obey and got behind the Clinton campaign, ***"millions of American lives would be at stake."*** What did Mr. Obama do? He boldly jumped into campaigning for Mrs. Clinton. The president's curse had fallen upon the people of the land. In the next section we will discuss in detail why the battle ensued. In the meanwhile, know that as long as the curse and sin is in the earth, spiritual warfare will continue. Our assignment as believers is to obey God, and take a stand against the powers of darkness and destroy the works of the devil in people's lives. We do this to save lives from destruction, and to bring the Blessing back into the earth. The devil comes to steal, kill and destroy. Jesus came to give us life and that more abundantly (John 10:10). It is our job as believers to lead people to that abundant life. When we do this, we are occupying the Kingdom on earth until Jesus comes.

Mr. Obama had drawn a battle line. I understood that the President of the United States had the power to harm me and my family, but I also knew what the word of God said (Romans 13:1-4). The powers that be *"are ordained of God." "For rulers are not a terror to good works, but to the evil."* The president is a minister of God to me, for good, not evil. Yet, evil was coming at me. This falls under the jurisdiction of the covenant. God will avenge me speedily. This I understood clearly. God also gave me peace in the situation. He showed me something that totally changed my perspective on the terror I was experiencing. The enemy was still threatening me with death, but I saw clearly that he had no power against me. Through God, I had power over the enemy. I had the power of setting the terrorist free. That is why God sent me on this particular assignment. God also gave me an open vision during the middle of the night. *I was looking at the stars and praying to the Lord. Then my spiritual eyes were wide open. The world around me was transformed*

111

*to a heavenly place. I saw a beautiful table fill the skies above me. The table was draped in a beautiful white cloth. It was covered with gold and silver cups and pretty wrapped gifts. At the center of this table were two beautiful candles stands that looked as if they reached to the heavens. This formal table looked very much like those found at wedding receptions, full of beautiful gifts. Then the Lord said, **"I have prepared a table before you in the presence of your enemies."** It was then that I knew God had a purpose for my enemies. It was as if I was standing at the victory stand to receive the gold medal after the Olympics. I won the battle over the enemy. Now he had to watch as God rewarded me before all the hosts of heaven. Indeed this was a new prospective for me.*

All of the spiritual warfare I had ever endured was all included in God's plan and purpose for my life. I thank God for my enemies. There's a scripture that is fitting, Romans 8:28. *"And we know that all things work together for good to them that love God, to them who are the called according to his purpose."* This experience of warfare me stronger and wiser than my enemies who are ever with me (Psalm 119:98). Somehow I was transformed by the renewing of my mind. My faith increased. My enemies made me stretch my faith muscles to new heights. Now I know that I can do all things through Christ, the anointing of the Holy One, that strengthens me (Philippians 4:13).

The Holy Spirit (the anointing of God) was the power that alerted me and carried me through treacherous waters. It was a supernatural transformation. It was an ambushment of the enemy much like what happened in the Bible to King Jehoshaphat (II Chronicles 20:20-25). When several kings came against them, God's people set themselves to fast and seek the Lord. They were told by the prophet to *"stand still and see the salvation of the Lord."* So they decided to send out the praisers before the army singing, *"Praise the Lord; for his mercy endureth for ever."* When they began to sing and praise, the Lord set ambushments against the enemy armies and they turned and killed one another. When God's people arrived to the battlefield it was full of dead corpses. All was left was an abundance of riches with the dead bodies which God's people stripped off for themselves. It was so much loot, that it took three days to gather all the spoil. The closer we get to Jesus' return, the more occurrences of God's supernatural power we can expect. The more we obey God, the more the devil will resist, but we win every time, if we don't give up the fight. It's not them against us. It is them against God.

It is not personal. It's Kingdom. God's Kingdom is moving mightily upon the earth, preparing for Jesus' return to set up His throne. It is the responsibility of God's people to demonstrate to the world what it is like to operate in God's Kingdom. It is not natural. God and His ways are supernatural. Not like the devil and witchcraft. They are **"knock-offs"** of the real deal. God is the Real Power, the only power that matters in this earth. In these last days God will face off with the enemy in the supernatural so that the world will know Who it is that hold All power both in heaven and in earth. This is a prophetic move of God to put things in place for a new Kingdom order in the earth. God said to **"expect transformations"** in our nation.

God's Kingdom message has always been about change. That is where God is drawing the battle line. The rulership of the nations must change. God is taking over. *"For the kingdom [is] the LORD'S: and he [is] the governor among the nations (Psalm 22:28)."* God is bringing healing and restorations to the nations. He wants all men to come into the knowledge of the truth about how much God loves us. Whatever is broken, lost, stolen or dead, God wants to restore in our lives. He initiates change to build faith in the hearts of men, especially in turbulent and uncertain times. The healing and restoration will begin in the house of God. *"Thou shalt arise, [and] have mercy upon Zion: for the time to favour her, yea, the set time, is come (Psalm 102:13)."*

The enemy has relentlessly battled against the people of God. Those who endure will *without fail recover all* (I Samuel 30:8). Those who endure are those who hold their ground against the enemy's retaliation. It's not the devil taking over. It is God taking back the world and the enemy is retaliating. The Lord showed me a brief *vision of witches going nuts pulling out all the stops against the people of God. Nothing they did was working. They were baffled.* CHANGE HAS COME! What worked before will not work in this season.

Likewise, it's not going to be church as usual for the Christian. Signs, wonders and miracles are the order of this day. Religion has drawn the battle line against God and those who choose to stay there will be lost. God is not trying to hurt people. He is going back to His way of doing things. God is a righteous judge. He plays strictly by His Book, but He is also looking at the hearts of men. There are many blocking the way to the Kingdom for others. They are not going in, which is their choice.

But, when they block the door keeping others from going in, God has a problem that will be resolved *"swiftly"* in this season. *"But woe unto you, scribes and Pharisees, hypocrites! for ye shut up the kingdom of heaven against men: for ye neither go in yourselves, neither suffer ye them that are entering to go in* (Matthew 23:13). *"* God is setting the captives free from the clutches of the enemy, no matter where they are being held. If that devil does not let them go voluntarily, God will take them down by force. This is the love of God in action.

God desires to prove his love to us. His ways of showing love are far beyond human comprehension. Be prepared to be **shaken** out of your comfort zone! His Spirit moves like a powerful wind upon those who love him. *God moves as he wills, upon whom he wills, whenever and where ever he wills.* He is desperately looking for a few good men and women who will allow the wind of His Spirit to lead them. *"Yes, there will be terrible resistance,"* says God, *"but to whomever trusts and obeys my every whim, there awaits unimaginable peace, love, joy and prosperity. Oh, you may have to venture into dangerous waters and unknown territories and uncomfortable places, but do not fear, you go not alone for I am with you to comfort and guide you all the way. So take a chance and plunge into the depths of my Spirit and experience not only a supernatural transformation in the way you look at life, but uncover the hidden treasures that have never been foreknown by men."*

This is God's challenge to each of us. He won't force us to change, but know for certain that with or without us, **supernatural transformation** is heading our way!

The Blessing Of Increase

What does it mean to increase? Is it about possessing more material goods, or gaining things of significant achievement? Is it about a job promotion, or about having more money? The answer to the question concerning increase may surprise you. We are going to look at increase from God's eyes. We will explore the original meaning of increase not according to man's standards, but according to God's word. Let us begin, at the beginning.

The Bible says that in the beginning, *"God created the heavens and the earth* (Genesis 1:1-2)*."* This verse lets us know that God created the heavens and the earth, but the next verse begins to let us know what God saw. *"And the earth was without form and void; and darkness was upon the face of the deep. And the Spirit of God moved upon the face of the waters."* The earth had no form. It had nothing in it. Darkness was all over the waters. This condition remained unchanged until the Spirit of God came on the scene. This was earth's **"null state."** When God showed up, the situation was about to change. That is why the Spirit of God was hovering over the deep. He awaiting the command of God. Once God spoke, the state of the earth began to change. *"And God said, Let there be light: and there was light* (Genesis 1:3)*."* This was increase coming upon the earth.

With everything that God commanded to come forth in the earth, He was commanding increase. Within seven days, the earth went from a dark and empty wasteland to a beautiful planet filled with color and animals and fish and fowl. *"And God saw every thing that he had made, and, behold, it was very good* (Genesis 1:31)*."* Not only did God increase the earth, but He also made everything to increase *"after his kind, whose seed is in itself . . .* (Genesis 1:11)*."* Everything God created, had within itself a seed, so that it could increase and produce more of its kind. So, He not only increased the earth, but God created all creation with the ability within itself to produce increase.

The last creation God made was mankind, whom He created in His own likeness and image. *"And God said, Let us make man in our image, after our likeness: and let them have dominion . . .* (Genesis 1:26). *"* God created man in his own image This is a mighty statement about how God created us. We look like God? How could this be? Look around. There are tall humans, short humans, male and female, humans of various sizes, shapes and forms. How is it possible that we look like God? It's not so much the specifics of our form that is like God, but the content, or ***"stuff from which we were made."***

God formed man from the dust of the ground, from dirt. Then He breathed His breath into the nostrils of man, and man became a living soul (Genesis 2:7). These dirt bodies were empty shells until God breathed into us *the breath of life.* Something that was inanimate suddenly became human. *"In the image of God created he him, male and female created he them* (Genesis 1:27). *"* This is increase. Dirt became fruitful in the Hands of God. Mankind increased with the increase (the Breath) of God (Colossians 2:19). The <u>real us</u>, that spiritual [breath] is just like God. It is the ***"God stuff from which we were made."***

Then the Lord commanded the dirt man and woman, to go forth in the earth, replicating God. Note that the seed to produce after their own kind, was also within them. Therefore they could fulfill the Blessing that God spoke over them saying, *"Be fruitful, and multiply, and replenish the earth, and subdue it: and have dominion . . .* (Genesis 1:28). *"* In other words, God was saying, as He made the dirt fruitful and multiplied its usefulness, do the same with all the earth. To the man God was saying, ***"Imitate Me."*** God didn't just make man in His likeness and image so that we would look good upon the earth. No! He made us that way so we could become ***"co-creators"*** with Him in bringing forth His will in the earth as it is in Heaven (Matthew 6:10). ***"Mankind was created for increase."*** We were created to look like God and to operate like Him in this earth. That means that Adam and Eve were in every way just like God. They looked like God. They spoke like God. They acted like God, walking in dominion upon the earth. They were the prototype for mankind. This is really something to wrap your head around, but this was God's original plan His human creation. Hang on to your hats and buckle your seat belts, we are about to boldly go where most Christians have never gone before.

116

By now, we all know how the story goes. Adam sinned and the curse came upon the earth. Pause. Even after the curse, God still wanted mankind to operate like Him. He never change His original plan for mankind. It is still God's plan for us today. Are you still breathing? How does one go from sinful man to operating like God? Or, put it this way. How can man go from operating like the devil in sin, to operating like God in righteousness? God had the perfect plan at Creation, but it would seem that sin flipped the script. Not so! Remember that Jesus was the Lamb slain before the foundation of the world. This was a pre-production move on the part of God. He knew Adam would sin, and wrote Jesus' sacrifice into the script. Sin was a minor issue for God. He wanted to stay on script with the Blessing; for mankind to operate like Him and producing what Heaven wants upon the earth. Salvation was written into God's original script. Men would receive salvation and become a new creature that is *"spiritually reconfigured"* to operate like God. Hence, mankind would be restored to their original *"co-creator"* position. *"For we are his workmanship, created in Christ Jesus unto good works, which God hath before ordained that we should walk in them* (Ephesians 2:10). *"*

Those who receive Jesus Christ as Lord, are *"re-positioned to increase"* (be fruitful and multiply, subdue and take dominion) in the earth according to God's righteous standards. Sin caused mankind to decrease from his former position in God. Salvation causes men to increase, not only to where Adam had fallen, but even further, to the place where they would have been if sin had never happened. This again, is increase, far beyond our human understanding. God planted in Adam, our faith waters, and God gives us the increase (I Corinthians 3:7). We who are saved become greater than Adam, with an even greater inheritance for the fullness of the earth has also increased. Can you imagine where you would be today if sin had never entered the earth? If there had been no sin, there would never had been the curse. Mankind would have steadily increased from creation to this very day. How man could have transformed earth's atmosphere over the billions of years, each generation increasing more than the previous! Could Earth even handle such production without it spilling over to the other planets in the universe? Talk about launching out into the deep.

The Bible tells the story of Simon Peter who had fished all night and caught nothing. Jesus steps on his boat and begins teaching the multitude. *"Now when he had left speaking, he said unto Simon, Launch out into the deep, and let down your nets for a draught (Luke 5:4-7)."* When Peter followed the instructions of Jesus, it brought such a multitude of fish that his net brake. He had to call his partners, and their ships overflowed and began to sink. This was a demonstration of increase even before the new covenant, before the Holy Spirit came to live inside of believers. Whether God is in your boat, or in your spirit, He will fill you till you overflow. That is how it was for Adam and Eve. Filled over the top with God, thinking His thoughts and acting like Him. They were one in spirit, soul and body.

God is a god of increase. He *"overdoes everything."* That is according to human perspective. When God, who is a very BIG god pours Himself into these simple dirt shells, we automatically go into *"overflow."* He fills our cups to overflow (Psalm 23:5). God makes His grace to **abound** [abundantly increase] towards us so that we always have **all sufficiency** in all things, so that we may **abound** [abundantly increase] in every good work. This is how God operates. He ministers *"overflow"* to us, giving us seed to sow and bread to eat. God, then multiplies our seed sown and increases the fruit of our righteousness. He enriches us in every thing which causes increased thanksgiving to God (II Corinthians 9:8,10,11). God is able to do exceeding abundantly above all we ask or think (Ephesians 3:20), according to His power that works in us. After salvation, God's power comes to reside within us. Therefore, we have the *"capacity to increase"* built within the new creature. The believer is *"rebuilt"* to receive the overflow of God and use it to replenish the earth. The Holy Spirit fills us, even to overflow; restoring us to the same stature as Adam [the last Adam]. With the endowment of the Holy Spirit, we increase.

This is why Jesus did not want his apostles going out in ministry until they were filled with God, the Holy Spirit (Acts 1:8), *the breath of life.* He wanted them to be *"full of God and fruitful,"* to bear fruit that remains. This is God's plan for our lives, but the devil has a plan to stop us from manifest the original plan of God for our lives. In the previous chapter we discussed the battle line being drawn. We need the power of the Holy Spirit in order to complete our mission. That devil refuses to comply with the legal order. He will not let go of what is rightfully ours without a fight. For our own protection, we must be equipped and maintain our connection with the Holy Spirit. We cannot go in our own strength nor our own wisdom. Jesus said it this way, *"Abide in me, and I in you. As the branch cannot bear fruit of itself, except it abide in the vine; no more can ye, except ye abide in me (John 15:4)."* If we want to increase God's way, we must abide in Him and His word. It was necessary that I lay a foundation of Biblical increase before we move on to the next level.

There have been many teachings about financial increase, the wealth transfer and prosperity. Much of what I have heard, is taken out of context of God's original purpose for man. In these end of last days, God is looking at **"what Adam lost and what Jesus restored."** He made this very clear to me. **"Salvation is about reclaiming the earth for the Kingdom."** It's not about heaven or hell. It is strictly about restoring everything that Adam lost. This is God's Kingdom mission that will be fulfilled in these last days. God created this earth for His purpose. As Psalm 24:1 says, *"The earth is the Lord's, and the fulness thereof; the world and they that dwell therein."* Sure, Adam lost it for a moment and satan took over, BUT Jesus bought it back. Now, God has ordained good works for us, **"works that are designed to take back everything"** in the earth for God' Kingdom. That means restoring mankind as sons of God. That means returning the fullness of the earth, which includes all of creation, the wealth and resources, back into God's Kingdom.

We established earlier that all of creation is groaning and travailing for the manifestation of the sons of God. Creation knows that when the sons of God take center stage, the curse will be reversed and all things will be restored back to God's original plan. Now, I'm going to say something that might shock and anger many a Christian, but God said something to me several years ago that corrected my thinking about the return of Jesus Christ. We are still taking about increase, God's way. What I am about to reveal renewed my mind and helped me to increase my faith.

Here is what happened. *"I will never forget the morning the Lord shook me awake with these words,* **"The Kingdom must be delivered up!"** *This was not God quoting scripture. This came in the power of a direct command from God. Immediately I got out of bed and picked up my Bible. I turned to I Corinthians 15:24-25 where it reads, "Then cometh the end, when he shall have delivered up the kingdom to God, even the Father;*

when he shall have put down all rule and all authority and power. For he must reign, till he hath put all enemies under his feet." Like most people, I had never considered that this scripture meant anything other than at some point Jesus would deliver up the Kingdom as the word says, but the Lord opened my eyes to see that we are seated with Jesus. We are His Body in this earth. We are called to deliver up the Kingdom. We must do it and prepare the way for our King. We must take up and finish what Jesus started. We go in His name.[1] This was a shocking revelation. We have been taught that Jesus is coming back, and everything will be all right and it will be all over. We are waiting on Jesus to return, but Jesus is waiting on us to establish the Kingdom by taking back the people and possession for God. It is a takeover (We will talk more about this later), it began with Jesus resurrecting with all power in heaven and in earth. He did this for us, so that we could arise as sons of God in the earth, imitating our Father and our big Brother, doing the works of God. We are created in their image. We have their word. We have the Holy Spirit. All is needed is for every believer to step into his or her position of authority and rule in the midst of our enemies.

This is also why there will be the greatest wealth transfer in the history of the world. All of earth's possession must be turned over to God's people, BUT not everyone will receive. Not everyone will believe. They will continue to sit by and wait for Jesus to break through the skies while the world and its people spiral out of control in darkness. WE ARE THE LIGHT OF THE WORLD. Get busy! Jesus has a job for you to do. People are suffering. They are confused. They are blaming God for things that wicked men are doing. Are you just going to sit by and let the world blaspheme your God? The wealth is transferring and so are the souls of men, but those who receive are those who obey the will of God for their lives. Understand that God, the Creator, created this earth and all it's wealth and resources for His sons. We are expected to be imitators of God like obedient children (Ephesians 5:1). Therefore, we must be sons and daughters of increase. The Bible says, *"The LORD shall increase you more and more, you and your children* (Psalm 115:14)*."* God wants us to increase; to profit in income, revenue, wisdom and deed. He also wants us to increase in love, in peace and joy.

---

1   Matthews, Paula. "The Blessing To Rule And Reign On Earth." *Living In The Faith Zone.* Atlanta: Spirit & Life Publications, 2019. 157-158. Print.

One must get into position to increase God's way. We cannot live nor think like the wicked men of the earth. We must live according to righteousness. In fact, the Lord said that in these last days, *"wealth and divine health will be signs of righteousness"* in His Kingdom. The wealth will represent the glory of God upon the righteous. We will see it, even in America. Righteousness will exalt the nation (Proverbs 14:34).

America has a significant part to play in God's magnificent wealth transfer. Here is what God has said. [Prophecy]: *"I am God and will not be mocked by any man; no matter how much wisdom and wealth he has gained. It all belongs to me, and I decide who has possession of the wealth. You evil rich men have brought this country to the ruin, but I have a people amongst you who have been given the plan to prosper America. I will take your wealth and give it to them. They have my heart for the people. They have my anointing to get my plan done in the earth. This my Kingdom hour to demonstrate my goodness and mercy to all mankind, and it will be done in America whom I have chosen for this demonstration so that all men can see that I am God and I have always loved my human creation; and have only plans to do you good and not evil. I love you, come to me and see the great and mighty plan I have for your lives."[2]*

This will be no ordinary wealth transfer, if ever there was such a thing. God is raising up millionaires and billionaires in the Body of Christ. These end-times will manifest *"the greatest wealth transfer"* this world has ever experienced. The Lord said He was raising up wealthy Black people in His Kingdom. This will be a significant *financial increase* for the Kingdom of God. These types of prophetic words were so prolific that one White pastor was talking about intermarrying into a Black family in order to get in on this wealth transfer. It wasn't until 2010-2011 that the Lord told me the wealth was not for Black people, but *"for those of African descent."* The Lord is *"recompensing"* the descendants of Africa for what they have suffered. This is significant for Black people in America who have been marching in the streets looking to the government. God has the plan already in place. If only they would turn away from the promises of politicians to hear what thus says the Lord.

2   Matthews, Paula. "God's Promise To Prosper America." *American Heritage 101.* Los Angeles: Spirit & Life Publications, 2012. 64. Print.

God says in His word, *"I call heaven and earth to record this day against you, that I have set before you life and death, blessing an cursing; therefore choose life that both thou and they seed may live* (Deuteronomy 30:19)."* If we want the Blessing of Increase, we must make the choice for life. Our African and Arab brothers are making that choice for God. They want to increase. Here is what God explained. The wealth transfer began during the **"shaking."** God began to identify why so much of the turbulence was happening on the continent of Africa and in the Middle East. He showed me that His glory had invaded the continent and that wealth and power was shifting in that place. There was a battle for the inheritance among the people groups (Jews, Africans, Arabs) who claim Abraham as their father. God said to Abraham, *"Neither shall thy name any more be called Abram, but thy name shall be Abraham; for a father of many nations have I made thee* (Genesis 17:5)."* Abraham was a barren old man when God called him the father of many nations. Today, many nations are at war with Israel because they all claim to be heirs of Abraham. They all want the Blessing of their father, but Abraham gave all that he had to Isaac (Genesis 25:5). Now, I want to spend a bit to time to show you how God's Blessing upon Abraham has caused the nations to be in an uproar. Eventually, we will learn that only Jesus Christ could bring the Blessing of the Lord, full circle to include every nation and every tongue, establishing worldwide increase for the Kingdom.

According to scripture Abraham had three wives. Sarah bore him Isaac. *"And God said, Sarah thy wife shall bear thee a son indeed; and thou shalt call his name Isaac: and I will establish my covenant with him for an everlasting covenant, and with his seed after him* (Genesis 17:19)."* Before Isaac was born, Sarah thought she and Abraham were too old to bear a child. Therefore she offered her Egyptian maid, Hagar to Abraham and she bore him a son named Ishmael (Genesis 16:15). *"And as for Ishmael, I have heard thee: Behold, I have blessed him, and will make him fruitful, and will multiply him exceedingly; twelve princes shall he beget, and I will make him a great nation* (Genesis 17:20)."* After the death of Sarah, Abraham married Keturah who bore him six sons, Zimran, Jokshan, and Medan, and Midian, and Ishback and Shuah (Genesis 25:1-3). The Bible tells us very little about all of these sons of Abraham. We do know that he sent these sons away and gave them gifts (Genesis 25:6), even lands in which they could inhabit.

Historian Josephus records of Ishmael and his sons. *"These inhabited all the country from Euphrates to the Red Sea, and called it Nabatene. They are an Arabian nation, and name their tribes from these, both because of their own virtue, and because of the dignity of Abraham their father."*[3] Concerning the sons of Keturah, Josephus wrote, *"they took possession of Troglodytis, and the country of Arabia the Happy, as far as it reaches to the Red Sea. It is related of this Ophren that he made war with Libya, and took it, and that his grandchildren, when they inhabited it, called it [from his name] Africa."* Josephus quotes another Alexander Polyhistor who attested to the same, saying *"'Cleodemus the prophet, who was also called Malchus, who wrote a History of the Jews, in agreement with the History of Moses, their legislator, relates, that there were many sons born to Abraham by Keturah: nay, he names three of them, Apher, and Surim, and Japhran. That from Surim was the land of Assyria denominated; and that from the other two [Apher and Japhran] the country of Africa took its name, because these men were auxiliaries to Hercules, when he fought against Libya and Antaeus.'"*[4]

It is difficult to accurately determine how these ancient lands translate into the modern topography of Africa. The earth has changed much since Josephus walked the earth from 37-100 AD. It interesting to see why so many people are battling in the many regions of Africa. Abraham increase in producing fruit (sons) in the earth, and they all were given lands to inhabit. Abraham's seed was increasing in the earth as God promised.

The Lord said that in these last days, ***"All of Abraham's son will get their portion in Christ."*** God put it all together for me. Because of all the division among the sons of Abraham, Jesus had to come set things back in God's order. What was that order? It began with Adam. If he had never sinned, everyone born of God would have had their portion [lands] in this earth. Sin caused division. First between God and man. *"Therefore the LORD God sent him forth from the garden of Eden, to till the ground from whence he was taken. So he drove out the man; and he placed at the east of the garden of Eden Cherubims, and a flaming sword which turned every way, to keep the way of the tree of life*

---

3   Josephus, Flavius."Chapter 12. Concerning Abimelech; And Concerning Ismael The Son Of Abraham; And Concerning The Arabians, Who Were His Posterity." *The Complete Works Of Flavius Josephus (Illustrated) Translated By William Whiston.* Kindle ed.
4   Josephus, Flavius. "Chapter 15. How the Nation Of The Troglodytes Were Derived From Abraham By Keturah." *The Complete Works Of Flavius Josephus (Illustrated) Translated By William Whiston.* Kindle ed.

(Genesis 3:22-24). " Then it was division between brothers, when Cain, the son of Adam, killed Abel his brother (Genesis 4:8). Adam invoked the curse. Because the man had dominion over the earth, sin and death reigned until another man Jesus Christ, was born of God to restore the Blessing. Prior to Jesus' appearance, God looked earnestly for a family in this earth in which He could give the Blessing of Increase. He found Noah and his sons Shem, Ham and Japheth. *"And God blessed Noah and his sons, and said unto them, Be fruitful, and multiply, and replenish the earth* (Genesis 9:1). " Not only did God Bless Noah and his sons, but He sent them forth to re-populate the earth after the flood (Genesis 10:32). Every people group we see in the earth today descended from the sons of Noah. Which means that the Blessing of God, the inheritance for the sons of God, was destined for all the people of the world. Only Shem was obedient. His brothers set up camp in the plain of Shinar and decided to build the Tower of Babel instead of taking the Blessing to the ends of the earth (Genesis 11). God came down and broke up their plans. He confused their languages and scattered their families upon the face of the earth. One way or another, God was going to get the message of the Blessing throughout the earth.

God found faithful Abraham who was a pagan and covenanted with him saying, *" . . . in thee and in thy seed shall all the families of the earth be blessed* (Genesis 28:14). " Jesus was the seed of Abraham. He came to earth to restore the message of the Blessing, first to the Jews (lineage of Shem). After His resurrection, Jesus told his apostles to take the message to Jerusalem, Judea, Samaria then to the utter most parts of the earth (Acts 1:8). The message wasn't meant only for the Jews. God wanted it to go to all the people of the world which included lineages of Shem, Ham and Japheth.

God was keeping to His original plan for man, even under the curse. Jesus' sacrifice on the cross was the only way to nullify the curse so that the Blessing would come upon the entire world. *"Christ hath redeemed us from the curse of the law, being made a curse for us: for it is written, Cursed [is] every one that hangeth on a tree: That the blessing of Abraham might come on the Gentiles through Jesus Christ; that we might receive the promise of the Spirit through faith* (Galatians 3:13-14). " Jesus was the only one who could bring together all the sons of God (both Jews and Gentiles) under the Blessing of God. Therefore, anyone who accepts Christ is also considered Abraham's seed and heir to the same promise (Galatians 3:29). Finally, the Blessing is increased, being propagated to all the nations around the world. In this *"end of the last days"* God has a people from every nation who will walk boldly in the promise of Abraham. They will rise up as *"giants among men,"* and run to the battle against the powers of darkness. When it is all said and done, they will be left standing, holding all the wealth and all the power of God's Kingdom, as rightful heirs of the Most High God. This will be the *"New Breed"* of leaders that Jesus is cultivating throughout the earth. They have been trained by the Holy Ghost *"to hear what others cannot hear and see what others cannot see."* Therefore they will be able to do what others could never do. These are little gods, who are walking in the power and boldness of their Father God. This is a powerful increase for mankind upon the earth. Ordinary men walking like gods in the earth? Hold on. We are about to increase your faith.

When Jesus claimed to be the son of God. The religious establishment of His day wanted to stone Him for blaspheme (John 10:31-39). Jesus simply said that He doing the works of His Father in the earth. He was attempting to bring the Jews into the increase knowledge of God. He was attempting to open the eyes of their understanding so that they would know the hope of God's calling for their lives. This was Jesus's way of showing them the *"exceeding greatness"* of God's power that was available to anyone who would believe (Ephesians 1:17-19). Jesus was our example. The Jews of His day did not understand that they had the Law, but in order to receive fully of what God had for them, they needed to *increase* in wisdom and understanding. Jesus came to bless them. They wanted to stone Him because He said *"God was his Father, making himself equal to God (John 5:18)."*

The Apostle Paul said to the church (Philippians 2:5-6), *"Let this mind be in you, which was also in Christ Jesus; Who being in the form of God, thought it not robbery to be equal with God."* Stop right here! Paul was telling Christians to think like Jesus. He was equal to God, but He walked as a man on earth. He did so to teach us how to walk humbly in the power and authority as gods (sons of God). The Jews stumbled at this thought; that any man could be equal to God. Jews didn't even speak the name of God, it was so holy. It would be unfathomable for them to even consider that a man would be so bold to say he is the son of Holy God. Stay with me. We are discussing the Blessing of increase. God wants to increase your capacity to receive all He created man to be in this earth. It's more than you can imagine, but it is possible. In a previous chapter, we talked about how God created mankind in His likeness and image, to be *"co-creators,"* imitating their Father in this earth. Again, we were created to look like God, to think and act like God, in order to walk like God in this earth. If it looks like, thinks like, talks and walks like God, then it is either God or His sons (and daughters). That means walking in faith and having perfect knowledge of what it means to be a son of God (Ephesians 4:13). Let's pause right here. God is King Eternal (I Timothy 1:17). What do you call the son of a king? A prince, an heir to the throne of His Father, but we have been made **kings** of our God. That means we have a (throne) dominion of our own right here on earth. We have jurisdiction over the earth as *"a chosen generation, a royal priesthood, and holy nation (I Peter 2:9)."*

Jesus, son of God came as Messiah (King). God seated Jesus at His own right hand in the heavenly places. He was given power *"far above all principality, and power, and might and dominion and every name that is named, not only in this world, but also in that which is to come* (Ephesians 1:20-21)." God named Jesus King of kings (Revelation 17:14, 19:16). Included under His dominion are all the kings of the earth. Got that? Now, let's increase in your understanding to another level. Are you saved? Then you have the same dominion that Jesus has. Read the Book! When you received Jesus, God raised you up and **made you to be seated with** Him [Jesus] in the heavenly places (Ephesians 2:2-10). In Christ, you are God's workmanship **created** (formed, manufactured) for good works that would rule and reign in the earth. With the abundance of God's grace and the gift of righteousness, we *"shall reign in life by one, Jesus Christ (Romans 5:17)."* Let's take it even further. The Bible calls the demons of darkness, "princes." They are rulers of darkness set over principalities in this earth. They are not kings. They are princes. Why? ***"Their father, satan the devil, is not a king."*** This is straight from the Holy Ghost. Here is the significance of that statement. Adam was earth's first king under God's dominion. When he lost the throne, it is assumed that whoever replaced him would also be king. ***"Not so, says God!"*** Look at what the Bible says. Satan, *the prince of the power of the air, the spirit that now worketh in the children of disobedience* (Ephesians 2:2)." Satan is not a king. He is a prince. He is under the authority of another. He is under our feet! God made us to be kings over the earth. Satan couldn't be a king, even if he wanted to. This is why he hates human beings so much. Even when he took the throne from Adam, that devil could never be king. The most he could hope for is becoming a prince of this world. That puts him under the dominion of the King Eternal. His desire was to *"be like the Most High God* (Isaiah 14:14)." This is not possible. Lucifer is not in man's class. He is in the angel class. Mankind is like God. *"For unto which of the angels said he at any time, Thou art my Son, this day have I begotten thee? And again, I will be to him a Father, and he shall be to me a Son* (Hebrews 1:5)?" Man is the only creation that God made in His own image and likeness. Man is the only creation that carries God's attributes. We alone were created to become His heirs. Sure, we were born in sin, placed under the dominion of satan the prince of this world (John 12:31) for a time. But when we became born again, we resumed our places as royal heirs to the throne of God in this earth. Those who are led by the Spirit of God, they are the sons of God, destined to reign in life, as an heir of God.

In these last days, we will see the ***"Restoration of God's Ancient Kingdom Dynasty"*** in the earth. This will be real Kingdom royalty such as the world has never seen before. We, who are belicvers have the title of kings of the earth, solely because our Father (King Eternal) is in Heaven. Our power, through the Father is both in Heaven and in Earth. Therefore we walk in His authority. That is exactly what Jesus said when He resurrected from the dead. He said *"All power is given unto me in heaven and in earth. Go ye therefore and teach all nations . . . and lo I am with you alway even unto the end of the world* (Matthew 28:18-20)." God has remnant of mighty warriors who are about to take center stage. These royal heirs of God who have been equipped to rule in the darkness. They will run to the battle. ***"There will never be another time like the time in which we live. There will never be another people chosen and equipped to excel in battle over the evil that has gripped the hearts and souls of men for thousands of years, and for those who faithfully accomplish their kingdom orders; they shall receive the Crown of Life. This is our INCREASE for going into combat and enduring the battle."***[5]

These mighty warriors have one ultimate goal; to honor God as Father, and Jesus Christ as King. The prophet Isaiah wrote about Jesus, *"and his name shall be called Wonderful, Counsellor, The mighty God, The everlasting Father, The Prince of Peace. Of the increase of [his] government*

5   Matthews, Paula."The Crown Of Life: Our Increase For Enduring The Battle." *American Heritage 101*. Los Angeles: Spirit & Life Publications, 2012. 71. Print.

and peace [there shall be] no end . . . (Isaiah 9:6-7). *"* This scripture says that *the increase of His government and peace there shall be no end.* In other words, the abundance and expanse of His dominion has no end. As we said before that the kingdoms of this world are becoming the kingdoms of our Lord and of our Christ. Wherever God's government rules there will be abundant increase in wealth and power. There will also be an abundance of peace. This is the word *shalowm* which means wholeness, welfare, protection, provision, everything necessary for sound human existence. Jesus alone was able to gather all the sons of God under His throne. This was God's vision for mankind from the foundation of the world. One family, a Kingdom Dynasty of righteous rulers upon the earth, ruling and reigning like their Father rules in Heaven.

Revelation chapter 21 describes the holy city, new Jerusalem coming down from Heaven. Then the Bible says, *"And I saw no temple therein: for the Lord God Almighty and the Lamb are the temple of it. And the city had no need of the sun, neither of the moon, to shine in it: for the glory of God did lighten it, and the Lamb [is] the light thereof. And the nations of them which are saved shall walk in the light of it: and the kings of the earth do bring their glory and honour into it. And the gates of it shall not be shut at all by day: for there shall be no night there. And they shall bring the glory and honour of the nations into it. And there shall in no wise enter into it any thing that defileth, neither [whatsoever] worketh abomination, or [maketh] a lie: but they which are written in the Lamb's book of life* (Revelation 21:22-27). *"*

Heaven is coming down to the earth, and who are the inhabitants of the holy city? The nations, *ethnos (Grk)* all the people groups of the world. These are those who *are saved,* from the various ethnic groups in the earth. These are the one whose names *"are written in the Lamb's book of life."* They are Blessed forever with the Father and the Son. This is the ultimate increase, the purpose behind everything that God has desired for His creation from the foundation of the world. God is gathering His family both in Heaven and in earth for His glory, and we shall be with Him forever!

YEARS 2016-2019:
THE KINGDOM ARISES IN POWER!

The Spirit Of Pharaoh Must Die!

The Lord began 2016 with a powerful prophecy:

"For those who are believing God,
It will be a year of restoration of all things; not just things we know about,
But things that were taken from previous generations, all the way back to Adam.
It's more than restoration of what we lost.
It's
The RESTORATION OF WHAT WAS PLANNED
FROM THE FOUNDATION OF THE WORLD"

This is the inheritance God wants to restore in these last days. God is talking about *"a magnificent acceleration from having nothing to having everything; from sin laden to having no sin at all; having every prophecy fulfilled."* These are the words God spoke to His people who were *"enslaved"* in the United States, unable to practice their faith as commanded by their Father in Heaven. This prophetic word was addressed to a people held captive in their own land. They were not free to worship Jesus as they choose. They were not free to live the abundant live Jesus came to give them. The country has laws restricting their right to life, liberty and the pursuit of happiness. People were even being forced to take jobs they did not enjoy because they were slaves to the America economic system.

Where was the American Dream their fathers enjoyed? Dreamers from other countries could come to our shores and realize their dreams, but ordinary Americans were being forced to give up their divine dreams because *"the powers that be"* did not approve of Christian efforts. All of this in the land they call *"free."* Is this really freedom? God had much to reveal concerning the economic slavery in America. *"Politicians say Americans need jobs! No! Americans need motivation, an impetus to live life with a greater purpose. In our economy, a job is no different from a welfare check. It's slave labor. People are being forced to do whatever is required, just to get paid. No one is being trained to give back into the economic system. Yeah, we talk about saving and invest-*

129

ing in America because we value our capitalistic market system, but our greatest resource is our people. We have to be willing to invest in Americans by instilling within them a sense of value in being connected to something bigger than themselves."[1] Unfortunately, people are connecting to the wrong source. Rather than taking hold of God, they are clinging to politicians who only want control over the masses. Then there are the Black people, who call themselves Christians, who bow to a certain political party as if it were the Savior. They are clueless to the fact that this same this same party was established as America's *"slave party"* from its inception, and continues the same mind-set even today. They have been bewitched by the devil, unable to discern truth from lies. These poor people are deceived by their own choice. They are cursed (Jeremiah 17:5). Christians of every ethnicity are deceived if they are looking to the world for answers. There are no answers outside of God. The world system is broken, and human wisdom cannot fix it. Even the politicians realize that the only way of survival, is to pit people groups against one another, and conjure up lies to stir public opinion. If the population is so busy fighting each other, they won't ever see the truth. If they cannot see the truth, then they can never be free. That is exactly what the devil wants. America needs to repent, if it wants to survive what is coming upon the earth.

At the time I heard these words from the Holy Spirit, there were many preachers speaking against the Babylonian system of the United States. They were referring to the political and economic systems of America. When God spoke to me, He included what He called **"the Babylonian church in America."** The Lord had me write a book addressing how the slave system of ancient Babylon had been the foundation of the Church. So the notion that the Church had been held captive by the systems of America is only partially true. According to God, **"it was the American Church that started the rebellion that led to the nation's captivity."** As the Church goes, so goes the nation. That is why God keeps bringing up II Chronicles 7:14. *"If my people, which are called by my name, shall humble themselves, and pray, and seek my face, and turn from their wicked ways; then will I hear from heaven, and will forgive their sin, and will heal their land."* Those calling themselves Christian, have to get prostrate before God and pray. We need to do like Moses and go before the Lord in fasting and prayer for the people of our nation. As

1   Matthews, Paula. "Chapter 4 Kingdom Economics." *American Heritage 101*. Los Angeles: Spirit & Life Publications, 2012. 48. Print.

Moses explained to those who rebelled against God in the wilderness. *"Ye have been rebellious against the LORD from the day that I knew you. Thus I fell down before the LORD forty days and forty nights, as I fell down [at the first]; because the LORD had said he would destroy you. I prayed therefore unto the LORD, and said, O Lord GOD, destroy not thy people and thine inheritance, which thou hast redeemed through thy greatness, which thou hast brought forth out of Egypt with a mighty hand. Remember thy servants, Abraham, Isaac, and Jacob; look not unto the stubbornness of this people, nor to their wickedness, nor to their sin: Lest the land whence thou broughtest us out say, Because the LORD was not able to bring them into the land which he promised them, and because he hated them, he hath brought them out to slay them in the wilderness. Yet they [are] thy people and thine inheritance, which thou broughtest out by thy mighty power and by thy stretched out arm (Deuteronomy 9:13-29)."*

These were the people whom God delivered out of Egyptian slavery with a Mighty Hand. Once they were free, they chose to deliberately turn away from the God who delivered them, to worship idols. This should have not been so surprising since the people had spent over many generations as slaves serving the idols of Egypt. They had not been freed very long before they wanted to go back to what was familiar to them. Even so, this rebellious behavior would become an established pattern with God's people that would continue throughout history. He would Bless them and they would experience a period of peace. Then there would arise a generation that forgot God. They would fall into the hands of their enemies and cry out for deliverance. God would send a deliverer and people would return to peace. The Book of Judges records the many times that the people turned from God and ended up in captivity, oppressed by their enemies. Is this not what we see in America? The issue is that we don't value what God has given us; thinking that the world has something better. We are so far removed from God that we think that our prosperity is about what we have done. The Bible warns us, *"But thou shalt remember the LORD thy God: for [it is] he that giveth thee power to get wealth, that he may establish his covenant which he sware unto thy fathers, as [it is] this day. And it shall be, if thou do at all forget the LORD thy God, and walk after other gods, and serve them, and worship them, I testify against you this day that ye shall surely perish. As the nations which the LORD destroyeth before your face, so shall ye perish; because ye would not be obedient unto the voice of the LORD your God* (Deuteronomy 8:18-20)." America had been rebellious so long, that we've gotten accustomed to sin. It has been legislated in our government. We have been indoctrinated to sin in our media. Politicians promoted sin because it brings in the votes. Americans don't recognize themselves as slaves. We think we are free, yet we are slaves to sin. Most, don't even want to be free. They don't believe they are slaves either. Mention slavery, and automatically people will think about the African slaves, or the sex trafficking that is degrading the vulnerable ones of society. ***"Slavery happens when an individual or a group, or even a government oppresses another either by great physical force or by overwhelming entanglements that binds another person to the point that they are unable to achieve positive results and unable to escape negative consequences."*** This is the definition that God gave me. The world system was built upon oppression, the slavery and victimization of the weak. Slavery is not about race. It's about greed. It's about wealth, money and power over others. The American system of doing business is based on greed.

God has a solution for all slavery. It's called ***"Repentance."*** Slavery did not begin with the Africans. It began in the Garden of Eden. When God Blessed man, He gave us dominion over everything that creeps upon the earth. God never gave us dominion over other human beings. When Adam sinned, the ground was cursed to produce *thorns and thistles* (worthless vegetation). Man would have to toil to find produce to eat from the ground. Consequently, mankind became a slave to working for his provision, or as some would say, "working for a living." This curse of slavery came upon Adam. God said, *"In the sweat of thy face shalt thou eat bread, till thou return unto the ground; for out of it wast thou taken: for dust thou [art], and unto dust shalt thou return* (Genesis 3:17-19)." If Adam had never sinned, there would be no slavery in the world. There would have been ***"co-laborers"*** working in partnership, but not slavery. Since the time of Adam, there have been servants, slaves, indentured servants and serfs. These were lower class people who made their living by serving those of the upper classes. In the Bible, the punishment for rebelling against God was to become a slave to your enemies. *"And he [God] said, Cursed be Canaan; a servant of servants shall he be unto his brethren* (Genesis 9:25)." We this throughout the bible. *"And if ye will not for all this hearken unto me, but walk contrary unto me; Then I*

132

will walk contrary unto you also in fury; and I, even I, will chastise you seven times for your sins ... And I will scatter you among the heathen, and will draw out a sword after you: and your land shall be desolate, and your cities waste . . . And ye shall perish among the heathen, and the land of your enemies shall eat you up (Leviticus 26:27-38)." Even in the Blessing of Abraham, God promises that in our rebellion, *"The LORD shall bring thee, and thy king which thou shalt set over thee, unto a nation which neither thou nor thy fathers have known; and there shalt thou serve other gods, wood and stone."*

God covenanted with Abraham saying that his seed would be enslaved for four hundred years, after which the Lord would bring them out with **great substance** (Genesis 15:13-14). This was to be a great wealth transfer from Egypt into the hands of God's people. The same is exactly happening in our generation. God wants to set His people free in America, like He did the Children of Israel who were enslaved in Egypt. In our day, Egypt is a metaphor for the world system. Oh, indeed God is bringing us out, but we are not coming out empty handed. ***"God is recompensing His people for what they have suffered while being held captive in Egypt."*** This was judgment against Egypt for what they did to the people of God. When the devil's time was up in Egypt, God forced Pharaoh to let His people go. It took God sending plagues against that nation, but eventually Pharaoh let the people go. Then God gave them favor in the sight of the Egyptians and the His people took all that nation had (Exodus 12:35-36).

What will happen in the world today, will usher in the greatest wealth transfer this world has ever seen. It will the spoils of the war between the gods. Almighty God is taking on all the idols of the earth, but the outcome will be that the wealth of the sinner will be given to the righteous (Proverbs 13:22). According to God, one of the first idols to go, will be the *spirit of Pharaoh*. When the Lord first began making this modern day comparison with what happened in Egypt it surprised me how history had repeated itself according to God's plan for these last days. To understand more clearly, the Lord took me through the Bible. We go back to the promise the Lord made with Abraham. *"Now the LORD had said unto Abram, Get thee out of thy country, and from thy kindred, and from thy father's house, unto a land that I will shew thee: And I will make of thee a great nation, and I will bless thee, and make*

133

thy name great; and thou shalt be a blessing: And I will bless them that bless thee, and curse him that curseth thee: and in thee shall all families of the earth be blessed (Genesis 12:1-3)." God promised to bless Abraham by multiplying his seed and the blessing them to be a blessing to every nation on earth. The Bible says that God keeps His covenant for a thousand generations (Psalm 105:8). It cannot change. If God's people are denied the opportunity to fulfill their part of the covenant *through no fault of their own*, then God will curse those who hinder His people. He will keep His part of the covenant no matter what.

Many Christians are quick to believe that the evil upon our nation is because of how we have treated the Jews. It's possible, but the Lord showed me that this is bigger than the Jews. It's about God's Kingdom agenda. Under the Blood covenant, those who put their faith in Jesus are considered the seed of Abraham. No longer does color, race nor nation nor creed matter to God. Whoever believes in Jesus Christ is qualified to receive Abraham's Blessing. Remember that Abraham was a pagan when God Blessed Him. He was not a Jew. Therefore, those who walk in faith like Abraham, are heirs of Abraham. *"For ye are all the children of God by faith in Christ Jesus. For as many of you as have been baptized into Christ have put on Christ. There is neither Jew nor Greek, there is neither bond nor free, there is neither male nor female: for ye are all one in Christ Jesus. And if ye [be] Christ's, then are ye Abraham's seed, and heirs according to the promise* (Galatians 3:26-29)." This is significant because Americans are taught that it is all about the Jews. No! It is all about Jesus Christ and what He has provided for all mankind under this *"new and living way."*

God Bless the Jews! They gave us Jesus. They may not recognize who He is, but today the Blessing of Abraham, is for all those who name Jesus Christ as their Lord. Salvation may have come through the Jews, but it is available to the entire world. The Jews will finally see Him, when the time of the Gentiles is complete. They were the first with the message, but they will be one of the last to have their eyes opened to see Jesus for who He really is. The Lord showed the spirit of Pharaoh, operating both in the church and in our government. ***"It's witchcraft."*** In fact, all rebellion to God is considered witchcraft, stubbornness is the same as iniquity and idolatry (I Samuel 15:23). These are spirits that want to take the place of God in our lives. They violate the first commandment. *"Thou shalt have no other gods before me* (Exodus 20:3)."* God didn't stop there. He said not to make any image or likeness of anything and call it god. In light of everything we have said about how mankind was made. What an insult to God if we, who are made in His image and likeness, would create an object and call it our God. Selah. Not only are we forbidden to make such an idol, we are not allowed to bow before it nor are we to serve it. Why? *"For I the LORD thy God [am] a jealous God, visiting the iniquity of the fathers upon the children unto the third and fourth [generation] of them that hate me; And shewing mercy unto thousands of them that love me, and keep my commandments* (Exodus 20:5-6)."

Pharaoh, like all ancient (even some modern day) rulers was a god in the eyes of the people. I've heard some people talk about certain celebrities calling them god. Before you go calling yourself or any human a god, consider this. You are just asking for a showdown with Almighty God. That is what happened with Pharaoh. God sent Moses and Aaron to the king demanding that he let His people go. Pharaoh was offended. *"And Pharaoh said, Who [is] the LORD, that I should obey his voice to let Israel go? I know not the LORD, neither will I let Israel go* (Exodus 5:2)." Pharaoh didn't want to let the people go because of money, because of what it would cost the nation, if the slaves did not work. Again, **"slavery is economic."** It had little to do with the fact that they were Hebrews. It was about Egypt using the people for slave labor. Instead of letting the people go, Pharaoh increased the workload and made it burdensome for the slaves. He wanted to dash their hopes of ever becoming free. This was the seed of Abraham, the people of promise under a ruler who had taken the place of their God.

Then came the showdown with the Almighty, but He didn't have to step upon the earth. God sent Moses. *"And the LORD said unto Moses, See, I have made thee a god to Pharaoh* (Exodus 7:1)."* Whoa! Remember how we said earlier **God is able to use anyone, at any time for any purpose He chooses.** Here we see that God made Moses a god over Pharaoh. God had something to prove in Egypt. *"Thou shalt speak all that I command thee: and Aaron thy brother shall speak unto Pharaoh, that he send the children of Israel out of his land. And I will harden Pharaoh's heart, and multiply my signs and my wonders in the land of Egypt. But Pharaoh shall not hearken unto you, that I may lay my hand upon Egypt, and bring forth mine armies, [and] my people the children of Israel, out of the land of Egypt by great judgments. And the Egyptians* *shall know that I [am] the LORD, when I stretch forth mine hand upon Egypt, and bring out the children of Israel from among them* (Exodus 7:1-5)." Pharaoh didn't know the Lord, but he was about to find out just who he was dealing with. You know the rest of the story. God brought the plagues that devastated Egypt to the point that they sent the slaves out and gave them their wealth. Now, flash forward to America where, according to the Lord, **"The war of the gods has begun."**

Americans have many gods. They worship the gods of celebrity; and sports "stars," movie "stars." They are our idols. The worship of idols is a favorite American past time. We are also a materialistic society. Many Americans worship money, possessions and note worthy accomplishments. A showdown is coming. These are the American idols that God is about to put away. These same idols have taken the place of the Holy Spirit in many churches. It is a spirit of Anti-Christ (anti-anointing) for sure. The True and Living God is not allowed in these types of churches. The same is in our institutions of higher learning, business and industry. In our government, there is a belligerent Anti-Christ spirit that suppresses any true expression of God. Now, one would expect such from the world because these people know nothing about God. BUT in the Church, you would expect leaders to honor God and His servants. In most cases, it is not so.

The Lord sent me to recover **"His leaders"** that the Church discarded. He said that **"they went to combat for the Kingdom, but were left to die on the battle field."** Make no mistake, these were those who obeyed the commission to *"go"* into all the systems (*kosmos*) of this world. God sent them as Light in the darkness. They preached the word with signs following. They were walking as the first apostles walked in the earth. However, they were not prepared for the extreme persecution that would follow. Their pastors and churches were suppose to back them up, but they didn't. These were **"burgeoning"** apostles and prophets, missionaries sent into the darkest places of America. God said they were left to die on the battlefield. I didn't know what that meant, until I went to retrieve them. My job was to minister healing and deliverance to these leaders and teach them how to overcome the persecution. Many were sent back to reconnect with their overseers. While in that assignment, a powerful opposing spirit rose up against me, even in my home church. Leaders attempted to keep me from obeying God. Finally, I was told to leave my church because I was a bad influence on my pastor. I was told that every time I showed up at the church, the senior pastor would start talking about how he wanted the other leaders to obey God. They knew what God said, but "they had other plans." They were not even allowing the pastor to obey. Demons had overtaken the church. God told me to shake the dust off my shoes because He had another assignment for me.

The Lord reminded me that I had a similar experience at an affiliated church. The pastor at that church called me into his office, and announced that he was going to stop me from obeying God. He kept yelling at me, "I am a great man. You have my gifts. Give me those gifts. They are for a great leader, you are a nobody." This man criticized me for obeying God. He was offended because of the miracles that were in my ministry. I tried to explain that it was the Holy Spirit that did the work. I simply obeyed God. That pastor didn't get it. All he could say was, "I'm going to stop you from obeying God." I left that meeting somewhat confused. His Bishop approached me, saying, "You are one of those people who obey God. Well, I am the man in charge of my church and I'm the one that decides if God is going to operate. You are not welcomed here." This was one of many leaders, that did not want God in their churches. They don't want the Holy Ghost. They don't want tongues or the gifts of the Spirit. Consequently, the congregation is not healed. People were not getting delivered from demons. Their prayers were not being answered and they didn't know why.

The Bible says that where the Spirit of the Lord is, there is freedom (II Corinthians 3:17). Pharaoh was keeping the people in bondage in God's churches. When the Spirit of the Lord came to set them free, the leaders shut it down. They belittled and persecuted those who want the real Jesus. Many Christians have, and continue to suffer similar persecution in American churches. The Bible tells us to *"Remember them that are in bonds, as bound with them; and them which suffer adversity, as being yourselves also in the body (Hebrews 13:3)."* The ones who are suffering the most, are those who are sent into the world for the Kingdom's sake. They have put their careers, their families and personal lives on the line for the Kingdom. They walk in the darkest of places in America, but no one recognizes them. Most of what the church recognizes is what goes on in the church building. There is also an erroneous belief in the church, that American Christians are not suppose to suffer. If they do suffer, the claim is that they are in sin. Most Christians have yet to obey God enough to merit persecution. Their obedient brethren are persecuted by the church and by the world, with no place to turn except to Jesus. In this season, God will raise them up in power and influence because Pharaoh in the church must die. This is only the beginning. Holy Spirit took me even further. He said that God has made specific promises for people groups around the world. Often they were people who received Jesus Christ as Lord, but who were persecuted and killed by a particular nation or group of nations. This happens often in the Middle East and in Muslim countries throughout Southeast Asia and Africa. Missionaries to these countries are often killed because their work for Christ upsets the wicked systems of those nations. When people are set free and began to experience the love and liberty in Christ, this upsets the nation's leaders because the Christian lifestyle deviates from their norm. These are oppressive, intolerance nations. Most of the fighting in these nations is spiritual. People are crying out to God to be freed and the governments, and rival religious groups are fighting to keep them in bondage. We see the same happening in America, although it's not as obvious as it is in other nations.

The Spirit of Pharaoh <u>reigns</u> in American politics as well. The story of Pharaoh and the enslavement of the Children of Israel is well known, but it's more than a story about an ancient civilization. It's the classification of a type of oppressive government system that was built upon the backs of slaves. The Children of Israel were set free, but the Children of God in America are still in bondage. The Lord showed me the plight of two groups of His people in America. The first was the plight of Blacks in our nation. He gave me a disturbing *vision* in 2016 which *I saw President Barack Obama and Presidential Candidate Hillary Clinton. These two politicians were in agreement as they stood on what looked like a huge door. I must have seen this same vision two or three times before the Lord showed that this door was part of a huge slave ship. The door on which Obama and Clinton stood was the door that leads to the bottom of the ship where the slaves were kept like sardines. They were standing on top of the door, keeping the slaves from coming out of that filthy dirty compartment. Under the door were the crushed bodies of Afro-Americans who were trying to push the door open to get free. Mr. Obama and Mrs. Clinton were arrogantly standing on the backs of poor Black people in America. I heard someone say, "We always do better under the Democrats." It was a symbol of severe oppression.* As a Black woman who had long admired both Mr. Obama and Mrs. Clinton, this was a sore disappointment, not just for me, but for all those sincere God loving people who believed *"the carefully crafted words"* of these *"shrewd politicians."* As a woman of God, I had to put aside my personal feelings, and obey My Master. Even the decision to include some of these detailed visions was not my ideal, It came from the Lord. He wanted me to be very specific, not to embarrass these leaders, but to show just how much God knows about what is going on *"behind closed doors."* People can be deceived, but God will not be mocked by anyone no matter their position. After seeing this vision multiple times, the Lord gave me a direct comparison between what was happening in America with what happen to the Jews in ancient Egypt. Much like it was in Egypt, America was built upon the backs of slaves who were taken from their homes, tortured, degraded and made to serve their religious master in this land. Neither the American government, nor the church has dealt with the issue of slavery to God's satisfaction.

The Lord brought it up and put it right in my face. *"The Spirit of Pharaoh still rules Blacks in America."* Here is how the Lord presented to me. This is the narrative I heard in the spirit. *"The slaves were granted freedom in the Emancipation of Proclamation of 1863, but their children were fruitful and increased abundantly, multiplied and grew exceedingly mighty; and the land was filled with them. Now there arose a new king over America who knew not God, and he said, 'Look, the people of the children of the slave are more and mightier than we; come, let us deal shrewdly with them, lest they multiply and it happen, in the event of war, that they also join our enemies and fight against us, and so go up out of the land.' Therefore, they set taskmasters over them to afflict them with burdens . . . and the more they afflicted them, the more they grew, and they were in dread of the children of the slaves."*

The Lord showed me this ugly picture of Black people still ensnared with the past evils of slavery, and unable to move into God's plan for their lives. They are kept on the welfare rolls and in poverty with little or no hope of a better life. Their ancestors were Africans of noble descent, who were demeaned and made to live like slaves in a strange land. The Spirit of God is calling them out of Egypt in this season, and Pharaoh is refusing to let them go because it is not good for the outcome of one political party. *"They offer them freedom, but have no intentions of setting them free."* Even in the Christian church in America, slaves were offered the freedom that Jesus Christ offers, but yet were not allowed to enter into that freedom. The government offers the freedom of our Constitution, but that freedom has yet to be executed on the behalf of specific people groups in our nation. Injustice is flowing from the cities of our nation and nothing is being done to stop it. We had a Black man in the White House who did not care. Then he wanted us to support his favorite candidate who cared even less about Black people. That is about to change. God has declared by His Spirit, *"My Hand is against both Mr. Obama and Mrs. Clinton. I will avenge my people in this hour. They shall be free to obey Me in this, the land that I have covenanted to love and protect. I cannot be stopped. No man can prevent me from carrying out My Will in America,"* says Almighty God.

It is astonishing that God talks about slavery in America amid the numerous prophecies about wealth and power being restored to Afro-Americans for what they have suffered. The Lord told me that even our *"relatives from past generations had prayed for God to restore to us what was stolen from them."* In these last days, God is answering the prayers of those who endured slavery in this nation. *"Even in this month of September 2020, God is calling forth millionaires and billionaires from among His people, more specifically from the people of African descent."* God will restore to them, everything that was stolen, not just back to their slave master, but all the way back to Adam. All the while, politicians are relying on poor Blacks to elect another "Obama" candidate. God would later call Mr. Obama's actions *"treasonous."* This is a serious conflict of interest before the courts of Heaven. God is calling the people to receive the millions and billions that has been laid up for them from the foundation of the world. Obama wants them to remain poor in order to win an election. The people are crying out to God. He will answer by sending His Strong Hand against these politicians. Pharaoh will die in our government, and the Kingdom will reign in the lives of God's people in America.

The Holy Spirit made yet another comparison. God remembered His covenant with Abraham (Exodus 2:24-25) and went to rescue the people from Egypt. In America, God remembered His covenant with the pilgrims on the Mayflower in 1620. We have evidence from the Mayflower Compact, that the Pilgrims covenanted to come here *"For the Glory of God And Advancement of the Christian Faith."* God will uphold this compact for His sake and for His glory. Unfortunately, it has become more difficult to practice our faith <u>in</u> America. As we said earlier, when

140

God's people are not being allowed to honor the covenant, through no fault of their own, God will intervene. He will curse that nation, or people who have prevented them from obeying God. America has started a cycle of death that only God can stop. Prayer was removed from schools, now violence prevails. God tells us to choose life and yet America is proud to give women the choice to kill their babies, born and unborn. There is a law that God put in the earth at the same time He Blessed Noah and his sons. *""Whoever sheds man's blood, By man his blood shall be shed; For in the image of God He made man* (Genesis 9:6).*"* The Lord said that *"**Americans have no regards for human life.**"* We should not be surprised that our young people are killing one another. American laws are forcing the nation deeper into death and the curse. Even so, God promises to keep His covenant forever for the faithful few who still believe. He told Abraham that his seed would be in bondage for four hundred years. After that time, God would bring them out when the sin of the Amorites (Genesis 15:13-16) was full. The same goes for America and the nations of this modern world. The enemy is allowed to sin only so much, before God will make him pay damages. Almighty will see that the enemy pays back everything he stole, even to the substance of his entire house (Proverbs 6:31). It's payday for the people of God!

There is one outstanding thing to notice about how God dealt with Pharaoh. The Bible said that *God hardened Pharaoh's heart* so that he would not let the people go (Exodus 10:1-2). Please understand that God's knows what is in the heart of man (Jeremiah 17:10). Whenever a person is arrogant enough to go head to head with God, He will let them. God will warn them like He did Pharaoh. God will give them many chances to change. God did that with Pharaoh. With every plague, there was a chance to repent, but Pharaoh would not. Over the years, God has shown the same attitude in Mr. Obama. I even heard the Lord say of the president, *"**He is killing himself.**"* The Lord loves us all, but He will watch us put a noose around our own necks, and let us jump to our deaths. God has sent messengers to Mr. Obama, just like He sent Moses, warning that *"**He would send plagues against our nation**"* if he did not let the people of God go. According to the Lord, *"**Mr. Obama arrogantly thinks he can overrule**"* what God says or does. There one final *vision* that I keep in prayer. In this *vision, my nieces and I were on assignment for God and Mr. Obama wanted to stop us. So he put us in what looked like a glass enclosure where we could not escape. Jesus*

141

showed up. An angel shattered the glass and it broke. Jesus pulled us out and Mr. Obama lifted his hand to strike us and was cut off before he could strike. Then I saw both him and his wife, each hanging by a thin string. Jesus was holding the other end of the strings. Jesus asked Mr. Obama what he wanted to do, come with Him or not. Mr. Obama said, "I'm not coming." Jesus cut the string and the man fell into hell. Then comes Mrs. Obama. Jesus asked her what she wanted to do. Her answer, "I want to follow my husband." Jesus cut her string and she fell into hell. Then the Obama girls automatically followed their parents to hell. Jesus never asked them what they wanted. We will continue to pray that the Obama family turns back to Jesus Christ. Even so, the spirit of Pharaoh <u>will</u> let God's people go, even if it means sending a plague of death against the country (Exodus 6:1). God will uphold His covenant for the generations of the upright; vengeance on some and recompense to others. God will expose every secret plot and scheme and He will repay them all. The Lord said that ***America owes God's people four hundred years of recompense*** (from AD 1620-2020). In addition, ***there is recompense due for everyone injured or enslaved, whether Black, Hispanic, Asian or Native American; for every person America enslaved, misused and abused, regardless of race, in order to perpetuate the power and greed of this nation.*** This is the hour of God's vengeance for all who are standing on their covenant. God will make good on His covenant and come down to set His People free. The battle of the gods has begun. God is about to overturn every oppressive spirit that has enslaved His people in this nation. The God of Heaven is about to show His Mighty Hand. ***"God will show what it means when He says, 'Touch Not My Anointed. Do My Prophets No Harm!'"***

Pharaoh will die and God's people will be set free . . . and, they are not coming out empty handed (Exodus 3:21). They are coming out with silver and gold. There will no feeble one among them (Psalm 105:37). This will be the greatest wealth transfer and healing flow, the world has ever seen. Those who walked as slaves will finally ride high like kings in this earth. Life on earth will be like Eden, as if we were never separated from our God. **<u>This</u>** gospel of the Kingdom shall be preached to all nations, and then the end will come!

Athaliah Will Be Slain With The Sword

For each chapter of any book that I write, I spend much time in prayer, seeking what the Lord would have me say. At least twice, I heard the Lord say the name *"Athaliah"* and then a face would appear. The last time I heard God say that name, He boldly showed the face of Hillary Clinton. It was then that I realized that it was her face God had been showing every time He spoke *"Athaliah."* So, I prayed in the Holy Ghost and the Lord reminded me of who Athaliah was in the Bible and how this *spirit* uses Mrs. Clinton.

The story of this evil queen is quite twisted. It is a story of a family dynasty that ruled by witchcraft, the worship of idols, sexual perversion and murder. It began with two of the most notorious rulers of Israel, King Ahab and his wife Jezebel. Their daughter was named Athaliah. Now, whenever the story of Athaliah is told, most people will talk about how she killed all of the heirs who were in line for the throne. The Bible says that her husband, Jehoram also killed his six brothers to secure his place on the throne of his father Jehoshaphat (II Chronicles 21:4). *"Shedding innocent blood"* in order to take the throne was the legacy of this family. God had already spoken a judgment of death upon the house of Ahab. Joram, the brother of Athaliah was king of Israel and Jehoram, her husband was king of Judah. Jehoram and Athaliah had a son named Ahazariah who reigned after his father's death. His mother influenced him to do evil in the sight of God like the house of Ahab.

God told the Prophet Elisha to anoint Jehu (servant to Joram) as the king of Israel replacing his master. *"Thus saith the LORD God of Israel, I have anointed thee king over the people of the LORD, even over Israel. And thou shalt smite the house of Ahab thy master, that I may avenge the blood of my servants the prophets, and the blood of all the servants of the LORD, at the hand of Jezebel. For the whole house of Ahab shall perish (II Kings 9:6-8)."* According to the word of the Lord, Jehu slew the sons of Ahab including Ahaziah the son of Athaliah. *"But when Athaliah the mother of Ahaziah saw that her son was dead, she arose and destroyed all the seed royal of the house of Judah. But Jehoshabeath, the daughter of the king, took Joash the son of Ahaziah, and stole him from among the king's sons that were slain, and put him and his nurse in a bedchamber. So Jehoshabeath, the daughter of king Jehoram, the wife of Jehoiada the priest, (for she was the sister of Ahaziah,) hid him from Athaliah, so that she slew him not. And he was with them hid in the house of God six years: and Athaliah reigned over the land* (II Chronicles 22:10-12).*"* Although she got away with murder and ruled Judah for seven years, the queen never knew that there was one heir who had been hidden from her sword. His name was Joash. When he was of age to rule, Jehoiada the priest gathered the captains and anointed Joash king of Judah. Athaliah heard the people cheering and found out that Joash had been anointed king. She cried, "treason." The guards took her out and slew her near the horse corral.

When making comparisons with Mrs. Clinton, it started to make sense. Like Athaliah, Mrs. Clinton was considered very controlling while her husband Bill Clinton was president. To this day many still compare Mrs. Clinton to Jezebel, but God says the spirit using her is Athaliah. Jezebel was a spiritual woman (witch), who thought herself a prophetess. She used beauty and sex to manipulate others. Murder was her last resort. Her daughter Athaliah was a cold blooded murderer. I was instructed that prayer was necessary because that controlling and murdering *"spirit of Athaliah has been operating through Mrs. Clinton,"* according to God. He wants to set the woman free from that evil spirit. This is a insanely dangerous spirit that kills its competitors and young alike. *"This is also the spirit behind abortion,"* where a woman will kill her young in order to preserve her own stature in life. It should then, be no surprise that Mrs. Clinton and her state of New York have recently passed an aggressive abortion law at a time when the Lord has pronounced judgment upon the nation for shedding innocent blood.

He explained that Mrs. Clinton, under the influence of Athaliah, is not past, committing murder to seize power, even if it means murdering a member of her own party, *"colleagues and constituents alike."* The Lord indicated something else about Mrs. Clinton just before the 2016 Election. In fact, the Lord showed me a *vision* about Mrs. Clinton. *It was brief, but I saw the Lord cut off her arm with a sword. She didn't seem to notice that anything had happened. But the Lord said that He cut off her power and influence over that election and she would not win.* The Democratic Party was so sure they had won that election. Even the polls had Mrs. Clinton winning, but God had already spoken against her. He had declared that she would not win. They tried to accuse the Russians of helping Trump win. That was not the case. If God said He was not allowing Mrs. Clinton to win. She was not going to win. Period. He cut her off! I also recall that after the election there was a rift between Mrs. Clinton and Mr. Obama. He was convinced that she lost because they did not run her campaign like he did. Stop! This was arrogance speaking and proudly puffing up his own accomplishments that only God allowed. Herein is the problem in America. We think our achievements are because of what we did. Sure, you work hard, but it is God who gives us the strength and grace to win. God had already told Mr. Obama that it was He who put the man in the White House. Mr. Obama did not win because of what he did. He won because God allowed him to win. This is how twisted people are in the world. They think it's all about them. No! America has a covenant with God. It's all about HIM and His purpose for us and our nation.

After this public disagreement was aired on the news, the Lord let me see that Mrs. Clinton was *"outraged"* by what Mr. Obama had said. In a matter of moments, the *spirit* of Athaliah came upon her. In the spirit, I saw Mrs. Clinton pick up the phone, and instantly I knew she had instigated a plot against the man. I told the Lord that I didn't want to see any more. People have no idea that there are demons out here, and then maybe they do know. These demons will join in on our emotions and take over if we let them. Athaliah is an insanely dangerous spirit. Her mother Jezebel was a seductive witch. Athaliah is a ruthless killer. She wants power and doesn't care what it takes to get it. Now, I understand that some people will be offended, but God does not lie about these things. In fact, some celebrities use to make jokes about how many people Mrs. Clinton has allegedly killed. There is nothing funny about being rumored to be a cold blooded killer. I never paid attention to those jokes until after God revealed the truth. And now, I definitely cannot deny that God has called the spirit of Athaliah and associated it with Mrs. Clinton. No more than I could deny that God said both Trump and Obama were called to be a Cyrus for our nation, or that the Spirit of Pharaoh is upon America.

Beloved, people are not our enemies. The demonic spirits are. That is why the Bible says that we wrestle not with flesh and blood (Ephesians 6:12). Most people have no idea they are possessed by demons. They may know that something is out of order, but after awhile some may believe that it is them, that it's normal. There is nothing normal about plotting murder, but politicians, like good church folk, are use to putting on airs. They are hypocrites to a degree, in that they do whatever is required to reach a desired end. They are not above lying, stealing, killing or destroying others. Why? It's what their father the devil does. *"The thief cometh not, but for to steal, and to kill, and to destroy* (John 10:10)." When people don't believe they can get something honestly, they cheat and try to obtain what they want another way. They don't realize that God would give them what they wanted if they would just asked Him. *"From whence [come] wars and fightings among you? [come they] not hence, [even] of your lusts that war in your members? Ye lust, and have not: ye kill, and desire to have, and cannot obtain: ye fight and war, yet ye have not, because ye ask not. Ye ask, and receive not, because ye ask amiss, that ye may consume [it] upon your lusts* (James 4:1-3)."

I will never forget getting a phone call from a woman who was training for ministry. She called me because all of a sudden her prayers were not being answered. The Lord immediately revealed to me that she was dabbling in witchcraft. While she was explaining her side of the issue, God was revealing that this woman had a man in her life and it was not a *"lawful"* relationship. It was this relationship that was causing part of the problem, but then the Lord revealed that this woman had been using charms to bewitch this man to marry her. When I asked her about it, the woman did not deny the fact that she went to a shop and bought charms to lure the man into a relationship with her. When I asked why she did it. She said, "I just had to have that man. I wasn't leaving this up to God." So, I asked her "Are you surprised that God won't answer your prayer if you are going to get them from the Voodoo shop? This is the kind of exposure God is revealing about politicians in America. "We have a covenant with God, and you expect to win an election by using witchcraft against God.?" They obviously don't know that it was God who pronounced the death sentence upon witches. *"Thou shalt not suffer a witch to live* (Exodus 22:18)."

Okay, in all fairness I have to say that the same type of behavior is happening in the Church of Jesus Christ. I could name the preachers that I know of personally who have *"worked roots"* on their congregations. I could name even more that tried the same mess on me and it backfired. Again, people turn to witchcraft in order to control people and situations that are out of their control. They are trying to be gods in someone else's life and they don't have permission to do so. Now, in the previous chapter we mention how the sons of God do the works of their father and they appear to the world like gods. It is because the spirit of God is at work in them, not to control people but to heal them and set them free from the control of the devil. Witchcraft does the opposite. It binds and controls people so that they are not free to live the way they desire. The Spirit of God comes upon believers and they do great exploits to help people. They are not God, but look like their Father here on earth. Technically speaking, the same happens for those who do the work of their father satan. They are operating like the god of this world (II Corinthians 4:4). Satan is not a god, but he perpetrates like one. The Bible also says the devil walks around like a lion seeking whom he may devour (I Peter 5:8). Satan is not a lion. He just acts like one. He is a perpetrator of deception. He looks like something that he really isn't. Those who are used by him take on the same. They look more powerful than they really are. In actuality, when they encounter the real deal, that is when the knock off is revealed. Not every one can see the counterfeit until it is compared with the real deal. That is why God said *"the war of the gods has begun."*

Human beings are ruled either by God or satan, but we are not independent souls in this earth. God didn't make us that way. ***"The human spirit is made to be occupied by God."*** That is what God breathed into mankind at creation. When Adam sinned, the Breath of God left the man. The spirit that ruled him was that of the evil serpent. We saw this when God removed His Spirit from King Saul. The Bible says, *"But the Spirit of the LORD departed from Saul, and an evil spirit from the LORD troubled him* (I Samuel 16:14). *"* We saw a similar thing in the madman of the Gadarenes. The Bible says that he had an unclean spirit (foul, perverted) and no man could bind him with chains. This man lived among the tombs and would cry night and day cutting himself with stones. Jesus cast out the devil and the Bible says, the man was found by the villagers, *"sitting, and clothed, and in his right mind* (Mark 5:1-15). *"* The spirit of Athaliah can also make one mad. Insanity hits the person and they lose control of their sense. I've encountered Athaliah with women and men on the job. One woman came to me and admitted that she plotted to kill me because I had the position she wanted. Earlier I mentioned that I had been fired from my job because I was a Christian. The company hired a young man who was determined that I was his wife. He was prepared to kill me to keep from being with another man. This was someone I had never met in my life. He was demon possessed. These people let their desperate emotions open the door to demons that tell them to kill to get what they want. This is how Athaliah operates. The Bible says there is only one way to deal with Athaliah. Jesus said it, *"for all they that take the sword shall perish with the sword* (Matthew 26:52). "* Does this mean that Mrs. Clinton must die? No! It means if she wants to live, she must let go of that spirit. Mrs. Clinton must repent and turn her life over to God. When anyone let's God take over their life, the devil has to flee. There are some people who don't want to be free. We pray that God shows them mercy before He lets the devil take their life.

In the Bible, it was the High Priest Jehoida who ordered Athaliah to be assassinated (II Kings 11:15). It it was the Prophet Jehu who kills Jezebel. He also killed Jehoram the husband of Athaliah in the name of the Lord (II Kings 9:23-24). Notice that God had the priest and the prophet execute vengeance upon the evil rulers, according to His word. This demonstrates the role of God's people, even in the political process. *"Let the saints be joyful in glory: let them sing aloud upon their beds. [Let] the high [praises] of God [be] in their mouth, and a twoedged sword in their hand; To execute vengeance upon the heathen, [and] punishments upon the people; To bind their kings with chains, and their nobles with fetters of iron; To execute upon them the judgment written: this honour have all his saints. Praise ye the LORD* (Psalm 149:5-9). "* God never meant for His people to put politicians above Him. We are ambassadors of His Kingdom. We are called to show the world how the Kingdom operates, in every area of life, even in government. When it comes to evil rulers, we have dominion in Christ. We pray for those in authority, then we do and say whatever our Father commands us to do and say concerning that individual.

While I am yet writing this book, America is in the midst of the 2020 Presidential Election. Once again there is an ***"overconfident spirit"*** in the atmosphere. The opposing party is planning wartime strategies to throw the nation into further chaos. God is not moved by what they are plotting behind the scenes. He will expose them all. They thinking they are fighting Donald Trump, but ***"they are about to find God Almighty standing behind the man."*** One would think that Mr. Obama of all people should understand. After all the plots that were against him,

God protected Mr. Obama in that office, even when he was disobedient. Witchcraft could not touch him. Plots of assassination did not prosper. God did that for Mr. Obama. How could he and Mrs. Clinton think that God would not do the same for Mr. Trump. God is no respecter of persons. He looking at *"the intents of the heart."* It's not about the man. It's about God. The Lord said, *"It's about whom America will serve."* God is taking over everything in this nation and in the nations of the world. Those who obey Him, will be left holding it all! Those who know God, don't have to worry about the opposition. God is carrying us to our wealthy place. He is carrying us to that place of destiny, regardless of what the enemy plots against us. Those who come against "His anointed," God will curse. *"Some will drop dead in public. Other will fall in their offices and in their political seats."* If indeed God has called Mr. Trump, His Cyrus. Then God has anointed the man. Don't touch him!

The Lord reminded me of what He said about Mrs. Clinton during the 2016 Election. It was the word of God that kept Mrs. Clinton from winning. Thus said the Lord, *"She will not win, again. This is My Plan and My Power says God. Anyone who defies Me will be destroyed in this hour."* Then the Holy Spirit spoke. *"This is the hour of America's greatest danger and God's Kingdom's greatest time to demonstrate His POWER! Power over death, Power over lack, Power to Rule in the midst of our enemies. "Occupation is certain, yet the enemy shall not prevail in his plot to destroy this nation, for I have a Blood Covenant with these My people in the land. Surely I shall uphold them by My Mighty Hand, and you shall see the entire world will come to know who I am, That Great I am, the first and last the beginning and the end, for I am and was and will always be the One and True God who loves My creation like no human ever could. I will raise and honor My people in the midst of utter destruction on these American shores. And I will restore this nation to My design, to My Glory that I purposed for her since the foundation of the world. Righteousness shall prevail in America for I have purposed it. I have spoken. Surely I will bring it to pass by My power in this the earth's final hours before the return of My son,"* says the Omnipotent One, the Almighty God of Heaven and Earth."*

The Holy Spirit added, *" President Obama was warned about the tragedy. He refused to head the warning. He didn't want to be upstaged. What is coming to America will upstage us all! Who wins the election*

149

is of no concern to God. It was the corruption and events that led up to the election that has caused our leaders to be judged guilty in the eyes of God. Instead of saving millions of American lives by allowing God's people to prepare to save this nation from harm. Mr. Obama hindered us in every way. 'Corrupt business practices of this nation's leaders have caused the entire nation to be judged guilty.'" "All the plagues are in place for Me to execute My judgment upon them. No one will escape My judgment," says God. Much prayer has gone forth for our nation and its leaders, even for world leaders. The Lord kept saying that our nation was *"at war."* We were warring with one another and warring with enemies abroad. This is sign of our woundedness. *In the spirit I saw destruction upon the Capitol building. In the background I saw the Clintons and Obamas taking cover for what they knew was coming. They set the stage and watched it all unfold. This is what they started.* This was the work of the devil using people who have hatred and woundedness within themselves. Their imperfections are highlighted for the whole world to see. It's shameful, the whole lot of them. Why are they even in leadership? If this is the best that America has to offer, no wonder are in serious trouble. No wonder God is demanding *"change in the nation."*

Chaos is being generated by our leaders who are deeply wounded in their hearts. When we pray for these people, God reveals what is going on in their hearts. God wants them healed before they destroy everything they have worked for. God said it earlier, *"our leaders are imperfect. They brought their flaws to the White House."* God knew they were not perfect when He called them to duty over the United States. God said, *"Men are not chosen because they are perfect, but because they were called to duty, with all their imperfections."* This is why we are commanded to pray *"For kings, and [for] all that are in authority; that we may lead a quiet and peaceable life in all godliness and honesty (I Timothy 2:2)."* The nation is out of sorts because the leaders are out of order with God. They can't see straight because the devil has them blinded. The only ones that have the power to open their eyes is the Church of Jesus Christ. It's our call to duty. *"To open their eyes, [and] to turn [them] from darkness to light, and [from] the power of Satan unto God, that they may receive forgiveness of sins, and inheritance among them which are sanctified by faith in me* [Jesus]." Why are we to do this? It's not about going to Heaven. It's about loving people enough to heal them and release upon their lives *days of heaven upon the earth.*

150

God did not create human beings to be possessed by demon spirits. We were created to be ruled by His Spirit, *the Breath of life*, so that we could enjoy this earth and every good thing God designed for our lives. Go back and read the Book of Genesis before Adam sinned. That is what God originally planned for our lives, abundant life, wealth, health, surrounded only by beauty and the loving presence of our Father. God loves us so much, sometimes I can hardly handle it. His love for us is overwhelming! That is what people need to know. That is what the Church needs to know. That is how we were designed to operate, in love for God and for one another. The love of God is no small thing. It's not weak either. When the love of God compels you, it will take you places you would never go otherwise. Look at me. I never had the desire to write a book in my life. Here I am today, the author of a couple of dozen of books published, with several more in the process. This was not my idea. Are you kidding me? I would have never even thought to write about the Church, or about the issues in the nations of the world. And, then to share my private conversations with God in prayer. Believe me, even to share what is in this book was not my idea. I have to obey God. Why? Because people need to know that God is watching us, that He knows what is troubling us. So that we know that He alone has the solution. Do you think it is easy sharing what God had told me about Mrs. Clinton? Not at all. Let me be very transparent here.

All my life, I have been surrounded by politicians. I grew up hating politics. I also grew up hating religion too. Something inside of me just didn't like either game, but I had a first cousin who began working for Hubert Humphrey's campaign in 1965. She fell in love with politics and made it her career, all the way to Washington, D.C.. Bea absolutely loved Hillary Clinton. It was always, ". . . Hillary this, and Hillary that." It was through what my cousin experienced first hand, that I began following Mrs. Clinton. She is a powerful image of what women can do in this male dominated area, but God appointed me to pray for her and her husband President Bill Clinton. The Lord opened my eyes back in the late 90's to see how the enemy takes the weakness of a leader and turns it against them. I saw the man's heart and it compelled me to pray more for his deliverance. God did that for the Clintons for the sake of their salvation and for that of the nation. Then during the 2016 Election, Mrs. Clinton was being attacked severely in her body. It was spiritual. God called me into prayer for her life. He let me know at that time, that even if she had gotten elected, the toll from the battle would have killed her. But, I also sensed in my spirit that Mrs. Clinton was willing to die for what she believed. Back then, she believed that she should have been elected president. In hindsight, God wanted to preserve her life *"for something greater."* She has to let Athaliah go. That spirit wants Mrs. Clinton dead. It's not God's plan, but the woman has to make that choice in prayer to God. If anyone has any notion that I get enjoyment in revealing things about Mr. Obama. You are dead wrong. It was God who told me to vote for Obama during the 2008 Primary Election in Los Angeles. God told me that His *"Hand was on Mr. Obama."* What I never revealed to anyone, not even my family, is that God also told me to *"financially support"* getting Obama elected. God called it my *"Kingdom seed for a change in America."* Never before had God told me to vote for someone and then send money to their campaign each month, but I obeyed God. To me, this was no different than any other seed God told me to sow. When I heed His voice and give of my money, or my time according to what the Lord says, I obey and let it go. I would do this for God, for any purpose. Period. This was not unusual in that sense. What made it extraordinary is that it was a seed sown in to the *"ministry"* of a political candidate. For what purpose? I still don't know the particulars. God never shared it with me, but I do know it was for a *"supernatural"* Kingdom result, a miracle even. This is how God operates. This is how miracles happen. Mary the mother of Jesus said it this way, *"Whatsoever he saith unto you, do it* (John 2:5). *"* You must hear something first, and it has to be the voice of the Lord Jesus.

Here a quick point that may help you discern the voice of the Lord. *Whenever God speaks, He will tell you something that sounds impossible for you to do*. It will also be something that is characteristic with Him and His word. It will also be something that will take you outside of your comfort zone. It will stretch your faith to new limits and new heights. Pray and listen for the voice of the Lord. It could be the voice of the Father, even that of the Holy Ghost. All three are God, just different persons. The Father is the Spirit. The Son is the Body. The Holy Ghost is the mind of Christ. Remember that every human being is created in this same image and likeness. We have a body. Inside that Body is our spirit and our soul. All three parts make up the whole. God may even speak through someone else's voice. Even that of a child. This is how you receive a miracle from God. Pray. Hear His Voice. Obey His Voice.

Now imagine how I felt when on a certain New Year's Eve, when in the realm of the spirit, I heard the count down. ***"3, 2, 1. Then I saw a guillotine come down and a head rolled to the floor. It was Mr. Obama's head."*** This is not God's plan for him. This is the result of the choices this man has made. God didn't let me hear this so I would gloat. No! He wanted me to pray for Mr. Obama's deliverance. I still pray for the Obamas and Clintons to this day. I know what these demons will do to them. They will use these leaders to destroy millions of lives and then those same demons will take these leader's lives. The devil does not play fair! He is was killer from the very beginning. He hates every human being because we have something he does not have. We have the dominion in this earth. He is not human. He is a spirit who desires to take dominion away from God so he can destroy every human on the face of the earth. That is why Jesus came to save us from the plan of the enemy. Sure God had a plan for us from foundation of the world, but when mankind bowed to satan, humans became servants of his evil plan. Jesus came to restore us back to the Father. God loves America so much that He is determined to do whatever is necessary to reach every leader, every man, woman and child with the good news about His Kingdom. That is why we pray. That is why we preach the gospel and tell people that ***"Change has come."*** As the angels sang when Jesus was born, *"Glory to God in the highest, and on earth peace, good will toward men* (Luke 2:14). *"* God is about to get the glory for bringing His peace upon the earth. We will see it in America. We will see it in the nations of the earth.

So, what about the 2020 Presidential Election? Who will win? Although I see no change in that office, meaning I don't see Mr. Trump being ***"ousted."*** God has not given me any specific word, but I see His miraculous hand on our nation. This is a highly prophetic time in our nation's history. God is calling the shots as He said. He is the ***"Director of It all!"*** I would not be surprised to see a ***"surprised ending."*** I know in my knower (spirit) that God has something up His sleeve. There is something that we don't know, that is coming forth before Election Day. ***"What's coming will determine the outcome of the election."*** This I know for sure. God is moving in a most unusual way. Even while writing this book, my spirit has been talking to God about what is coming. Nothing has yet been revealed to my spirit, but twice I heard my spirit say to God. "I am ready."

What about Joe Biden? Pray for his soul. This man has been heavy on my heart ever since he announced his candidacy. Immediately, I knew he was not right. He didn't sound like himself. His eyes were glazed over as if he wasn't there. It was as if he was under a spell, under someone's control. This was not the Joe Biden of the past. Something was definitely different, even errie about the man. Then one evening, out of the blue, the Lord said, concerning Biden. ***"Obama is the puppet master."*** So, I began praying for the man's deliverance from what was obvious either witchcraft or brainwashing of sorts.

Then a week later, the Lord wakens me in the middle of the night with a *vision. I see Mr. Biden in his office. No one else was with him. He was standing next to a table which had an oblong tan colored box on it. Mr. Biden goes to the table and opens the box. There was a relic, or talisman so I thought. It was big, V-shaped with a long handled. I could not tell if it was wood or metal. I heard Mr. Biden say to himself, 'This will give me the advantage in the election.' When he picked up the relic, a powerful spirit immediately over took his body. It began killing him. What surprised me, was Mr. Biden's reaction. He was not afraid of that demon spirit. In fact, that evil surge overtaking his body felt like power. He enjoyed it, even though it was destroying his body from the inside."* As I prayed in the spirit for Mr. Biden, I was angry at the Church in America. World leaders want power, but they are going about it the wrong way. They are going to the devil because the Church at large has refused to operate in the power of God. They have religion, but that turns people away from God. And yet, religion is not from God. It is devilish. It kills when God desires to heal the hearts of men.

It's time for the Church to return to its roots, to the example of the first Church that operated in the word, with signs and wonders following. They spoke and the word of God cause multitudes to come into the Kingdom. People were hungry for the word. They came to hear the word preached and God healed them. We saw this in Jesus' ministry where He healed them all (Matthew 12:15). We saw great miracles in the ministry of the apostles as well. *"And by the hands of the apostles were many signs and wonders wrought among the people (Acts 5:12)."* People are in search of miracles. That is why we see so many leaders going after witchcraft. They need a miracle from God. Too many Christians are ignorant about the power of the Holy Ghost. God is the only power that heals. He protects and provides for us supernaturally. Jesus told us to go into the world and cast out demons. It does not matters that they are leaders over our nation. All humans need God. They need His love, His protection and His wisdom in navigating this life, especially in the *"perilous times."* The Bible talks of men and women who *"resist the truth: men of corrupt minds, reprobate concerning the faith. But they shall proceed no further: for their folly shall be manifest unto all men* (II Timothy 3:8-9). *"* Certainly people are going to resist *the truth,* but if they want to succeed in these last days, they are going to have to do it God's way or die. It's **"Do or die!"** God is trying to save lives, not destroy them. That's the devil's program.

If every Christian would earnestly pray for those in authority we can get them saved and delivered. When we see world leaders going to satan to get power, it is designed to destroy the nation. This is opening the gates of hell, against America, the same gates that Jesus declared, *"would not prevail"* against the Church (Matthew 16:18). The Church needs to repent for allowing Athaliah, Pharaoh, spirits of witchcraft and divination from ruling in this country. Oh yeah, God said that the relic Joe Biden had was a *"divining rod."* He wasn't looking for water. He was summoning up demon spirits in **"water witching."** God said, **"He will die."** Mr. Biden opened the door of death for himself and for his family. If he were to be elected to office, Mr. Biden will that same spirit of death upon the nation and upon everyone who is associated with him. That devil wants us all! The only thing that can stop Him is Almighty God working through His people to destroy the works of the devil. That is why we pray. Now if Mr. Biden decides not to part with this demon, then God will let the devil have the man.

Again, like Mr. Obama and Mrs. Clinton, God is trying one last time to get their attention. He does not want either to be killed, but I saw assassination coming to them both. As the Bible says, *"He that killeth with the sword must be killed with sword* (Revelation 13:10). *"* It is not God's desire that they be killed. It's the choice that they have to make, but as long as they are alive, there is a chance to repent. God can, and will save them, if they want to be saved. *"Say unto them, As I live, saith the Lord GOD, I have no pleasure in the death of the wicked; but that the wicked turn from his way and live: turn ye, turn ye from your evil ways; for why will ye die, O house of Israel* (Ezekiel 33:11)?*"* God wants men (and women) to repent so that they can live, but the choice is theirs. These leaders have blood on their hands, only God can help them. So, what about President Trump? I'm so glad you asked. Evangelical Christians have made a spectacle of themselves in a manner that has alienated the people they were ordained them to reach. Yes, God called the man. Yes, like Mr. Obama, God called Mr. Trump *"His Cyrus,"* for the season. The Lord told me that He chose Mr. Trump because *"he was the only candidate who would fight for America in righteousness."*

In other words, President Trump is, the only candidate who would hear and obey God when America's trouble comes. While writing this chapter, *I saw the glory of God come upon Mr. Trump*. The fear of God came on me. God has prepared the stage. He said, *"The battle of the gods has begun."* The election, is not about a man or a woman. It is about *"which God will America choose?"* This is personal to God. This is not about a political party. It's about whether we as a nation will continue in rebellion against Almighty God.

According to God, there will be bloodshed in our nation, but in the end America will be where He destined her to be from the foundation of the world. We've said it before and will continue to declare the word of the Lord for this nation. *"America shall be saved!"*

Dress Rehearsal For The Grand Finale

[Prophecy]: *"This earth and its inhabitants belong to Me," says God. "There will very soon be a changing of the guard. Stewards must be found faithful. Faithful to their assignment. Faithful to their call. That has not been so with the Church. I have another people who are after My heart and My desire. They will excel in the promise in these last days. They will accomplish all My will. They will glorify Me and honor Me before all men. They will show the world My love, My compassion and let them know who I am, as I desire to be known. I Am God. I change not! I set the stage. I choose the actors. Those who don't like the part, I have changed. The performance date has been set. The venue chosen. It's time to take center stage in this My Grand Finale before My Son returns. This is it! Take your places now!!" Says the Faith God, Directory of It All!*

After God spoke those words to me. I went into prayer sometime after midnight. The Lord set the tone of the *opening scene* of the performance. God said, *"Danger has increased!"* In the spirit I saw another level of danger come upon the nations of the earth. Jesus reminded me that darkness was going to increase before He returns. He said to me, *"No evil shall befall you."* The Lord said it again, *"No evil shall befall you."* Immediately I began praying in the spirit for the safety of my family, the cities, and the nations of the earth. Sometime later I could hear my spirit saying to the Father, "I will do all thy will." Again, my spirit said to God, "I will do all thy will in the earth!" Something was happening in the spirit. I had no understanding, but my spirit began saying, "My time as come! My time has truly come!" What did that mean? It has come time for me to step onto the stage, but not before being reminded of a warning.

According to the Lord, I have been hidden on purpose for such a time as this. The Lord said to me, *"You have an enemy."* Indeed. There is one person who has a habit of going into the spirit realm to send terrorizing threats to me and my family. Mr. Obama would love to stop God's people from doing what we are called to do in this country. God is telling me that it is my time to step out. I'm going to obey God, no matter what. The plan God gave me is for the nation's refuge from *"the whirlwind"* that is coming to our shores. As God said, Mr. Obama didn't want to be *"upstaged,"* but what is coming *"will upstage us all."* My assignment was to save millions of American lives. Mr. Obama was told that if he did not stop his political interference in this nation, *"millions of Americans"* would lose their lives. Therefore, because of his plots against the people of God, Mr. Obama has made himself the *villain"* of this American story. The man is *"off script,"* doing what he wants to do, but the Director is watching his every move. God, the Creator is also a *"Master of Improv."* He has people waiting in the wings, who have been trained in how to respond to the schemes of the evil villain. They are not ignorant of his devices (II Corinthians 2:11). They are simply resting in the Lord and waiting patiently for Him to give them their cues. They are not fretting because those who *seem* to prosper in their villainous ways. They are not angry. They are not quaking in their boots. These Holy Ghost trained performers know that the Director makes the final decision on what happens on stage. The performers on stage have some creative latitude, as long as it flows in the same spirit as the written script. However, if one proves to be too difficult to work with, they will be replaced. *"For evildoers shall be cut off: but those that wait upon the LORD, they shall inherit the earth (Psalm 37:7-9)."*

God said it in the prophecy. *"Those who don't like the part, I have changed."* Beloved, each of us is a seasonal performer. The Bible tells us that God has made this world and all that is therein. *"And hath made of one blood all nations of men for to dwell on all the face of the earth, and hath determined the times before appointed, and the bounds of their habitation (Acts 17:26)."* We can be easily replaced in the performance of life. I say this from experience. In the past, God taught me how to obey Him, through what I suffered. Even hanging with the wrong people can get you fired. God told me once that if I didn't stop hanging with a certain friend, who was distracting me, He would replace me with *"someone more faithful."* I want to be counted among those whom God finds faithful. I also want to receive my inheritance that God has laid up for me. In other words, I want everything that God sent Jesus on earth to give me. I want it all, in Jesus' Name. Therefore I stay before the Lord, seeking His Director's notes. Are there any changes in the script? What performers have written out of the script? Are there any deleted scenes? Is there a change of venue? Where is the staging area? As a performer, these are just a few of the things I need to know if I want to

158

do my job. The answers to these questions come by the wisdom of God. It comes from spending time with Him and keeping that line of communications open both day and night. God is about to promote those who *"hear what others cannot hear and see what others cannot see. Therefore they will be able to do what others could never do."* These are God's star performers. They stand out because they go the distance with Him. *"They desire to live life to the fullest, to experience all that God has for them in this life."* Knowing God and His Son Jesus Christ, is the highest knowledge available for mankind. This is where the *spirit of wisdom and revelation* enters the picture. We pray for God's *wisdom* and He responds in *revelation*.

The Holy Spirit began ministering to me about the purpose for the wisdom of God. Many in the Church in America have been taught that God does not speak to us any more; that the Holy Spirit is not necessary because we have technology. This is not true. Why would the God of the Bible speak to every generation upon the earth except for us? From Genesis to Revelation, God was speaking to men on earth. We are after all created in His image and likeness. Jesus only spoke what the Father told Him to speak (John 12:49). He also said that when He speaks God's word, the Father will do the work (John 14:10). This is how miracles are manifested. Again, we must hear the wisdom that comes from the mouth of God. As Jesus said, *"Man shall not live by bread alone, but by every word that proceedeth out of the mouth of God (Matthew 4:4)."* Whatever God speaks by His Spirit, He will absolutely bring it to pass in your life, if you hold on to that word with patience. God's word will not come back to Him without accomplishing what it was meant to do. *"So shall my word be that goeth forth out of my mouth: it shall not return unto me void, but it shall accomplish that which I please, and it shall prosper [in the thing] whereto I sent it (Isaiah 55:11)."*

God is always speaking. His wisdom is all around us, but are we listening? The Lord gave me a *vision* of the people of the earth. *I saw the wisdom of God, everywhere around us, everywhere we went. It was in the streets, and the bars, everywhere people were. The wisdom of God was there, but few were listening. There were so many loud voices competing for our attention. Many more alluring voices such that when men heard the wisdom of God, they would shut it down in favor of another wisdom; what they heard people say, what they saw people do. Some even argued with God's wisdom and cancelled it out because of what they felt with their senses. They chose sense knowledge over God's wisdom, with some measure of success, and then failure followed. The wisdom of God came only to make them wealthy (Proverbs 8:21), to bless them (Proverbs 10:22) without toil. Very few heard, and they were the wealthiest among men. They did not follow the crowd with sense wisdom: They were looking for what others could not see. They wanted to hear what others could not hear. These are the ones whom God seeks to make them wealthy.*

I keep hearing these same words, **"Whatever He says, do it."** Remember that God is the Director of what is getting ready to happen in the earth. It's **"His Grand Finale,"** which means we have to know our part. We must learn our lines. The Lord told me years ago that the script for our lives is downloaded to us from Heaven. *"The script is written on our hearts by the Holy Spirit."*[1] It may come as a vision, or dream. It may even come from the audible voice of the Lord directing you to a particular scripture. Regardless of how it comes, if we want to keep our part in God's production, we must find His script for your life. Begin by making Jesus the Lord of your life. If God is the Director of the Finale, you want to be on the same page. Therefore you must be born again. Pray. Ask God to forgive your sin and make Jesus the Lord of your life. Ask Him to fill you with the Holy Spirit. Now, ask the Holy Spirit to show you God's plan for your life. Take note of every detail that He shows you. Every detail is important. If the Holy Spirit did not give you the plan, seek God on your own. Start is by reading the Bible and committing what you read to prayer. The Holy Spirit may direct you to a specific passage in the Bible. If not, then the Gospel of John is a wonderful place to begin. Rehearse what you have read and heard. Meditate on it day and night. As the Bible says, *"This book of the law shall not depart out of thy mouth; but thou shalt meditate therein day and night, that thou mayest observe to do according to all that is written therein: for then thou shalt make thy way prosperous, and then thou shalt have good success (Joshua 1:8)."* The wisdom of God for our lives, is **the script we must follow** in these days. *"I[Wisdom] lead in the way of righteousness, in the midst of the paths of judgment: That I may cause those that love me to inherit substance; and I will fill their treasures (Proverbs 8:20-21)."*

---

1   Matthews, Paula. "STEP 1: You Must Be Born-Again." *Seeking And Enjoying The True Treasure Of This Life.* Shaker Heights: Spirit & Life Publications[SM], 2013. 41. Print.

God's wisdom is available to anyone. It can be found when one seeks righteousness and justice. The Bible says that Jesus is made *"wisdom"* for us (I Corinthians 1:30). He will lead us along the path of righteousness for His name sake (Psalm 23:3). This is how He restores us. God's wisdom not only brings restoration, but it also brings wealth, in abundance until it overflows. If we are faithful to God, we will abound with Blessing (Proverbs 28:20).

The wisdom God reveals also gives us words to speak. For example, God been saying for years that He was ***"putting an end to racism."*** The devil keeps using words and scenes of suffering to keep people chained to an old script. If people buy into that story line, they won't be able to inherit what God has for them. This is why people need to find God's script for their lives. People are oppressed because they are hearing negative speech about who they are, and about what they can have. They find themselves rehearsing these evil scenarios until they become a self fulfilling prophecy. It is just as easy to speak good things about yourself as it is the bad things. To find those good things, you will have to turn to God. Find out what God's word says about and put that word in your mouth. Let His word be the prophecy that is fulfilled in your life.

God says that your are fearfully and wonderfully made (Psalm 139:14). God knew you before you were in your mother's womb and He set you apart and ordained you for His purpose (Jeremiah 1:5). God's thoughts toward you are for good and not evil (Jeremiah 29:11). There are many scriptures that will lift you up while the world and the media is tearing you down and dashing your hopes. Your hope and expectation must be centered in God alone. He wants to do you good for all of your days, and for all eternity. Repent to God for the evil you have spoken. Then put His word in your mouth. Watch it manifest! We are in a highly prophetic time period. We are about to see our words manifest quickly, both the good and the bad. So it's best to have a "good" script to read in order to bring forth the good things God has for your life.

This world and the nation has been telling people who they are and what they are entitled to receive. God's inheritance for us is greater than anything we could ever imagine. *"Now unto him that is able to do exceeding abundantly above all that we ask or think, according to the power that worketh in us* (Ephesians 3:20). *"* You're not going to find His script by listening to the world. You have to hear it from God directly. What God has for your life and for my life, is hidden in a mystery. That is why the Bible says, *"Eye hath not seen, nor ear heard, neither have entered into the heart of man, the things which God hath prepared for them that love him. But God hath revealed [them] unto us by his Spirit: for the Spirit searcheth all things, yea, the deep things of God* (I Corinthians 2:9-10). *"* The Holy Spirit knows where all the good things are hidden. He will show them to you. Don't let anyone tell you different. Let God be true and every man a liar (Romans 3:4). No matter what evil you see, **"strive to see the good,"** and when you find it, put that in your mouth. Speak only what God speaks. Believe in the Lord and you shall be established (secure and faithful). Believe in His prophets and you shall prosper (II Chronicles 20:20).

Now that you have the script, ***are you dressed for the part?*** Have you put on the new man? As a son or daughter of God, you have a certain authority in this earth (John 1:12). Jesus is our example to follow. The Bible says that *"as he is, so are we in this world* (I John 4:17). *"* Jesus demonstrated how to walk in the authority of the Father. Pray that God gives you *"the spirit of wisdom and revelation in the knowledge of Him* (Ephesians 1:17). *"* Pray also that *"the eyes of your understanding"* would be enlightened so that you may *know the hope of His calling* for your life; that you would *know the riches of the glory of His inheritance in the saints*; that you would *know the greatness of His power available to you* who believe. It's according to the working of His mighty power. God has so much in store for you as His heir. Pray that the Holy Spirit reveal all that belongs to you so that you may be clothed with all the richness of His glory. Then, it is time to present your body for Kingdom services, a living sacrifice, and renew your mind with the word of God (Romans 12:1-2). Don't be conformed to the ways of this world any longer. You are not only the heir of God and joint heir with Jesus, but you are also a citizen of the Kingdom. This is an entirely different government than this world. It is important for you to read the Bible to learn more about this new Kingdom. It is equally important to be a part of a Bible teaching church so that you can learn more about this *"new way"* of living in the earth.

The final dressing you will need in your wardrobe is the *armor of God* (Ephesians 6:10-18). You need to be strong in the Lord, and in the power of His might. There are hecklers and naysayers out there. There are people who will hate what God is doing in your life. They may speak evil against you and persecute you. You need *spiritual armor* to be able to stand against the schemes of the devil. You have an invisible enemy. It is not the people who come against you. Our enemy is not flesh and blood. It is the devil and his demons. We war against principalities, against powers, against the rulers of the darkness of this world, against spiritual wickedness in high places. Only God can protect us from these demonic forces. That is why He gives us His armor. Therefore, we take by faith, *the whole armor of God.* We open our mouths, put on the armor of God and take a stand against the devil in this evil day.

*"Stand therefore, having your loins girt about with **truth**."* You must remain firm on the word of truth, especially that which God reveals directly to your spirit. Stand boldly on what you know to be true. Put on *"the breastplate of **righteousness**."* Protect your heart and emotions by maintaining integrity and right standing with God. Even if you sin, don't stress about it. Confess it to the Father and repent. God is faithful and just to forgive you sin and cleanse you from all unrighteousness (I John 1:9). Remember, you are no longer a sinner, but the righteousness of God in Christ Jesus (II Corinthians 5:21). You are a new creation. *"And your feet shod with the preparation of the **gospel of peace**."* Stand firm on the truth of the gospel and how it changes lives of the poor, how it heals the brokenhearted and sets the captives free. God sent the gospel come to open blinded eyes and to set free those who have been bruised; to proclaim the favor of the Lord, a day of vengeance of our God to comfort all that mourn (Isaiah 61:1-2). More than anything, take *"the shield of **faith.**"* Stand strong in faith so that you will be able block every thing the devil may throw at you, the wicked schemes and the fiery darts of criticism, witchcraft, evil visions and dreams. Believe in God and don't take the devil's suggestions. Don't take the bait! Retaliate with the word of God in your mouth.

Then *"And take the helmet of **salvation**."* Keep before you all that Jesus has done for you, and the benefits of salvation. *"Bless the LORD, O my soul: and all that is within me, [bless] his holy name. Bless the LORD, O my soul, and forget not all his benefits: Who forgiveth all thine iniquities; who healeth all thy diseases; Who redeemeth thy life from destruction; who crowneth thee with lovingkindness and tender mercies; Who satisfieth thy mouth with good [things; so that] thy youth is renewed like the eagle's* (Psalm 103:1-5). *"* Bless the Lord who daily loads us with benefits (Psalm 68:19). He is the God of our salvation. Take up the *"sword of the Spirit, which is **the word of God**. "* If the enemy tries to convince you of something that is untrue, respond with *"It is written (Matthew 4:1-10)."* That is exactly what Jesus did when the devil tempted Him in the wilderness. Satan came at Jesus with the word of God. That devil knows the word, but you have the Mind of Christ. Let the Holy Spirit give you words to speak. Finally, pray in the Spirit, always watching and praying for the saints. You have a common enemy that would like to divide and conquer the family of God. It's like Jesus said to Peter, *"Simon, Simon, behold, Satan hath desired [to have] you, that he may sift [you] as wheat: But I have prayed for thee, that thy faith fail not: and when thou art converted, strengthen thy brethren (Luke 22:31-32)."* That devil would like to sift us all, but we must repent for disobedience to God. Then we can be converted, not just for ourselves, but also for our brethren in the faith.

Now that you are dressed, it's time to take your places. Do you know where and when to enter the stage? Where is your mark? Do you know how and where to exist off stage? Since you are born again and filled with the spirit, allow the Holy Spirit to give you your cues. Move only when He prompts you to move. Speak only when He urges you to speak. Let the Holy Spirit help you remember your script. Jesus said, *"But the Comforter, which is the Holy Ghost, whom the Father will send in my name, he shall teach you all things, and bring all things to your remembrance, whatsoever I have said unto you (John 14:26)."*

Places everyone! God wants the actors center stage for the opening scene. This is a dress rehearsal. Stay on script no matter what happens out there. The devil will try to distract you with wars, rumors of wars, with famine and earthquakes, with hurricanes and wild fires and economic upheavals, pandemics and protests and political rhetoric, but the show must go on! Instead of saying, "Break a leg," I say to you, "Break the back of that devil!"

Go forth in the Name of Jesus. Remain faithful to your Kingdom assignment and your call. Go after God with your whole heart, and you will glorify the Father and honor Him before all men. Walk in love at all times. Show the world your Father's love, His compassion and let them know Who He really is, as He wants to be known. God is love.

YEARS 2020 AND BEYOND:
THE YEARS OF MANIFESTATION
God Will Be Glorified In The Earth!

If there is ever a theme that God is speaking in these end of the last days, it is about His Glory being seen in all the earth. The scripture is clear, the time is coming when God's glory will cover the earth (Psalm 72:19). *"For the earth shall be filled with the knowledge of the glory of the LORD, as the waters cover the sea (Habakkuk 2:14)."* There are numerous scriptures that talk about how the glory will cover the earth, but what God is saying today, is that *"the time is now. The glory is here!"* What God wants us to know is, that the entire world is about to recognized the glory of the Lord. It won't just be a "church thing" or something that is done in isolation. God is about to put His Glory *"up front and center"* and every eye will see it, and only the spiritually blind would be able to deny that it was God.

According to the Spirit of God, *He was glorified through His Son, and will be glorified again through His People who are called by His Name.* There is a powerful scripture reference that demonstrates what we are about to see in this season. It begins in the Book of John with the story of Lazarus, whom Jesus raised from the dead, and the glory of God was seen. This is such a powerful story. I know that we touched on this story in Volume I of **The War Journal**, but God has revealed so much more about this story that is relevant this particular season. It's as if the things God revealed back in 1999, are finally coming to pass in this season. So, if some of these stories seem familiar, they are. God is revealing even more about how this story parallels where we are today.

Jesus raised Lazarus from the dead, Jesus knew His time on earth was up. He said, *"Father glorify thy name."* The Father answered, *"I have glorified it and shall glorify it again (John 12:28)."* God will be glorified in His saints. As Jesus said, we will do "greater works" than He did. *"Verily, verily, I say unto you, He that believeth on me, the works that I do shall he do also; and greater [works] than these shall he do; because I go unto my Father (John 14:12)."* Jesus went to the Father and sent the Holy Spirit, the anointing power of God. He is the Father within who does the work (John 14:10). Therefore, it behooves us to take a closer look at one of the greatest miracles Jesus performed in His ministry. We need to understand the circumstances in which this miracle was performed, and know that the Holy Ghost Spirit Church will perform such works, and even more. The Bible says that they that know their God shall be strong and do exploits (Daniel 11:32). This is where we need to be in the Church. We have to know our God, not just head knowledge of Him, but intimate experiential knowledge of the Father. This requires spending quality time with God and His word. It begins with relationship. God wants us to truly know Him. That is why He calls us family. He desires a close relationship with His human creation. ***"The purpose of the Glory, is to reveal the person and character of Almighty God."*** We saw the glory of God earlier, in the story of Pharaoh who asked a question God had to answer. God didn't just speak through Moses. He answered Pharaoh with plagues against that nation.

Pharaoh said, *"Who is the LORD, that I should obey his voice to let Israel go? I know not the LORD, neither will I let Israel go (Exodus 5:2)."* The Bible says that God *"made known his ways to Moses,"* his acts to the children of Israel (Psalm 103:7). God make His ways known to His servants the prophets, but His acts are manifested first of all to His people, and then to the world. The acts of God are His miracles, signs and wonders. These are the things that capture the attention of human beings causing them to pause and acknowledge the presence and authority of Almighty God. In Egypt, it took God bringing devastating plagues, before Pharaoh and the Egyptians realized that God had all power. They were so tormented by the plagues that the people gave away their wealth and desired that the Children of Israel leave that nation. They would have done anything to make the plagues to cease. This is how the glory works. It forces the hand of the enemy to do right by the people of God. The enemy is punished while God's people get blessed. God made Himself known to Pharaoh and the entire nation. No longer could He say, *"I know not the LORD."* Pharaoh learned a tough lesson about the Lord. Afterwards, he did let Israel go. The glory is manifested in whatever way is necessary for God to reach a people. With Egypt it took being barraged with plagues. With Lazarus' sisters it was not so.

Jesus had a personal relationship with Lazarus and his sisters. His friend Lazarus was sick. His sisters sent word to Jesus, but before Jesus arrived. Lazarus died. When He finally shows up, Martha, the sister of chides Jesus saying, *"Lord, if thou hadst been here, my brother had not died."* Martha knows Jesus is the Son of God. She knows He is a holy man, but her first reaction was directed at Jesus, her brother's friend. Then in the same breath, she offers what seems like a religious appeasement. *"But I know, that even now, whatsoever thou wilt ask of God, God will give [it] thee."* Now imagine you are Jesus. Your best friend has died. God sent you to raise him up. His sisters know you as the Healer. They are thinking that you could have stopped what you were doing long enough to come minister healing to your friend so that he could live. What Martha was really saying, "If Lazarus was important to you Jesus, you would have been here." But, she caught herself and attempted to regain her faith in the power God had granted Jesus.

"Knowing the ways of God requires ignoring the reactions of men." The ways of God are far above ours. His thoughts are not like our thoughts (Isaiah 55:8-9). When you are attempting to perform a miracle, don't expect people to understand anything you are doing or saying. Otherwise you may become frustrated and lose the anointing to do the work. Martha was obviously conflicted about her brother's death. She knew Jesus had the power, but she also realized that God could do whatever he desired in that situation. Here is the thing. God has no limits, but humans do. To see the glory of God, we have to renew our minds to think outside of the box. You have to see things with the Mind of Christ.

God is eternal. Life and death are the same in eternity. They have no significance except on earth. They are only important in the time cycle of human life. Eternity it timeless. Souls will continue to live, either in the eternal life of God, or in the eternal death of hell and damnation, but every soul will live forever. So, the idea of death or life on earth is of no significance to God. Like Jesus said to His disciples when the sisters sent a messenger telling of Lazarus' death. *" Our friend Lazarus sleepeth; but I go, that I may awake him out of sleep* (John 11:11)."* That's just how God views death on the earth. Therefore, God is not moved by the fact that someone died. He can raise them up. The miracles of God bypass life, death and even time itself. It didn't matter to God that Lazarus had died. It didn't even matter to God how long he had been in the grave. Jesus came to raise him up. There are no impossibilities with God. He has no constraints. This earth is His creation. He made the laws of the universe, so God can bend the laws of nature, even those of this earth, anyway He chooses. All we must do is obey and God is glorified for doing the impossible in the midst of men. The issues will always be the naysayers, unbelievers and religious people who run their mouths in unbelief. If you want to perform a miracle and see the glory of God, you have to ignore the *"hecklers in the theatre."* Believe me, they are everywhere. They cannot hear what you are hearing from God. They cannot see what God is showing you. They are trying to reason it all. It's not possible to reason how God operates. I recall a pastor that I worked with who was convinced that every miracle of God had a rational explanation behind it. Really? When Jesus multiply the two fish and five loaves of bread to feed the five thousand, where did the twelve baskets of leftovers come from? This is a miracle that I have seen in my lifetime more than twice. The first time was when I was in college. A couple of friends and I were stranded after a bitter snow storm and none of us had enough food to make a meal. I asked everyone to bring what they had in their pantry to my apartment. God was going to make sure we had plenty to eat. As I can recall, we had one chicken, a handful of potatoes, a canned vegetable and I had a bit of flour enough to make biscuits. We had a feast and ate till we were full, and we had enough left over to keep us going until the roads were clear for us to drive. In that case, I had only cooperation. Those girls did not know how to cook on the fly, so they trusted me wholly and God got the glory.

Again, I was at a friend's home and the wife was too busy with the infant to cook. So I offered to fix dinner with whatever she had planned to do. Everything was already on the counter, all I had to do was open boxes, pour and cook. The wife said, to me, "Go ahead and cook, but it is never enough for everyone to get full." Why did she have to say that. She didn't know who she was talking to. It is my habit to pray a blessing over whatever I am cooking, and that meal was no exception. I fixed what the wife wanted and they wanted me to join them at dinner. Not only did they get full, the kids were stuffed. One even said, "that was the best food I've ever tasted." Oh, yeah, there were plenty of leftovers. God multiplied that food. Where did it all come from? I don't know and really don't care. I just know that when it was Blessed of God, He brought the overflow from Heaven. We simply cannot reason what God does. It is beyond human comprehension. I glad it is beyond us because if it weren't people would be trying to prove that they can do what God does. You can't let people like that get into your eyesight, they can block a miracle. You cannot let people's reasoning, their fears or emotions move you to do or say what God has not told you to do or say. This is God. It is supernatural. It is outside of the human scope of understanding. That is why Jesus did not go to Lazarus until He knew it was in God's timing. Sure He felt the pain and suffering of Martha and Mary, but He had to obey God. Even as I write, God is bringing to my mind such a situation. Some of you may have heard me give this witness before. I was training certain ministers in prayer and intercession. They had successfully created a prayer room in the inner city right across from a building where the local crack heads and druggies hung out. People were coming in for prayer and getting miracles, some of the most unusual miracles were being happening. Families were prospering because God had moved into the neighborhood.

One day, the minister in charge of the prayer room called me complaining that she needed money. Now mind you, there was food miraculously appearing in her cabinets. The neighbors had been showing up with grocery bags getting food from her kitchen. No one was shopping for food. It was just appearing in her cabinets miraculously. The minister said she was grateful for those miracles, but she needed money. It never occurred to her that the same God that put food in her cabinets could also put money in her pockets. The glory of God was in that place, and God was about to prove it. While she was complaining, the Lord tells me that all the money she needed was in her apartment. The minister didn't take me seriously. I told her exactly where God said it was, in a huge jar of coins in her living room. Again the minister told me that only coins were in that jar. She began to get testy with me. I hung up the phone and drove over to her apartment. I walked through her door and asked for a wire clothes hanger. This minister was full of unbelief, but I knew what God had shown me.

I went into her living room and picked up the huge jar. I put the clothes hanger into the jar and pulled out bills. I handed the bills to her and kept pulling more out of the jar. Time went on and there were so many bills in that jar that the woman got emotional and knew this was God. Why? Because she never puts bills in that jar, and no one has come into her apartment to put bill in there either. All she could do was repent for her unbelief and give glory to God for doing the impossible not once, but twice in miracles for her. God made food and money appear in this woman's home. Because she was faithful to handle His business and set up a prayer room, God was faithful to provide all she needed supernaturally. This is how God was glorified and her faith was increased. That is why God did not heal Lazarus, but allowed him to die. This was to increase the faith of the people. It was a demonstration of the power of

God over death. I also believe that it was a rehearsal of sorts for the resurrection of Jesus Himself. Martha and Mary were upset over the death of Lazarus due to sickness, but the sorrow of losing Jesus in a brutal execution was soon to come. They would have to have faith that if God would raise Lazarus, surely He would raise His only begotten Son. The people needed to see the glory of God at another level to also build their faith, even for their own resurrection in the last day when the saints will arise from the dead. This is the *"blessed hope"* of all believers (Acts 24:15; Titus 2:13).

Now, concerning Lazarus' death Jesus told Martha, *"Thy brother shall rise again* (John 11:23)*."* Martha was quick to respond, *"I know that he shall rise again in the resurrection at the last day."* Here we go. Jesus is talking about raising up Lazarus right then and now. Martha is regurgitating her religious recitation of scripture. She has head knowledge, but Jesus is talking about the glory bringing about the reality that if Jesus is here today, then resurrection is available right now. Jesus puts it right in Martha's face. *"Jesus said unto her, I am the resurrection, and the life: he that believeth in me, though he were dead, yet shall he live: And whosoever liveth and believeth in me shall never die. Believest thou this?"* After hearing, this Martha tried to have faith, but obvious this too went over her head. *"She saith unto him, Yea, Lord: I believe that thou art the Christ, the Son of God, which should come into the world. And when she had so said, she went her way, and called Mary her sister secretly, saying, The Master is come, and calleth for thee* (John 11:25-27)*."* The conversation was too deep for Martha. She needed a diversion, so she walked away and called Mary her sister. I can just imagine that if Martha was in the American Baptist tradition, she would have held up her index finger and walked away. She could not stretch her faith to follow what Jesus was saying. This was also the end of the conversation as far as Jesus was concerned. When Mary showed up, Jesus simply said, *"Where have ye laid him?"* Sometimes it is better to show the power of God rather than explain scripture to people. The Lord told us that He would confirm the word with signs following (Mark 16:20). Jesus spoke, but now it was time for a demonstration of the word.

The Bible says that when they directed Him to where Lazarus was laid, Jesus wept (John 35). I believe that Jesus wept for a number of reasons. Sure He felt the mourning of those who came to comfort Martha and Mary. Then there also had to be sadness at the unbelief of Lazarus' sisters. These were friends of Jesus. They would have been privy to Kingdom secrets and miracles that others may not have seen or heard of and yet they still had unbelief. This sadness could also be for His own death and resurrection that was soon approaching. The resurrection of Lazarus would be the most significant miracle in Jesus' ministry. It would bring much attention to Him, causing the enemy to come to take His life. He knew that the Jewish leaders wanted to stone Him. Raising Lazarus would be the one miracle that would give them the motivation to execute Jesus.

Once at the grave, Jesus said, *"Take ye away the stone."* This was the command that would demonstrate who had faith in resurrection. Martha barked, *Lord, by this time he stinketh: for he hath been dead four days."* Remember how Martha said to Jesus earlier, *"But I know, that even now, whatsoever thou wilt ask of God, God will give it thee* (v22)." Her belief was being tested, only to realize that it wasn't as strong as she thought. Jesus said to Martha before He raised her brother Lazarus from the dead, *"Said I not unto thee, that if thou wouldest believe, thou shouldest see the glory of God* (John 11:40)?" Lazarus had been in the grave four days and Jesus came to raise him up. It is the glory of God to do the impossible in the midst of men. The glory is based on God's purpose for Lazarus' life. Jesus had told Martha from the very beginning that her brother's sickness was not unto death, but for the glory of God. Sickness and death don't come from the Father. They come from the thief who comes to steal, kill and destroy (John 10:10), but God allowed it for a demonstration. Lazarus died, but it was not God's plan that he remain dead. God wanted to get glory out of raising Lazarus from the dead. The Bible does not say what caused Lazarus' sickness. Clearly it did not matter to God because that was not Jesus' concern. His assignment from the Father was to raise Lazarus from the dead. This was to be a sign and wonder to those in Bethany the town of Martha, her sister Mary and their brother Lazarus. It was also to be a demonstration of God's power for the disciples as well. When they realized that Lazarus was dead, Jesus said to them, *"And I am glad for your sake that I was not there, to the intent ye may believe; nevertheless let us go to him* (John 11:15)."

This resurrection was a dramatic demonstration to help the disciples and all the onlookers to believe. It would seem that there were many unbelieving followers of Jesus at that time. God had to show His glory so that they might believe. Think about it. How many so called Christian are followers of Jesus Christ? Of those followers, how many actually believe? It's one thing to know the scriptures like Martha did, but it's quite another to recognize the living and breathing Word of God who is with you. Martha and Mary knew Jesus. He spent time at their home. He fellowshipped with them. He dined in their home. This was a close relationship, and yet they did not fully understand who Jesus was, nor did they recognize the power that He possessed. Isn't this just like so many Christians? They say they believe, but when their faith is put to the test, they back up and back down.

The issue with so many Christians is that we think we know how God ought to answer our prayers. We know what we want and just assume God wants the same thing. Not only that, but we want to tell God how to do His miracle. The miracle that Martha desired was healing. That was something they had seen Jesus do numerous times. But God wanted to take their belief far beyond healing to the "blessed hope" of resurrection. That is the ultimate miracle for any believer. Now, Martha was a bit peeved at Jesus because her prayer was not answer in the way she desired. Again there are Christians who have done the same thing. If God does not answer their prayer just so, they get an attitude. Some even turn against Him. As if God's answering their prayer, the way they want it answered is an indication of His love for them. This is how many Christians think. "God, this would not have happened if you really loved me." That is the attitude Martha was demonstrating. BUT, God wanted to be glorified. When confronted with the idea of her brother being resurrected on the spot, Martha was indignant complaining about how the body would be stinking. Who cares if he stinks? God wants to get the glory in the man's death and resurrection. God wants to prove that you don't have to wait until that "great day" you can have resurrection today.

Likewise, there are Christians who are awaiting the glory of the Lord to come when Jesus returns in the power and glory of the Father. They are quoting scriptures of some event in the future, and Jesus is trying to do a miracle now. He wants to use something that has gotten sick or died in our lives as a demonstration of His resurrection power. It is all so that the Son is glorified in the Father. People today hardly believe that Jesus was a real person. They know the Bible stories, but some think they are just fables. No! God is real. Jesus is real, and He wants to be glorified, so that the world will know that God really sent Him. This was the issue Jesus had with Martha and Mary. He wanted to raise their brother from the dead so that those with Him, and those with the sisters in their mourning, would know that God heard His Son, and that this was a demonstration before all these people, that the Father had sent Him. When Jesus cried with a loud voice, *"Lazarus, come forth!"* He walked out of that grave bound in grave clothes. Jesus said, *"Loose Him, and let him go."* When Lazarus was loosed, so was the faith of those onlookers. They had proof that God heard Jesus' and that He heard the cries of Martha and Mary too. In His faithfulness to them, God was also glorified.

Jesus put His life at risk coming to Bethany. The Jewish leaders wanted to kill Him. Perhaps that is why Jesus waited as long as He did before going to Lazarus, not because His life was in danger, but because He wanted to complete the miracle in God's timing. Who knows? If Jesus had gone to Lazarus early, news could have got out about His whereabouts and it could have hindered God entire plan. It also had to be a frustrating time for Jesus to get the message of the sickness and ultimate death of His friend. The disciples were confused as to why Lazarus was sleeping. Then Martha attacked Him with nonsense about her brother not dying if Jesus had come like she asked. Then there was Mary and the mourners with her. By this time, surely news had traveled that Jesus was in town. His haters had just enough time to stage a plot to take His life. That meant that Jesus had only a short window in which to raise Lazarus from the dead. It would be sort of a **"grand finale"** of miracles before His execution. And so it was.

Jesus raised Lazarus from the dead. Imagine the commotion it caused with the Jewish leaders and that whole town. As the Bible says, *"Then many of the Jews which came to Mary, and had seen the things which Jesus did, believed on him. But some of them went their ways to the Pharisees, and told them what things Jesus had done."* And, they plotted to take Jesus' life. They put the word out that if anyone knew where Jesus was, to show the authorities so they could take Him away. But, Jesus did not hide from them. He continued obeying the Father, in plain sight. Several days before Passover, Jesus and his disciples came to Bethany and had supper with Lazarus and his sisters (John 12:1). The town's people heard that Jesus was there and they came not only to see Jesus, but to see Lazarus whom He raised from the dead. This caused the Jewish leaders to want to kill both Jesus and Lazarus. The Bible says that *"On the next day much people that were come to the feast, when they heard that Jesus was coming to Jerusalem, Took branches of palm trees, and went forth to meet him, and cried, Hosanna: Blessed [is] the King of Israel that cometh in the name of the Lord* (John 12:12-13)." Because of this miracle, Jesus was glorified and hailed as King! Jesus knew that all this fame would lead to His death. He knew it was time to be glorified. He said, *"Father, glorify thy name."* The Bible says *"Then came there a voice from heaven saying, I have both glorified it, and will glorify it again. The people therefore, that stood by and heard it, said it thundered: other said, An angel spake him* (John 12:28)." God spoke from heaven as a witness to the people, that this was the glory of God in their midst. This was no ordinary man. This was no ordinary situation. This was the Son of God.

Likewise, we are in a season like no other. God was glorified in His Son, and now He will be *glorified again* in His people. He will resurrect everything that has died in their lives. In doing so, God will show forth His glory and the people will praise Him, both saint and sinner. They will know Him as a **"Good God."** The world will see the **"good works"** of His people and will be drawn to Him. They will hear the word of God spoken by His people and they will see miraculous signs and wonders to follow. Their *light* will shine ever so brightly and draw men to Christ, but there will be many naysayers and haters. Oh, they will see bona fide miracles, but it's the notoriety that bothers them. Everybody in the world wants to be *king of the hill*. They wanted to make their names great, but God exalts **"no bodies"** who He will make their names great and He will get the glory for their deeds.

The world is about to learn that promotion does not come from the east or the west, nor the south. **"Promotion comes from God."** In this season, God will put down one and raise up another (Psalm 75:6-7) whom will do all of His will. This will anger the political and religious "pharisees." They will plot to take your lives. They will plot to hinder your assignment, but God has got your back. God has commanded, **"Loose them and let them go!"** This is happening even as we speak. God is shaking the world in order that His will be done in the earth and in the lives of His people. He will rain down fire from Heaven. God will send plagues if He has to, but that devil <u>will</u> let His people go. We are in a **"kairos Moment"** in time. This is God's appointed season to do all of His will in this earth. Anyone in His way, will be removed, even by force. Hence the **"shaking"** we see and will continue to see around the world. All God's people need to do is move forward in their assignments, no matter what comes against them. If they obey God, He will do the rest. In fact, God is bringing judgment upon those who refuse to let us go. He is telling His people to state their case against the devil. ***Almighty God: "Bring forth your case!" To ME, Every knee shall bow And tongue shall take oath!"*** Jesus is returning soon. The Church and the world has to be ready. Everything that can be shaken, will be shaken until all that remains is that which belongs to the Kingdom of God.

Here is the prophetic word God spoke about 2020 and beyond:

"I have glorified My Name in the earth through

My Beloved Son, and I will glorify it again through

My People who are called by Name," says God.

"For The Winds of My Spirit

Shall purify them and purge them from all iniquity."

"I am sending A Wave of Healing and Deliverance

To mend their bodies and their souls.

For My Purpose Alone shall I do these things.

No man shall get the glory, for I do this by My Spirit Alone."

"This is My Time to purify the sons of Levi,

My Time to set them aside for this final season of earth's

Captivity to the evil one."

"I will sovereignly set them free

For the purpose of demonstrating to the world

Who I am,

The Healing Balm in the Land of the living."

"I will strengthen them in My power

And they will take Healing And Deliverance

To The Nations of the world."

"I will be glorified," says God.

"For they shall bear much fruit that shall remain forever
As a praise and an honor to My Greatness."
"I share My glory as they Glory in My Divine Power."
"I will glorify My Name through them.
For they are Vessels Of Honor unto Me."
"They are my sons and daughters led by
My Spirit to do good works that honor Me.
Such works as have never been seen before by any human."
"This is My Hour to showcase
Who I am in the lives of people whom I love.
I will do great things on their behalf that will stun the world.
For I am Great and have Great things to give,
If only they would listen and obey My Voice."
"Yes, I will do this thing in the earth NOW,
For It is My Time to Shine through My People.
For yet darkness has a little time,
But MY GLORY HAS NOW ARISEN UPON MY PEOPLE
And they shall Glorify Me, now and forever,"
Says Almighty God.

"Look unto me, and be ye saved, all the ends of the earth:
For I am God, and there is none else. I have sworn by myself,
The word is gone out of my mouth in righteousness,
And shall not return,
That unto me every knee shall bow, every tongue shall swear."
Isaiah 45:22-23

The Winds Of Change Have Come!

Jesus said that everyone is born again is like the wind (John 3:8). On the surface, this might seem an odd comparison at first, but further exploration will reveal that *"The Wind"* holds a significant part in the life of every believer. The Bible describes a conversation between Jesus and Nicodemus, a Pharisee, a ruler of the Jews of that day. He had heard Jesus speak earlier that day, and came to the Lord that night with questions. *"Rabbi, we know that thou art a teacher come from God: for no man can do these miracles that thou doest, except God be with him (John 3:1-2)."*

Being a religious man of reputation, Nicodemus approaches Jesus with a compliment, but the Lord was not impressed. He immediately responds by letting this ruler know that he cannot gain favor with God by compliments. Jesus said, *"Verily, verily, I say unto thee, except a man be born again, he cannot see the kingdom of God."* Nicodemus knew about the coming of God's Kingdom, and probably assumed that his leadership position in the synagogue qualified him for entry. Jesus threw him off of his religious conjectures, and the ruler responds by attempting to elevate himself in the conversation by stressing the impossibility of a man being born again in his mother's womb. This was said, as if to demean Jesus after He did not receive the gracious compliment of a noted Pharisees. Jesus was not about to stroke this man's ego. Neither was He going to make light conversation to be politically correct in the face of this man of stature.

If Nicodemus had heard Jesus teach, then he should have been ready to be hit with the truth. Perhaps that is why he came to Jesus at night, as not to be seen by his peers and to get the Lord's undivided attention. So, he had Jesus' attention, but Nicodemus was not quite ready for such a spiritual encounter with the Lord. Such is typical of religious people. They can battle you with scripture and what the Bible says, but when you begin talking about an intimate relationship with the God of miracles, they begin to backtrack. Unless it can be read in a book and studied, they find it hard to believe, and yet God is a Spirit (John 4:24). He desires those who will worship Him in spirit and in truth. Therefore, if Nicodemus was a real worshipper of God, then He had to be man enough to receive the truth that Jesus spoke. And so, he listens as Jesus continues to speak. *"Verily, verily I say unto thee, except a man be born of water and of the Spirit, he cannot enter into the kingdom of God."* This comment is significant because Jesus said that one had to be born again to recognize (see) the things of the kingdom. Now, He was saying that you had to be born of both the water and of the Spirit or you could not even enter into the Kingdom of God.

Imagine what was going through the mind of this ruler of the Jews. The Jews had been taught that Abraham being their father qualified them to automatically enter the Kingdom. Jesus just upset the religious theology. One can be in church. You could even be a leader of the church, but that does not qualify you to enter into the Kingdom. This is a spiritual Kingdom. Flesh and blood cannot enter into it. You must be born again, meaning, you must be born of God's Spirit. A spiritual transformation must take place if you want to enter into the Kingdom.

At this point, one can only assume that Nicodemus was speechless, but he may have indicated surprise, even shock at what Jesus said. The Lord continues, *"Marvel not that I said unto thee, Ye must be born again."* Jesus then makes a sharp departure from talking about becoming born again. *"The wind bloweth where it listed, and thou hearest the sound thereof, but canst not tell whence it cometh, and whither it goeth: so is every one that is born of the Spirit (John 3:8)."* This must have been so ridiculously impossible to Nicodemus that he could no long keep quiet. He responds, *"How can these things be?"* Finally, he has to admit that Jesus is talking far above this ruler's understanding. This in itself is a demonstration of how the wind of the Spirit blows. It cannot be reasoned by human intellect. It cannot be studied in a book. This is the wind of the Spirit in operation and Nicodemus has no response.

Jesus continues, *"Art thou a master of Israel, and knowest not these things? Verily, verily, I say unto thee, We speak that we do know, and testify that we have seen; and ye receive not our witness. If I have told you earthly things and ye believe not, how shall ye believe, if I tell you of heavenly things?"* Nicodemus had no understanding. Perhaps he was even confused about what Jesus was saying. Again, this is how it is for the born again believer. You cannot perceive what they say or what it means. The words they speak from God, are spiritually discerned.

This was a wonderful example of how the wind of the Spirit moves, but let's take a look at what is going on from God's perspective. The Lord spoke a word to me in season. I heard it once and took note of it. I heard it twice and it got more of my attention. Then one evening, I heard Him speak, *"My Winds are here, get ready to set sail."* Immediately I thought about Jesus' conversation with Nicodemus. I just knew that the Winds of God were about to blow, taking me to my divine destiny. I needed to get ready. It takes discernment to know that it would not necessarily be a wind in the physical sense. Perhaps God would send a series of supernatural events designed to cause His people to move into their positions of destiny. Maybe it is something that would cause us to set sail on a course of victory. In any case, one who is born of God's Spirit would know within their spirit when it is time to set sail.

The *"Wind of God* (the Ruwach, breath, mind, spirit)*"* resides within the heart of every believer. How is this possible? Like Jesus told Nicodemus, you must be born of water and of the Spirit. It is a supernatural process by which the human heart is converted into a receiver for the Spirit of God. We saw in an earlier chapter how God took dirt and breathed His Breath, *the Breath of Life* into the nostrils of man and mankind became a living soul. This *Wind of God* is the same Breath of God, but notice that it is not being breathe in the nostrils, but upon the heart of man. When Adam sinned, mankind did not physically die. As long as he had breath in his lungs, the man could live. What left the man, was the Breath of God which was the heart and mind of God. The natural breath remained, but the spirit, that which was God Himself, departed from man. He is a Holy God. He cannot remain in a place where sin exists.

What remained inside of the man was empty space where God once lived. Man still had a soul. He still had a body. His human spirit was void of God's Spirit giving instructions, and downloading information on how to function in the earth. God was man's teacher, but after sin, man had to figure things out for himself. He was left to work through this life by his own wits. Once man was born again, his heart was re-configured to receive the Holy Spirit of God, who is deposited inside of every believer. This *Wind of God* becomes the power that directs our steps in this life. The *Wind of God* blows where He wishes. If we want what God has, then we must go with *the Wind*. We must let the Spirit lead us to our divine destiny. This is how Jesus operated. This is also what He was attempting to explain to Nicodemus. The difference between this ruler and believers of Jesus Christ today is the Holy Spirit. Nicodemus and other followers of Jesus, did not have the Holy Spirit until after the resurrection. Before Jesus went to the cross, He told his disciples, *"If ye love me, keep my commandments. And I will pray the Father, and he shall give you another Comforter, that he may abide with you for ever; Even the Spirit of Truth; whom the world cannot receive, because it seeth him not, neither knoweth him: but ye know him; for he dwelleth with you, and shall be in you* (John 14:15-17)." The Spirit of Truth (Holy Spirit) comes to reside within the heart of the believer at salvation, but those who are not born again cannot see Him or the Kingdom. They cannot even know the Spirit (Wind) of God without being born again. The Holy Spirit was with the disciples, but after the resurrection, He would come to dwell within every believer. And so it is today for everyone who receives Jesus as Lord of their lives. The Holy Spirit comes to lead them into all truth. Jesus showed us how to operate in the Holy Spirit. The Bible says that the sons of God (Romans 8:14) are those who are led by the Spirit of God. Every believer has the authority to receive on the level of a son (John 1:12). It is through obedience to the Holy Spirit that one is positioned to receive the fullness of their earthly inheritance.

God has many good things set aside for His own people, yet they cannot receive unless they allow the Holy Spirit to reveal these things to them. Remember that *"eye hath not seen, nor ear hear, neither has it entered into the hearts of men, the things that God has reserved for those who love him* (I Corinthians 2:10)." These things are revealed by His Spirit to our human spirits. Discernment comes from the Holy Spirit giving God's people eyes to see, and ears to hear what God has for them. We are in a season in which God is about to release *"the precious fruit of the earth* (James 5:7). This is the season of the latter rain. This shall be the greatest harvest we have seen on earth. Therefore we pray once again, for all believers, the same prayer that apostle Paul prayed for the Church,

"That the God of our Lord Jesus Christ, the Father of glory, may give unto [them] the spirit of wisdom and revelation in the knowledge of Him. *The eyes of your understanding being enlightened; that ye may know what is the hope of his calling, and what the riches of the glory of his inheritance in the saints* (Ephesians 1:18)."

180

We know that the Wind of God is His Spirit, but when God talks about the WINDS, this refers to the effect of the Wind (Ruwach) upon the earth. Like the natural winds cause the leaves and trees and everything to move, so does the Spirit of God do so much more as He moves through His people. When the Spirit of God moves, it causes a supernatural flow that cannot be stopped. The *Wind of God* causes the laws of God's Kingdom to supersede every law in the universe. These *spiritual* winds are sent to propel us to our divine destiny. They will do whatever is necessary to get us where we are supposed to be. They can do it the easy way, or the difficult way, as long as we get where God wants us. They can come as a simple wind or as a volatile storm of severe magnitude.

I recall the story of Apostle Paul who was imprisoned and determined to appeal to Caesar (Acts 26:32; 27:1-44). They took Paul and the other prisoners and set sail for Italy from Jerusalem. When they reached Sidon and went through Cyprus. The Bible says that *"the winds were contrary."* When the sailing became dangerous, Paul obviously sensed something in his spirit and spoke up. *"Sirs, I perceive that this voyage will be with hurt and much damage, not only of the lading and ship, but also of our lives. Nevertheless the centurion believed the master and the owner of the ship, more than those things which were spoken by Paul* (v10).*"* They ignored Paul, but later there arose what the Bible calls *"a tempestous wind, called Euroclydon* (v14).*"* This was a whirlwind, or hurricane, so powerful that it had been given a name. Then they became shipwrecked and Paul spoke again. *"But after long abstinence Paul stood forth in the midst of them, and said, Sirs, ye should have hearkened unto me, and not have loosed from Crete, and to have gained this harm and loss. And now I exhort you to be of good cheer: for there shall be no loss of [any man's] life among you, but of the ship. For there stood by me this night the angel of God, whose I am, and whom I serve, Saying, Fear not, Paul; thou must be brought before Caesar: and, lo, God hath given thee all them that sail with thee. Wherefore, sirs, be of good cheer: for I believe God, that it shall be even as it was told me. Howbeit we must be cast upon a certain island* (v21-26).*"*

Here is a story of what happens when the *"winds are contrary."* This was not the *"Wind of God"* propelling Paul to his destiny with Caesar. This was a storm sent to kill him and the other passengers. It was sent to prevent Paul from completing his assignment. What saved the passengers and the crew was the fact that God wanted Paul to witness to

Caesar. This is why people need to know specifically what God's assignment is for this season. Again, this is the importance of seeking the wisdom of God. Then when the storms come and everyone is thinking they are about to die, you will know that no harm will come to those around you because you have destiny to fulfill. If you know what God wants you to do, if you know what He promised would happen, you have a very powerful weapon to use against the enemy. This weapon alone will strengthen your faith in turbulent times in the world. As the Bible says, *"this is the victory that overcometh the world, even our faith* (I John 5:4)."

There is yet another story that Lord put on my heart to share. It's in Mark Chapter 4. Jesus was teaching by the seaside. He entered into a ship and sat on the sea. He taught the Parable of the Sower and many other parables as well. *"And with many such parables spake he the word unto them, as they were able to hear [it]. But without a parable spake he not unto them: and when they were alone, he expounded all things to his disciples. And the same day, when the even was come, he saith unto them, Let us pass over unto the other side* (v33-35)." That same evening, after Jesus taught, he said, *"Let us pass over unto the other side."* Then they sent away the multitude and took the ships out. Here comes another storm. *"And there arose a great storm of wind, and the waves beat into the ship, so that it was now full. And he was in the hinder part of the ship, asleep on a pillow: and they awake him, and say unto him, Master, carest thou not that we perish* (v37-38)?" What is wrong with this picture? Jesus was asleep. It should have been obvious to the disciples that if there was serious threat to their lives, He would have already dealt with it. If there was a problem, Jesus would have been awake, but He was asleep on a pillow. Jesus was sleeping comfortably, and why not? He had been hours teaching the multitude. Jesus needed a nap. He had something even bigger than that storm to deal with on *"the other side."*

Jesus had been teaching all day. There was a purpose for Jesus telling them to go to the other side. He had another assignment to fulfill. This was not a sightseeing trip. This was not for fun. It was a Kingdom work Jesus had to fulfill on the other side of the sea, and He needed to rest. Didn't those disciples learn something that would strengthen their faith? Obviously not. They were afraid for their lives and decided to pester Jesus. "Master, don't you care we are all going to die?" That is what they were saying. It sounds a lot like what Martha said after her brother died, "If you had cared and had been here, my brother would not have died." Such whining unbelievers! How could they spend so much time with Jesus and still have no faith? So, Jesus got up and *"rebuked the wind, and said unto the sea, Peace be still. And the wind ceased, and there was a great calm. And he said unto them, Why are ye so fearful? how is it that ye have no faith? And they feared exceedingly, and said one to another, What manner of man is this, that even the wind and the sea obey him (v39-41)?"* Again, we find a situation in which Jesus had a purpose to fulfill and therefore could have a peaceful sleep even in the midst of a storm. What waiting for Him on the other side of the sea was the madman of Gadara, whom God wanted to be made free. That storm was sent by the enemy in order to stop Jesus from arriving at the Gadarenes.

This has been a useful tactic of the enemy. He will send storms, even viruses to send fear so that you won't complete your Kingdom assignments. That happen when COVID-19 hit the earth. Many Christian panicked like the rest of the world and thought it was the end. Not so! God had already told me what was to happen in 2020. I was expecting great manifestations of God's promise and when the virus hit, it was strange. I thought it was a hoax. It was not real, but yet there was evidence of something being real. God said to me, **"Wage a warfare."** I reminded what Paul told Timothy. *"This charge I commit unto thee, son Timothy, according to the prophecies which went before on thee, that thou by them mightest war a good warfare; Holding faith, and a good conscience; which some having put away concerning faith have made shipwreck (I Timothy 1:19-19)."* Oh, I took out every prophecy the Lord had given me and began speaking them into the atmosphere and waging war against that virus. Then the Lord opened my eyes further to see how our **"waging a warfare was more than standing on prophecy."** It is directly connected to why we pray for all men and for those in authority.

Here is how the scripture reads. Paul tells Timothy to stand on the prophecies for his life and why it's important, and immediately He says, *"I exhort therefore, that, first of all, supplications, prayers, intercessions, [and] giving of thanks, be made for all men; For kings, and [for] all that are in authority; that we may lead a quiet and peaceable life in all godliness and honesty. For this [is] good and acceptable in the sight of God our Saviour (II Timothy 2:1-3)."* We pray for and intercede because we have a prophecy to fulfill. We speak to the storms because it is the will of God, and these are the signs, wonders and miracles, the good works that men will see and glorify our Father in Heaven. Hear this. ***"the turbulence is coming because the enemy wants to stop the move of God in this earth. God is unstoppable."*** If God is unstoppable, then we latch onto Him and we'll be unstoppable too! Then we ***"take what the enemy meant for evil and use it against him."*** We continue on our course. We keep speaking the prophetic words given to us. We continue to pray for all men and especially for those in authority. WHY? So that we can lead a quiet and peaceable life in all godliness and honesty. Put it right up in that devil's face. *"But as for you, ye thought evil against me; [but] God meant it unto good, to bring to pass, as [it is] this day, to save much people alive* (Genesis 50:20).*"*

Okay. Let me calm down a bit to finish this teaching. I could get really fired up in the Holy Ghost, but the Lord has already told me to release this book and I'm not quite done writing. Now, let's return to talking about God's Winds of Change. He told us to get ready to sail. Before one can sail, they must have a ***"sea-worthy"*** vessel prepared for the voyage. What's your assignment? What did God tell you to prepare? There are many vessels, but not all are capable of going where the Lord wants to take His people in this season. When Noah built the ark, he wasn't just building a boat to sail on the waters. This was not to be a luxury cruiser. This was no time for a family vacation. God declared His season of judgment, and He commanded Noah to build an ark for protection from the destruction God was sending upon the earth (Genesis 6:13-22). Once again, God has declared **this** to be HIS Season, not to destroy all flesh, but to save them and preserve them from the wrath to come (I Thessalonians 1:10). This is a season of judgment, but only for the purpose of getting us prepared for Jesus' return. After that event, the Church will be taking out of the earth and the wrath of God will be unleashed upon the earth with full power.

In our day, the glory of God is in our midst. The enemy is attempting to distract us by causing all manner of evil to pop up. He wants us to miss out on what the glory will bring, but as long as we are faithful to God, that devil will be forced to back down. The same glory that he is attempting to block will be the very *Wind of God* that destroys him. God made a covenant with Noah, that He would never destroy all flesh, like He did with the flood (Genesis 9:11). Instead, God sent His Son, Jesus Christ to save all men. So, what is the wrath that is coming to the earth?

It is the wrath of God against the sin and evil that our adversary the devil, has brought upon our lives. God created this earth for His own pleasure. It was to be the inheritance for His earthly children (Psalm 2:8). God created this earth as a place in which His sons and daughters could reign. They were to reign in righteousness, with the Blessing, as rulers over their own domain. Adam, the first ruling heir, decided that he could do better all on his own. Little did Adam know. Mankind was not created to do things, apart from God. They were never meant to go on their own. We discussed how it was God who breathed into man the very breath that we breathe (Genesis 2:7). To operate apart from God meant that His Breath, the Holy Spirit, the powerful Ruwach of God, had to be removed from Adam. God's Spirit is holy. He will not reside inside of sinful men. All human beings are born in sin and without God's Spirit in this world. They have no innate spirit (breath or wind) in which to live as God originally created us to live.

We were originally designed to *live, and move and have our being* (Acts 17:28) in the Ruwach (Wind, Spirit) of God. Sin relegated us to be disconnected from God's Spirit and bound to the curse. Righteous living under the Blessing was God's plan for mankind for all eternity. Instead, Adam cursed mankind to sin and to death. Righteousness no longer ruled. The earth, its people, and all its possessions fell under the authority of satan, the adversary. God, being a good Father, was determined to restore mankind and the earth back to righteousness, but He gave man dominion over the earth (Genesis 1:28). God is a Spirit. He could not step out of Heaven and give the earth back to man. Even so, there were no righteous men on earth. God still continued covenanting with mankind to restore the Blessing. We talked about how God covenanted with Noah and His sons. The Blessing went through Noah's son Shem down the generations to Abraham. No matter how many covenants God made with His people, nothing was adequate to remove the curse.

God had to come down Himself, in the form of a man (Philippians 2:7). Jesus agreed to be the Lamb of God that takes away the sins of the world (John 1:29). Jesus bore the curse for us, so that the Blessing could be restored to our lives (Galatians 3:13-14). " Jesus came to restore everything that Adam lost. Although the adversary has had influence since Adam fell, the Bible reminds us of earth's true owner. The earth is the LORD's (Psalm 24:1)! The earth, and everything in it belongs to God. In these last days, He is taking it all back. Wrath is coming because this will be a violent taking over. Jesus came the first time to save mankind from the wrath that is to come. God is *"putting away all unrighteousness."* Righteousness will be restored in this earth. God does not hate sinners. He hates sin because it results in death. Jesus is coming very soon, and whatever is not cleaned up will be burned up! He is a consuming fire (Hebrews 12:29). God will not change His plan to restore the earth. In this season, it is vital that we seek the wisdom of God in everything. God said, *"Turn you at my reproof: behold, I will pour out my spirit unto you, I will make known my words unto you* (Proverbs 1:20-23).*"* God is not withholding information from you. He is trying to release His wisdom so that you will know how to live in these last days.

The Holy Ghost *"shaking"* is about to increase to the utmost degree. The Lord has commanded His people to build **arks of protection**, just like Noah did prior to the flood. These may not be arks in the physical sense, but they are institutions and projects for Kingdom living in these turbulent last days. They will be *"a refuge from the storm."* God wants the world to be prepared for this dramatic shift in ownership from world governments to Kingdom authority. The transition will create turbulence like this world has never known. The world will resist the change, but they will not win. Jesus will reign over the nations of the earth.

His will be a righteous reign, full of peace and prosperity, full of Heaven's bounty flowing down into the earth. This is what God wants the Church to demonstrate now. Even with all of the ugly things that Jesus said would happen before He returns, there is one bright note. *"The gospel of the kingdom shall be preached in all the world for a witness unto all nations."* No matter what happens in the world, there will be the preaching and demonstration the power of God's Kingdom.

This is what Jesus did on earth. He taught the Kingdom, and demonstrated its power over sickness, disease, lack, even over death. Jesus calmed the raging storm. He brought the dead to back life. He opened blind eyes and caused the lame to walk again. This was the power of the Kingdom then, it is the power of God's Kingdom available to believers today. This power is the *Wind of God* moving in each and every situation that came against God's creation. We don't know how the Wind does what it does. How did the lame walk? How did blind eyes open? How could the Wind even bring the dead back to life? Just ask Ezekiel.

The Bible says that God took Ezekiel by the Spirit and set him down in the midst of the valley which was full of very dry bones (Ezekiel Chapter 37). *"And he said unto me, Son of man, can these bones live? And I answered, O Lord GOD, thou knowest. Again he said unto me, Prophesy upon these bones, and say unto them, O ye dry bones, hear the word of the LORD."* Notice how God commanded the prophet to prophesy to those dry bones. Prophecy is the word of God that is from the *"Breath of God."* This is the *prophetic* word that proceeds out of the mouth of God (Matthew 4:4). Man does not live by physical bread alone. God has the *"bread that cometh down from heaven, that a man may eat thereof, and not die (John 6:50)."* Jesus taught us to pray "give us this day, our daily bread (Matthew)." This bread to eat and the word of God to live by each day. ***"The prophetic word is manna from Heaven that gives life."*** As Jesus said, *"The words that I speak unto you, they are spirit, and they are life (John 6:63)."*

So, when God told Ezekiel to prophesy over those dry bones, it was ***"manna from Heaven"*** that was to come into those dead bones give them life and raise them up. Here are the words that God in Heaven gave the prophet to speak. *"Thus saith the Lord GOD unto these bones; Behold, I will cause breath to enter into you, and ye shall live: And I will lay sinews upon you, and will bring up flesh upon you, and cover you with skin, and put breath in you, and ye shall live; and ye shall know that I [am] the LORD (v5-6)."* Let me take a moment and say something to every reader. You will notice that this book is full of prophecy. There is a reason for that. God is sending His ***"manna from Heaven"*** just for you. He wants to breath life into you. God wants to raise you up to that place where He has ordained you to be since the foundation of the world. You can read the Bible. Hey, you can read it all day long, but it has no life, until it begins to speak to you. This is the ***"living word of God."*** There is life in the word, but it has to be activated by your faith.

The Bible says that faith comes by hearing, and hearing by the word of God (Romans 10:17). We briefly discussed this earlier in the book. In order to have faith in something, you must have heard or seen something. If you hear it enough times, you will begin to believe. That's what it means by *"faith comes by hearing."* That is indeed the first level of hearing. Now, the more you hear, something begins to happen inside of you. There is an ***"awakening"*** that occurs. Almost like an "ah ha" moment when it all begins to *click*. You are hearing on another level, to the point that it is no longer surface hearing, but a certain *knowing* occurs within you. That is how faith is developed, and when it does, ***"faith brings with it hope and great expectation."*** This is why meditation in the word of God is a good thing. These are words of life spoken by God to bring life to human beings. God gave Joshua the formula for prosperity and success. *"This book of the law* [word of God] *shall not depart out of thy mouth; but thou shalt meditate therein day and night, that thou mayest observe to do according to all that is written therein: for then thou shalt make thy way prosperous, and then thou shalt have good success* (Joshua 1:8)." Did the formula work? Absolutely! Joshua was able to conquer enemy territories and give out inheritances to the people of God.

Now, this was faith in God's word. A person can also develop faith in the words of the devil. Meditate on evil and it will begin to take root in your heart, causing you to receive words of death. Take for example what the media has been feeding people since COVID-19 came upon the nation. Every day they are telling how many people got the virus and how many died. Notice that they don't tell you how many are recovered or have had miraculous healings. They are not telling many success stories. Why not? They want to control people with fear and death. So, the people are developing a fear of death, but no hope in living. This is how you know the words are from the devil. Remember that the thief comes to steal, kill and destroy, but Jesus came to give you life and that more abundantly, even in the midst of a virus. READ THE BOOK! Again, Jesus said that there would be pestilences (Matthew 24:7) in these last days, but don't be deceive. It's not the end of the world. It's not the end of your life, unless you let it be the end. This is the time for the good news of the gospel to take center stage. Cut off that news and open up the Bible. Begin filling your heart with the promises of God. Read your protection in Psalm 23 and Psalm 91. If you aren't saved, turn to the back of the book and read the Salvation Prayer and get saved. Then let the Holy Spirit minister life, the *"Breath of Life"* into your life.

So, what happens when Ezekiel prophesies to those dry bones? *"So I prophesied as I was commanded: and as I prophesied, there was a noise, and behold a shaking, and the bones came together, bone to his bone. And when I beheld, lo, the sinews and the flesh came up upon them, and the skin covered them above: but [there was] no breath in them (v7-8)."* The prophet speaks and "there was a noise and a shaking." Isn't that what's going on in the world today? The prophets of God have been speaking to get the Church to arise and the world has been shaken by the *"Sound of Heaven."* Heaven has a sound, a voice like none other. Earlier we talked about how rulers over nations have issues with prophets speaking the word of God over them because the *"weight"* [sound] of God's authority is greater than theirs. They don't like something in the atmosphere speaking more powerful than they speak. That is also what causes the persecution of the Church in America. There are government leaders who realize that God's voice and authority is greater than theirs. In certain states, these leaders are trying to shut the Church up and shut it down completely. Why? They don't like what, or how God is speaking. That's why there is a *"Shaking"* going on in America and around the world. In the meantime, God is resurrecting the dry bones of His Church in the land. Physically they came together and fasted and prayed, bone to bone, but like those dry bones Ezekiel saw, *"there was no breath in them."*

Then God tells Ezekiel to prophesy again, this time the prophet was told to speak to the wind. *"Then said he unto me, Prophesy unto the wind, prophesy, son of man, and say to the wind, Thus saith the Lord GOD; Come from the four winds, O breath, and breathe upon these slain, that they may live (v9)."* This is phenomenal if you consider that God did not Breath His breath into the flesh like He did at creation. Notice why. These were dead things, corrupted and slain in the cursed world system. Although God was bringing them back to life, they were yet sinful men in that Jesus had not come to make a way for mankind to be *"regenerated back into the stature of Adam."* That would come later after the resurrection, when the Holy Spirit would come upon and reside within born again men on the earth. It would be the only way the Breath of God could enter and *"quicken"* [bring to life, revitalize] earthly men. For these slain men, the only "wind" available to breathe life back into them, was that which was already in the earth. Therefore, God had the prophet to command the four winds of the earth to fill the bodies of the slain with breath. *"So I prophesied as he commanded me, and the breath came into them, and they lived, and stood up upon their feet, an exceeding great army (v10)."* What a powerful story about healing and restoration of that which was dead. This is the same power of the Kingdom of God that Jesus demonstrated in His earthly ministry. We saw it demonstrated again with the first apostles of the early Church. Could the same thing happen today? I'm glad you asked because God gave me a *vision* of this exact same thing. *In this vision, I saw God raising up a powerful army of believers from the lowest places of the earth. I saw gang bangers, crack heads prostitutes, wicked politicians and evil preachers and the like. It was as though they were suddenly awaken to what was happening around them. God had opened their eyes to see the lack of leadership to help the nations.*

Some of these people never knew God, oh, but they have heard about Him. Like Gideon, some of them are questioning, "God, if you are real where are you?" "Where are all those miracles you did in the Bible?" "Where is the God of the Bible?" God will respond to these voices. He will appear to them and raise them up much like Ezekiel prophesied to the dry bones. God will raise up these leaders from the deadness of this life, even the dead in the Church. Together they will form a remnant of believers who will perform the greater works. They will do great exploits and honor God!

Where is this remnant today? Like the vision showed, some are hidden away in the lowest parts of the earth, nearly dead. God will raise them up with the same words He gave to Ezekiel to speak to that *"exceeding great army."* God would have His prophet say to them, *"Thus saith the Lord GOD; Behold, O my people, I will open your graves, and cause you to come up out of your graves, and bring you into the land of Israel. And ye shall know that I [am] the LORD, when I have opened your graves, O my people, and brought you up out of your graves, And shall put my spirit in you, and ye shall live, and I shall place you in your own land: then shall ye know that I the LORD have spoken [it], and performed [it], saith the LORD (v12-14)."*

This is indeed what God is doing in America in this season in the earth. He will continue **"awakening"** His exceeding great army in the earth. This is the Church that has been hidden away because of persecution and threats of death. It is time for them to arise and shine because the glory of the Lord has risen upon them in this hour. As God said, they must first be healed and restored, but then they will build the arks and demonstrate the power of God's Kingdom over whatever comes against mankind in these last days.

Whether it is war, famine, pestilences, or earthquakes or treacherous winds, God's Kingdom has a solution that will be demonstrated in the earth as a witness to all nations, and then the end shall come. No longer will God's people just read those Bible stories like they are fables and tales.

In these last days, believers will walk as giants among men, doing great exploits in earth. They will do such great works, that men will glorify the God of Heaven for having sent Jesus to earth! It's time for the Body of Christ arise and run with God's vision. God's Winds are Here!

"The Winds Of Change Have Come!"
Get ready to set sail into your divine destiny!

"My covenant
Will I not break,
Nor alter
The thing that is
Gone out of my lips."

Psalm 89:34

CONCLUSION

America's Covenant And The Hope Of Glory

America has a Blood Covenant with Almighty God. This covenant was made by our forefathers for our protection and provision, for the preservation of our nation. God will Bless us, if we return to Him and His purpose for America. Otherwise, our enemies are given permission to destroy this land utterly. Politicians are playing with people's lives. Make no mistake about it. According to God, America is *"at war."* There is a *"violent end coming"* to the political game playing. Thus says the Lord, *"The end is now!" "No witch shall stand before Me to obstruct My Holy Ones." "I will recompense them swiftly. It's their time to shine. Darkness shall not prevail!!"* The political leaders of the land, have caused the people to sin against God. The enemies of this nation are coming. God is using the storm that the enemy planned against them. The season of lies and deception and the curse is over for God's people. They are finally being set free, even if it means destroying the entire world system that is operating in America.

The Lord let me hear our enemies shouting "Death To America!" Yet, God said that His *"Judgment is Here."* America's enemies have been attempting to get the people to accept death. That is why they sent COVID-19. It was rehearsal for what is to come. The enemy wants to condition people by programming their minds with daily statistics from the news media about death. The devil gives suggestions in a repeated methodological fashion. It is a slow process of programming fear and death in the hearts of people. The Lord gave me a powerful *vision* describing what was going on with the so called "pandemic." *I saw this larger than life arena that had a huge stage. On the stage was a performance that had captured the attention of the entire world. The Lord pulled back the scene and I saw a puppet master hovering over the stage, pulling the strings of every performer. Then I heard the Lord say,* **"The performance is being narrated by the news media."** *Wow! It hit me. Very few people could see the puppet master and even fewer heard his voice behind the script the news people were reading. This was a deception extraordi*naire *indeed, but why?*

God explained that there was *"something more extraordinary"* was going on in the world that the puppet master (that old devil) could not stop. All he could do was use deception to distract the people of the world. Then the Lord showed me *"something more powerful going on outside of that arena." Money was being transferred. Power was being transferred. Homes and properties were being transferred. Miraculous healings were taking place. God was answering the most impossible prayers, but only a few saw what God was doing, therefore only a few could receive this tremendous Blessing. Those who were captivated by the stage performance never saw the Blessing. They were too wrapped up in the actors performing on the stage.*

Here is what the theater audience never realized. *"The performance was a set up, a distraction, to keep the people from seeing and enjoying the powerful move of God to Bless His people."* God has a plan to Bless us and the devil wants to stop us from receiving. The devil cannot stop God. His only recourse is to *"deceive the whole world* (Revelation 12:9). *"* That's his job. He's on it, and so are the faithful remnant of believers who see the truth behind the performance. Blessed are their eyes to see and their ears to hear, what others cannot see or here. These are people of faith. They are in position to receive during this great move of God. It began with the word that they heard from God. They believed God and put His word in their mouths. The Bible says *we shall have whatever we say* (Mark 11:23). If they had repeated what the performers in that arena were saying, they would have had that as well. People don't seem to understand the relationship between what they say and what happens to them in life. This is a highly prophetic season. Our words are quickly coming to pass.

"Life and death are in the power of the tongue." Those who love it will eat the fruit of it (Proverbs 18:21). We live and die by the words we speak. In the vision, the words of the puppet master were words of death. The words of God are words of faith. They are words of life that bring forth the Blessing of the Lord. God says, *"The Blessing is here!"* This is a *"new era to promote the Blessing in the earth! The season of the curse with its lies, and deception is over! Those who want it will be dead!"* God has declared a new season for The Blessing. He goes on to say, *"My Will is done in America . . . bondages will be broken off of the nation!"* Then I saw redemption throughout the earth, for all who wanted to be free. For them, all things will work together for

194

their good, but they have to see it to receive it. They will have to ask the Lord to open their eyes to see what He has within The Blessing for their lives. It is for the entire world. Few people are experiencing The Blessing in the world because they are mesmerized by what the news media is reporting. Even those in the Church are captivated by the news and not by the Father's word of faith. They are speaking what the news is saying and therefore have manifested the curse instead of the Blessing. Our nation is at war. It cannot be prevented. The world leaders are waiting in the wings to take war to the ultimate level of destruction. We can not afford to be distracted by the media. We must change the script, if we want America to survive. The Lord said that *"the only salvation"* for our nation *"is the word of faith;"* taking God's promise for America and putting those words in our mouths. That is what our forefathers did. That is why we recited the Pledge Allegiance daily in our schools. It was a reminder of who we were as a people. We were *"under"* the Blessing, the grace and purpose of God, our One and Only True Authority. This land will never be truly free until we return back under God's authority. It's time for Christians to mobilize.

Overnight I heard the Lord say, *"War is here!"* I was asleep, yet my spirit responded. Out of my spirit came, "In your presence is the fullness of joy. At Your right hand are pleasures for evermore (Psalm 16:11). " The Holy Spirit said *"Where are you seated?"* I am seated together with Jesus in the heavenly places (Ephesians 2:6). Jesus is seated at the Right Hand of the Father (Ephesians 1:20). It hit my spirit. *We are seated where there are pleasures forever more!* There may be war in the world, but I am in God's presence, seated together with my big brother at the Father's Right Hand. My expectation is not for destruction. He redeemed my life from destruction (Psalm 103:4). I'm appointed for pleasures forever more. That is what I am seeking, the pleasures God had for me in these last days. The Blessing of the Lord makes one rich, without adding sorrow to it (Proverbs 10:22). This my portion in this life. This is also the portion for everyone who believes. This is the *word of faith* in action. *"The word is nigh thee, [even] in thy mouth, and in thy heart: that is, the word of faith, which we preach* (Romans 10:8). " I heard from the Lord. I believed in my heart (spirit) what He said. I confessed it with my mouth and it shall come to pass in my life. This is how we got saved. We believed in our hearts what God did in the life of Jesus, that He raised Him from the dead. We confessed with our mouths that we desired Jesus to Lord over our lives. This is how to use the *word of faith*. We hear it. We believe it in our hearts. We confess it. Believers in Jesus Christ can no longer say what the world is saying and expect this nation to flourish. We must honor God's word. We must live by faith, not in what the news is saying, but in what God is saying to our hearts. We must stand on the word of God above all things, if we want to receive His Blessing on our lives. We can no longer see ourselves as Americans first. This is not God's order for our lives. Our primary allegiance should be to God's Kingdom purpose. He alone must be our first allegiance. **"When God is first, all other relationships will flow in harmony."**

That is why when He was asked, *"Master, which is the great commandment in the law?"* Jesus responded, *"Thou shalt love the Lord thy God with all thy heart, and with all thy soul, and with all thy mind. This is the first and great commandment* (Matthew 22:37-38)." It all begins with love. It's the *royal law* of God's Kingdom. We have a **"covenant of love"** with God the Father and His son. *"For God so loved the world, that he gave his only begotten Son, that whosoever believeth in him should not perish, but have everlasting life* (John 3:16)." We love God first and foremost, because He first loved us (I John 4:19). According to the Lord, **"too many Christians have never believed in the love"** of God. They have church. They have religion, but no love. Here is the issue. The Bible says that, *"God is love* (I John 4:8)." Those who have religion, and no love, also have no God. Christianity is all about love. In fact, Jesus said that the world would know us by our love for one another (John 13:34-35).

So, where is the love in the American Church? The Church has the reputation of being hateful and unloving, especially to unbelievers. This is not the heart of the Father. There is hatred and division among denominations, among various people groups, among the sexes. Jesus prayed that we *"all may be one,"* as He and the Father were one (John 17:21). We must know and believe the love God has for us. Then we will love one another with that same love that God has for us. We can in turn, minister that love to our families, to our communities and to the people of our nation. Love heals. It delivers from oppression and sets people free. Our government cannot do that. It cannot love people, nor set them free. It's an institution void of love. God's government is a spiritual institution, called **"His Family"** and we are all about love, not human love, but sacrificial love. We believe in laying down our lives for a friend (John

15:13). It doesn't mean dying physically like Jesus did, but it does mean dying to our selfish desires to help someone in need. This is drastically different from the world, where people are self-centered, thinking very little, if anything about others. People have a sense of *"entitlement"* and it's every man for himself. When the Lord spoke about war, I saw something in the spirit. I saw the destruction brought on by our selfish ambitions, but there arose what God called *"women of valor."* There were ordinary women taking the lead in the fight, and we won the battle. The women protected their families, their neighborhoods and cities. These were women of valor, women of virtue as found in the Bible. *"Favour [is] deceitful, and beauty [is] vain: [but] a woman [that] feareth the LORD, she shall be praised (Proverbs 31:30)."* These women had a love not only for family, but for community and for people in general. This love sprang from a heart full of the love of God, not wanting others to suffer. They arose valiantly to the battle and it was won.

This is just one of the stories that will be working during times of trouble in our nation and around the world. There is darkness, deep darkness in the world. Every form of evil is emerging on the scene. Gross darkness is on the people (Isaiah 60:2). There is even a *"perverse race among the people of God."* The Body of Christ must take a stand against abortion, and sexual immorality of all kinds, including prostitution and sex trafficking. In the absence of godly leaders both over the Church and the nation, these spirits have been allowed to creep into homes of the innocent. The word is being preached but not many are paying attention. Rebellion is the order of the day. Many Christians are doing what is right in their own eyes, in lieu of standing on their covenant. The Lord said that *"war was necessary to purge sin out of the camp."* It will be a fierce battle, but it is the only way to get that perverse spirit out of the Church. *"Whoso walketh uprightly shall be saved: but he that is perverse in his ways shall fall at once (Proverbs 28:18)."*

The perverse spirit in the Church is also dominate in the nation. People have publicized what President Trump did in his past. It's shameful what leaders continue to do in their public offices. It is far worse than what they accused Mr. Trump of doing. Some years ago, the Lord had me do an article on the Sexual Deviance[1] in the Obama Administration. From the increasing number of military rapes, the FBI hiring prostitutes

1   Matthews, Paula. "Sexual Deviance Marks The Obama Administration." Scribd, Scribd, 10 Oct. 2016, www.scribd.com/document/327117713/Sexual-Deviance-Marks-The-Obama-Administration.

before a presidential visit and even the alleged adultery of Mr. Obama while in office. What is amazing is that no one was trying to deal with these issues. They were swept under the carpet. The victims who sought remedies were harassed and threatened. Now these bold leaders are attempting to take over this nation by seizing the White House. They actually believe that God has no power to stop them. But, God said that He is *"ambushing the enemy"* in this season. In fact, the Lord isn't even treating this like a real war. He said, *"it's a set up"* and has been from the start. Witches cannot see what God is doing, no one can. They can only see what God allows them to see. The enemy is cut off and doesn't even know it! Praise God! The Kingdoms of this world have become the kingdoms of our Lord and our Christ!

God is determined to heal, deliver and restore America. When God says, *"Let My people go!"* And the devil resists, the only option is for Him to send the plagues, even death. It will happen suddenly and swiftly. *"God cannot be stopped!"* The angels are in full motion. People are moving and obeying from the North, South, East and West. It's God's appointed season. It's like a *"super atomic supernatural freighter going at maximum speed."* If you are blocking the tracks, you die! If you are trying to prevent someone from receiving from that freighter, you die! It's not going to stop! The Kingdom is moving at maximum speed and the devil cannot stop it. *"The darkness comprehendeth it not* (John 1:5)." God said, *"it is time for the crash"* of the train on the track of *Everyday Life in America* that we discussed in an earlier chapter. God is upholding His covenant with the remnant of believers in the land. Amen.

This is a season of God's judgment. No one will be excluded, beginning with believers. But, if we judge ourselves, we will not be judged. *I was in the spirit, seated on the walls of this nation, watching like a sentinel. For what? Enemy missiles, air strikes, other enemy tactics, and the like. I saw them all. I even saw a nuclear weapon detonate over the Eastern United States. Everything and everyone was gone.* I cried out to God for mercy upon our nation. I refused to believe that My Father in Heaven would allow the enemy to destroy us without the gospel message ever being demonstrated. The Church does not know God. The world does not know God. All they know is religion. I wanted them to know Him before leaving this earth. God heard my prayer. He has given us grace for this season, but I also saw something else. Witches were desperately pulling out every stop. Nothing they did would work. God could not be stopped. Then I saw the apostasy. I saw many people leaving the Church. God said *"it was happening even now."* These are those who were never in the faith. They were in the Church as onlookers and bench warmers awaiting their passage to Heaven. They were not equipped to handle what was coming upon the nation. Truth is, they were never in the faith at all. They were tares among the wheat. Their hearts were never converted. They never received the Lord. They did not desire to retain God in their knowledge, ever learning but never coming into the knowledge of the truth. God will turn many over to a reprobate mind to do as they please. They have a form of godliness but deny the power of God to change their lives. We were warned to stay away from these *"traitors,"* lovers of pleasures instead of God. They will no longer be a hindrance to the Church of Jesus Christ.

Then I had a most unusual *spiritual occurrence* after praying for America. It was something I was prompted to do by the Holy Spirit. It began when I heard a man in Nigeria give a testimony about praying for his village. In the spirit this man saw a wall surrounding the village that was holding captive the people. When a prophetic word was released, the walls around that village fell down, setting the entire community free. Dr. Paul Eneche, Sr. Pastor of Dunamis International Gospel Centre, Abuja, told everyone to repeat the following prayer to tear down the walls that held Nigeria captive. Now, I prayed this same prayer with the congregation. I stood in agreement for Nigeria, but I also included America as well. Here is the prayer: *"Every wall of captivity, of oppression, of terrorism, every wall of bloodshed, of kidnapping, every wall of ritual killings, surrounding Nigeria [America], Oh you demonic wall. In the Name of Jesus, Crumble! Collapse! In the Name of Jesus Crumble, Collapse, Scatter! Now! Every wall of destruction! Every wall of death, Crumble! Collapse and Scatter! Now! In Jesus' Name."* Then we all prayed in the spirit until released.

Immediately after the prayer, In the *spirit, I saw the walls in our nation's capitol fall! Then I saw Nancy Pelosi, standing in what appeared to be an empty House Chamber. She was wearing all white. Not only was the room empty of people, but everything had been demolished, the walls, the seats, and the platform. It all had been destroyed. It looked as though a tornado had come through the capitol and destroyed everything in sight.* Then I knew in my spirit, ***"the battle against the White House had been settled."*** It was never about the man in the White House. It was about God. People don't seem to understand that God is serious in these last days. His judgment is upon us all! The courts of Heaven have passed sentences upon the wicked. It is either *"God's will or theirs"* but He cannot be stopped. *"They will be stopped, even by force if necessary."* God said this about the political game playing, but it also goes for those *"playing church." "There will be many tragic ends,"* says the Holy Spirit, *"so that people will learn to fear God and His Church in holiness."*

We are in the time in which God has commanded Isaiah 45 to come forth! *"Woe unto him that striveth with His Maker* (Isaiah 45:9)*!"* God will have salvation for His people and devastation for their enemies. Even God will do this for America. There have been atrocities against the people of this nation from a previous Administration that God calls *"treason."* He said they were *"conspiring against America to divide and harm the people to benefit their personal kingdoms."* God said, *"Judgment is here!"* God has no favorites, but people do. They are about to see their idols fall in shame and humility. I did hear the Lord say twice, about Barack Obama, that his legacy will be that of *"international shame."* Mr. Obama has worked his plan of control and manipulation far enough. God said, *"he is done!"*

Beloved, this is *"God's chosen season to work His will in the lives of His people, for His purpose alone!"* It's time for God's people to turn their hearts back to the Father in repentance. It's time for the leaders of this country to repent and turn back to what is best for the people according to God's standards. It's time for all of us to repent and prepare for the coming of the Lord Jesus Christ. Here is a prophecy. *The works of man has ended. It is My time,"* says God, *"to perform the greater works through my faithful servants in the earth. Oh what a time, it shall be. Righteousness will flow from the hills to the valleys, peace like a river upon the earth. This is it! My time of Jubilance as righteousness returns in the earth!" "It's time to arise and shine My people. Your day has come to be prospered in the earth. Arise now my sons and daughters and do all I have commanded for this hour. I am with you. You shall not go alone. I will never leave nor forsake you,"* says God your loving faithful Father. *"Purify your hearts, My people. Draw nigh to Me. Forsake all others and follow Me, now! It's your time to arise and shine. My Glory is upon you now!"*

God said that His glory is upon us now! We have the covenant to protect and provide for us, but the glory is the manifestation of our identity as sons of the Most High God. The glory that manifests in these last days will serve to *"uphold the covenant"* while we manifest the Blessing the earth. Like God told Abraham, *"I will Bless you and make your name great, and I will bless those who bless you and curse those who curse you."* God knew that the enemy would try to stop us from operating in the Blessing. The glory insures that we can go about our Father's business while the angels are assigned to watch our backs, cursing those who try to hinder us. This is part of *"the Kingdom benefits package."* Let's take a look at how the glory is designed to work. It was the genius of God to put His Spirit (the glory) inside the hearts of obedient men. Imagine the entire Kingdom of God residing within a person's heart. That means we can have all that God has. We can be all God is, and do all that He can do. With man this is impossible. But God in us is *"the hope"* of a glorious transformation for our lives, for our neighbors, our cities, the nation and ultimately for the entire world.

Recall the beam of light *vision* from **The War Journal Volume I.**[1] *The Lord showed circular beams of light coming from heaven to the earth. These beams of light were the glory of individual believers sparsely located all around the world. New beams appeared in seemingly random order all over the earth. Then some of the beams began to enlarge in diameter to the point that they appeared to connect to other beams. The Lord said that the beams increased in size according to the obedience of the believer. The more obedient the believer, the larger the glory beam appeared from heaven. As one obedient believer connected with another obedient believer, the glory of those believers seemed to be woven together into an even larger beam of light. This weaving of beams multiplied in the earth blocking out all signs of darkness in their midst. This began happening all over the earth. The final result was the appearance of one solid beam of light coming from heaven and covering the entire earth, just as it was in the beginning when God created Adam. The glory in the earth appeared as the fullness of God flowing directly from heaven, destroying the darkness and unhindered by the sin of man.* This is how the glory appeared at the time of Adam. As the prophet said, *"For the earth shall be filled with the knowledge of the glory of the LORD, as the waters cover the sea* (Habakkuk 2:14).*"*

---

1   Matthews, Paula. "The Love Of God Manifested." *The War Journal (1999-2010) Volume I.* Los Angeles: Spirit & Life Publications, 2010. 88. Print.

Now, contrast what we see happening in America today. Men are speaking and plotting evil and spreading it around the world to create more evil; to tear down the unity of men, and turn brother against brother. This is the work of the evil one to bring our nation down. But, America has a covenant with God. He will not allow this nation to be destroyed, for the sake of the *"handful"* of true believers in these United States of America. God has a faithful remnant in the nation who know and live the truth of God's word. We are standing earnestly in intercession for America. Father Abraham interceded for Sodom when God threatened to destroy that city. *"And Abraham drew near, and said, Wilt thou also destroy the righteous with the wicked? Peradventure there be fifty righteous within the city: wilt thou also destroy and not spare the place for the fifty righteous that are therein* (Genesis 18:23-24)?" Abraham asked if God would spare the city for forty righteous. Then he asked to spare the city for thirty, and then for twenty righteous people that live there. For the sake of Abraham, God said He would spare the city. God said, *"I will not destroy it for ten's sake* (Genesis 18:25-32)." If God would spare the wicked city of Sodom for ten righteous people who live there, surely He would spare America, with whom He has covenant, for the sake of the handful of righteous that live in our nation.

The story of Sodom parallels what we see in America today. God threatened to destroy Sodom, but before He did that, He sent angels to spy out the situation in the city. These angels had the power of saying yea or nay concerning the plight of Sodom. But, when the men of that city came to force sex on the angels, that was the axe that cut off any chance that Sodom would be saved. The angels told Lot to take his family and whatever they brought with them out of that place. *"For we will destroy this place because the cry of them is waxed great before the face of the Lord; and the Lord hath sent us to destroy it* (Genesis 19:12-13)." This was a wicked city. It had no covenant, and yet God was determined to show them mercy. God would do the same for America, if we repent and turn back to Him. This does not mean that there won't be some cities destroyed. The Lord had me move from a place that was like Sodom. He told me to take everything I had out of there. He warned that if I left anything there, it would also be destroyed. That was years ago, but I will never forget the *vision* the Lord showed me about what was going to happen in that place. *I saw God step out of Heaven. I watched as His foot hit the ground and shook everything in sight. Then He put His Hand in the clouds and pulled out something so powerful that it caused build-*

ings and towers to be destroyed. Huge craters were left in their place. People were disintegrated, their bodies left in a smoldering pile of ashes. It was like the scripture says, *"For the wind passeth over it, and it is gone; and the place thereof shall know it no more* (Psalm 103:16). *"* The Great and Terrible God showed up and dealt with His enemies. This is the glory. The supernatural grace and power of God comes on the scene. The wicked are judged while the righteous are Blessed.

This is the same glory that resides within the hearts of the believer. When we speak and obey the instructions of the Lord, it is the Father within that does the work (John 14:10). It's sounds crazy, but it's true. God gave me a demonstration about what He put in my mouth. The Lord showed a *vision* in which *a family was being threatened by the enemy. They came to me for prayer. I didn't have to pray. The Lord had a prophetic word that came out of my mouth. All I recall saying, is, "God won't let that happen. He will take care of this situation before the people make it to their destination." Then the Lord showed me what happened when I spoke those words. The plane that was carrying those who threaten this couple, had plane hit the side of the mountain and the passengers were killed.* After that vision I became very careful with how I spoke. God said, ***"this is what I have put inside of your spirit."***

Years ago, the Lord explained why He had to put His glory inside of the hearts of men. It had to do with His covenant promise never to destroy the every living creature by water ever again (Genesis 9:11). The glory had to be returned to the earth, but sin was the issue. The glory and sin could not inhabit the same place. So, God had to find a place within the hearts of men that was vacant. Adam's sin left a vacancy in the hearts of men, that only God could fill. Therefore, at salvation, the Spirit of God, the anointing comes to fill that vacancy and resides within man. That anointing is every bit of God, His provision, His power, His glory, all of God and His Kingdom is in the anointing. He could not put it in every man, but only those who invited Jesus in their hearts. Since mankind has dominion, any spirit has to have permission to enter their bodies. God is a Spirit. Like Jesus said, He standing at the door knocking, but we have to let Him in (Revelation 3:20). Satan on the other hand, breaks down the door of people who are unaware. He and his demons take over. People can also have open doors in their hearts or emotions, even their intellect that can also allow the devil entry. For example, if one is hurt and wants revenge, the devil can come to take over. If they are lustful and go after people, that devil comes in. If they are prideful and arrogant it is an invitation for the devil. In fact, anytime we do anything that God has told us not to do, we open the door for the devil. But, for the born again believer, *"God put Himself inside of us."* It is referred to the treasure in earthen vessels (II Corinthians 4:7). This is no place for demons. The Bible talks about *"Christ in you, the hope of glory* (Colossians 1:27).*"* This is one of the greatest revelations we will see unveiled in these last days. God will make known the vastness, *"the infinite array of riches"* He has planned to glorify mankind and this earth. When we obey the Spirit of God, the glory is released into the atmosphere, changing our lives to reflect the beauty, the abundance and opulence of Heaven. This is why Jesus came, to recapture Heaven's glory upon this earth; to bring back all the glory Adam experienced in Eden for mankind to enjoy. It is the manifestation of the days of Heaven upon the earth.

"The Kingdom of God is the operation and government of God upon the earth." As sons and daughters of God, we have to uphold the government of our Father in this earth, creating what He desires in the earth. This is how Adam operated; man, co-creator with His Father, God Creator of the heavens and the earth. As long as God's Breath was in man, He could create what the Heavenly Father desired, making earth a replica of Heaven. This was God's plan for man at creation. That is *still* God's plan for the born again man. Earth was established as a territory under the domain (ownership and governance) of God, created to be ruled by the righteous sons of Almighty God. These are the kings of the earth, gods under the authority of their Father. We witnessed this superhuman transformation in the life of Moses. God made Moses a god (Exodus 7:1) to Pharaoh. Was Moses really a god? Yes, in word and deed only. He was sent by the Lord to Pharaoh, which made Moses an emissary of God. His obedience and presence before the king, was liken to God Himself appearing before Pharaoh. This was the glory (essence and power) of God upon the life of Moses.

Now consider the born again man or woman. They are *"regenerated back into the stature of Adam,"* as the man was at creation. These are sons of God *"by nature of the new birth."* They are born of God's Spiritual DNA. *"I have said, Ye [are] gods; and all of you [are] children of the most High* (Psalm 82:6). *"* This is a supernatural transformation that is available only for the born again man or woman. You're not God, but as His son or daughter, His glory, His essence and His power resides within you. That means, when you act in obedience, the God (Christ) in you becomes activated and does the work of God the Father in your life and ministry. Then you begin speaking like God. Jesus said, *"Is it not written in your law, I said, Ye are gods? If he called them gods, unto whom the word of God came, and the scripture cannot be broken; Say ye of him, whom the Father hath sanctified, and sent into the world, Thou blasphemest; because I said, I am the Son of God* (John 10:34-36)*?"* People who witnessed the preaching of the word and the manifestation of miracles recognized the "god-like" quality in the servants of God. This is what happened to Jesus. It also happened to the apostles. When they operated in obedience to God, people thought they were gods. Here is an example.

Paul and Barnabas were in cities of Lycaonia where they were preaching the gospel (Acts 14:6-11). There was a man who had been crippled from his mother's womb, never having walked. This man was listening to Paul preach, and *"perceiving that the man had faith to be healed,"* Paul said in a loud voice, *"Stand upright on thy feet. And he leaped and walked."* When the people saw what Paul did, they said, *"The gods are come down to us in the likeness of men. And they called Barnabas, Jupiter; and Paul, Mercurius, because he was the chief speaker. Then the priest of Jupiter, which was before their city, brought oxen and garlands unto the gates, and would have done sacrifice with the people.* (Acts 14:11).*"* Barnabas and Paul heard about this and were outraged, saying, *"Sirs, why do ye these things? We also are men of like passions with you, and preach unto you that ye should turn from these vanities unto the living God, which made heaven, and earth, and the sea, and all things that are therein* (Acts 14:15).*"* This was a pagan culture that served idols. They saw the "god like" things that the apostles did and would have hailed them as god is they had not prohibited them.

Our goal as believer is to imitate our Father, who is not like the gods of this world. We must be obedient to Him while letting people know that it is His power not ours doing the miraculous works. Again, it's not you, it's your Father doing the work. The ultimate accomplishment is for people look at you, and they see the Father. Here is another example from the book of Acts. Paul was among prisoners and crew of a ship that was wrecked. They escaped and landed on the island called Melita. Paul had gathered a bundle of sticks, and when he laid them on the fire, a viper came out of the heat and bit him on hand. The island natives thought that Paul was a murderer who escaped death at sea, but that vengeance would be served when the viper would kill him. Paul shook the viper off and felt no harm. The natives kept observing Paul thinking that at least he should have swollen and fell down dead suddenly, *"they changed their minds, and said that he was a god* (Acts 28:1-3). *"* Think it not strange that when signs, wonders and miracles begin in your life that people will say, "They think they're god." No! You're not god, but the sons of God doing the work of your Father in the earth. The glory is released as we walk by faith. This is the manifestation of the sons of God. Our Heavenly Father always wanted a family. Now He has one both in Heaven and in earth. Our job is to represent Him and His interest in this earth. This is why Jesus came in the first place.

God sowed His only begotten Son in this earth, in order that He may receive a harvest of sons. Adam was God's firstborn son. When Adam turned from God, the Father has been in search of a family in which He could give an inheritance. Throughout the Bible, everyone who obeyed God was considered a son, but God chose Israel and made them His own (Acts 13:17). He called Israel His *"firstborn* (Exodus 4:22). *"* He chose them to be in His family the same way that every believer in Jesus Christ is grafted into the family of God. The major difference between Moses' generation, and ours since the resurrection of Jesus, is that the Spirit of God resides within us like it did with Adam. That means we have **"the power within"** us to do the works of God. We are in every sense, predestined and spiritually empowered to walk as gods (sons of God) in the earth.

At salvation, a **"super** (over and beyond) **human transformation"** takes place. As the word of God says, *"Therefore if any man be in Christ, he is a new creature; old things are passed away; behold, all things are become new, and all things are of God* (II Corinthians 5:17-28). *"* No longer is one human, but a god-infused man. It is a transformation that takes place the sub-human level; hidden from man's sight and manipulation (I Corinthians 2:9). It's God invading the soul of man, changing him into the image of Christ, who is the express image of the Father. This is the glory of God hidden inside of the born again man waiting to be manifested in the earth. The glory is the reflection and essence of the Heavenly Father. To be in the glory of the Father is to be in His very presence, as if He were total manifested in a physical being. Jesus gave us His glory for one purpose. According to scripture, Jesus said, that it would be proof that He was sent by the Father (John 17:22-23). The glory is proof (evidence) that God is among us, manifested and operational in the lives of men. Jesus came in the glory of the Father, so we could see God. Jesus sent us in His glory so that people could see Him and the Father in us. That is why Jesus prayed that we would be one, as He and the Father are one. It all serves as proof that the same God that did miracles in the Bible, did indeed send Jesus and now Jesus is sending us into the world to do the same works. ***"The glory's sole purpose is that men would know God and His miraculous love for us."*** God is Spirit. He can't just show up in person and introduce Himself. He sends us as His representatives, to show the world just how wonderful God is. His glory can be seen on us. We saw that with Moses as well.

When Moses went to the mountain top for forty days and forty nights, he was saturated in the glory of God who visited with him. When Moses came down from the mountain, he came down with two things: 1) The Ten Commandments; The Law (instruction from God), 2) The glory (brightness) of God reflected on his person. The man was changed in knowledge and appearance. This was evidence of God's presence upon an unsaved men. Then came Jesus, the only begotten son of the Father (John 3:16). *"And the Word was made flesh, and dwelt among us, (and we beheld his glory, the glory as of the only begotten of the Father,) full of grace and truth* (John 1:14)." Jesus came in the glory of the Father. He also came as a man. This raises the question, "How can a man be also god?" The transformation is sub normal. It is done on a level man cannot see, touch, hear or imagine, but the result of such a man was manifested in supernatural signs, wonders and miracles. This is the glory (endowment) of *"Emmanuel"* God with us (Matthew 1:23). We have this same hope of glory, as the sons and daughters of God.

In **The War Journal Volume I**, we described how the glory is both the judgment and love of God. This pursuit of glory has been an ever increasing unveiling of a great mystery. Ah, but Solomon saw it! It is the glory (honor) of God to conceal a matter. *"It is the glory of God to conceal a thing: but the honour of kings is to search out a matter* (Proverbs 25:2)."* This means, that what matters to God is concealed in a mystery beyond human comprehension. Human eyes can't see it. Neither have our ears heard it. The human heart can't even conceive of it. Yet, God placed eternity (a longing to know) in the hearts of men (Ecclesiastes 3:11). This indeed is a great mystery. God created man for Himself.

Man turned away from God to do his own thing, and yet the longing, yearning to know our purpose remains until satisfied.. No matter how we stray from our Creator, because He created us for His purpose, it is the knowledge of His purpose that draws us back to Him. We cannot begin to touch our purpose, nor the things of God, without being touched by Him. This touch comes in the form of being born again. Then the Kingdom (domain, governance, righteousness) is revealed from glory to another level of glory (II Corinthians 3:18), as men have faith to believe what God says by His Spirit. The Kingdom is ours at salvation. It is placed inside of our hearts, but the process of manifestation comes through faith. You must believe to receive. Again, God's glory is precious, therefore it is concealed.

So, how does one unlock the mysteries that have been hidden specifically for the kings of the earth? The Bible says that God hides *"sound wisdom"* for the righteous (Proverbs 2:7). This redefines who God identifies as kings. Not every ruler over a nation is qualified, but a righteous ruler will seek to unlock the wisdom of God for the sake of the people he serves. This concealed wisdom is revealed to those who honor what God honors. We need to understand the nature of God's glory. It is revealed for a specific Kingdom purpose. God gave it to Jesus, who gave it to us (the believer). Therefore every believer has a specific Kingdom purpose (assignment) in which to reveal the glory of God. Christians are waiting for God to send His glory. We mentioned, *"Christ in you* (believer)*, the hope of glory* (Colossians 1:27).*"* The glory within us is revealed when we walk by faith. So instead of looking for God to send His glory, we just need to release the glory from within by obeying the assignment and call upon our lives.

According to God, too many Christians see the glory as the Spirit of God that comes upon you tingling the flesh and causing them to manifest in dancing, spinning or flailing. The more glory one gets, then they are not just flailing, but are being slain in the spirit, even falling down as if dead. The glory of God is like the wind. We can't see it, nor can we know it's direction. We just know that it was here. The glory operates much like the wind. You cannot see it, but we see the effects! It's a force that causes things to move. We mentioned how it moves men to dance, but the more or stronger the glory, the more powerful the force. Jesus said, Everyone who is of the Spirit is like the wind (John 3:8). Think about the wind. It can be a gentle breeze. It can also become a powerful typhoon. The same glory that tingles, can also destroy. Christians desire the glory, but if they are not rooted and grounded in the word of God, and in the love of God; they could be destroyed. It's as if they do not realize that the glory of God can be manifested in the nature and character of God in our lives. It's a supernatural transformation we don't understand. Consider this. The Bible has many names of God, but is this really Him or His glory? Did God come down in the flesh to reveal himself? No, not until Jesus came. When Jesus did come, He demonstrated how to *"abide"* in the Father's word and His love. We discussed how God is Wind (Spirit) among men. We describe God according to how he interacts with us, His creation. If you don't interact with Him, what's in the Bible are simply words, stories of which you have no connection. But in these last days we are about to see what some are calling *"The Greater Glory."* It will manifest around the globe.

God is about raise up a company of people who carry *"His DNA."* Again, I saw it in the realm of the *spirit*. I saw what looked like a DNA strand arising in the earth. It was like it had a life of its own, and it was recreating the lives of mankind. I didn't see the source of the DNA, but in my heart I knew that it was somehow connected to the Blood of Jesus. This particular DNA was spiritual, not physical, even though it would produce physical results. What I saw was the restoration of God's original plan, and it had to do with recreating the lives of man in this earth. This particular strand of DNA was that of royalty. It came directly from the Heavenly Father. I saw restoration, not just natural restoration, but a supernatural restoration all the way back to Adam. This was not creation. In a sense it was re-creation.

We have talked about restoration, but as I saw the DNA strand, it looked like the first creation had been halted for a long season. The spiritual DNA picked up where the original one left off. It was as if there has been a hiccup in God's plan, an abruption of the flow of the breath of God (Spirit) in the lives of men. *"That condition is now over,"* says God. *"Restoration has begun in earnest."* We must be led by the Spirit in order to receive. Our worship and praise is the supernatural door (portal). Prophetic prayer gives us the instructions. Paul and Silas prayed and praised and the prison doors opened from the foundations (Acts 16:25). Our praise opens every door that God has set for us since the foundations of the earth.

The glory will manifest returning all creation back to God; back to His original plan and purpose under the Blessing. The glory will deliver and restore the people of God, putting them back on the path of their divine destiny. *"But upon mount Zion shall be deliverance, and there shall be holiness; and the house of Jacob shall possess their possessions* (Obadiah 1:17)."* Everything must be restored back to God before Jesus can return. It is the assignment of the saints (believers) to deliver up the Kingdom (I Corinthians 15:24). Many are waiting on Jesus to return, but all of Heaven is waiting on believers to begin walking by faith. It is not the time to be looking for Jesus to break through the clouds to take you home. No! There is much work to do in this earth. God is glorified when we bear much fruit that remains (John 15:8).

God said the *"shaking"* in the earth was caused by the sons of God as we obeyed our Father. As the sons and daughters of God, we will continue to walk in our destiny, manifesting the glory of the Lord all around us. Our Father has given us the land, every place the soles of our feet shall tread. Like the people of God who marched around the walls of Jericho, as we walk out our destinies so shall the walls of the wicked cities fall. Like the lepers who walked and the enemy heard a mighty army, so shall it be as we walk in the forbidden places of the earth. Each step we take will cause the earth to tremble and the enemy to flee. We see people marching in violent protests, anarchy in the streets. God is about to set them in order. He said *"they are marching to their deaths."* The Bible says that the steps of a good man are ordered by the Lord, and He delights in his ways (Psalm 37:23). Praise God for the legacy of Dr. Martin Luther King, Jr., a prophet of God who stood on Kingdom principles and led the people in nonviolent protests. They walked for God's justice for all mankind, and changed the world.

Like Dr. King, we follow the example of our Lord Jesus Christ who walked the Via Dolorosa to be executed on the cross. His mighty steps and acts of obedience caused the earth to quake, the dead to arise from their graves, and the veil of the temple to be torn in two. His words and His steps have been causing this earth to quake ever since. Before Jesus returns, the *"shaking"* will increase. His glory is coming to destroy everything that is out of order with God. *"The only refuge is the Kingdom of God."* We are about to witness the removing of things that are shaken, so that which remains will stand forever. The writer of Hebrews said, *"Our God is a consuming fire* (Hebrews 12:29)."*

According to God, these are *"the end of the last days."* This is the word that was prophesied by the Prophet Daniel, *"And in the days of these kings shall the God of heaven set up a kingdom, which shall never be destroyed: and the kingdom shall not be left to other people, but it shall break in pieces and consume all these kingdoms, and it shall stand for ever* (Daniel 2:44). *"* We who have received Jesus Christ, have received a Kingdom that cannot be shaken. Let us receive that grace by which we may serve God acceptably with reverence and godly fear. For in our obedience to God, we release the glory that blesses us and makes us a blessing to the entire world.

What saith the Lord in conclusion? *"Your warfare is over,"* says God. *"The warfare has ended,"* declares Almighty God. *"Comfort ye, comfort ye my people, saith your God. Speak ye comfortably to Jerusalem, and cry unto her, that her warfare is accomplished, that her iniquity is pardoned: for she hath received of the LORD'S hand double for all her sins* (Isaiah 40:1-2). *"* The Lord has avenged us speedily (Luke 18:8). He has recompensed us for all we have suffered. The world will fear and tremble for all the goodness and for all the prosperity God has given to us (Jeremiah 33:9), who are faithful to His word.

What next? The Lord said it in two words, *"Get Busy!"* People of God, it's time to be about our Father's Business!

"And the glory of the Lord shall be revealed,
And all flesh shall see it together,
For the Mouth of the Lord hath spoken it."
Isaiah 40:5

Salvation Prayer

It's time to make a change. Begin by giving your life to Jesus. Make Him the Lord of your life. All it takes is one simple prayer.

Dear God,
I repent for sinning against you and your destiny for my life. I renounce satan, all witchcraft and idolatry. I want Jesus as my Lord. Cleanse me from my sin. Fill me with Your Holy Spirit, and I will live all the rest of my life for you. In Jesus' Name I pray. Amen.

If you said that prayer and meant it in your heart. You are a citizen of God's Kingdom and a beloved member of the family of God. That means you qualify to operate as a king and priest for Almighty God.

Let the Holy Spirit teach you. Let Him give you the words to pray and speak. Let Him guide you into all truth.

Find a Bible teaching church and begin to fellowship with like-minded saints. Begin reading your Bible and letting the Lord minister directly to your every need.

Welcome to the Family of God!

Prayer For The Healing & Restoration Of The Nation

Dear God in Heaven,

We come to You, standing in the gap for the Church and for the people of the United States of America. You said in Your word (II Chronicles 7:14), *"If My people, which are called by my name, shall humble themselves, and pray, and seek my face, and turn from their wicked ways; then will I hear from heaven, and will forgive their sin, and will heal their land."*

Father, You also said, *"My covenant will I not break, nor alter the thing that is gone out of my lips."* We repent for not honoring Your covenant in obedience to Your word. We ask for Your forgiveness right now. Cleanse us from our sins as we humble ourselves before You.

God, our nation is in peril of losing all of the blessings you have bestowed upon us. We repent on behalf of the leaders, the men and women who have selfishly used this nation for corrupt purposes. We repent for their actions that would have left us defenseless before our enemies, if it had not been for Your covenant.

Turn Your heart towards your people now, and hear our cry. Our nation is in bondage to sin because of our rebellion against You. The leaders of this nation have caused the people to turn from You to worship idols and witchcraft. Forgive us Lord. Those in the household of faith have been sorely persecuted for speaking Your word. Some are facing threats of death and jail time all because they are obeying your command. Hear our cry, Oh, Lord. Forgive our sins. Remove the curse from our midst. We want Your Blessing upon our lives now.

Avenge us speedily from the wicked. Recompense us for all we have suffered at their hands. Release us from this captivity of sin so that we can fulfill Your will for our lives and uphold the covenant that was sealed in the Blood of Jesus. *(continued)*

As we pray for those in authority over our nation, we ask that you pull down those leaders who refuse to obey Your will. Raise up leaders who have Your heart for the people of our nation. Give them the plan of healing and restoration so that we can live a quiet and peaceable life in all honesty and godliness.

Lord, restore to us, Your peace that passes all understanding. Restore love, joy and prosperity to Your people in the land. Let them stand tall far above the wicked in the land. Give them ears to hear what others cannot hear. Give them eyes to see what others cannot see. Give them a heart of wisdom and obedience to carry out all You would have them to do for the benefit of this nation.

Lord we ask that You come down from Heaven and grace us with Your presence. We love and honor you. God the Healer and Restorer of our souls.

In Jesus' Name We Pray
Amen

BIBLIOGRAPHY

Matthews, Paula. *American Heritage 101*. Shaker Heights: Spirit & Life Publications, 2012.

Matthews, Paula. *Living In The Faith Zone*. Atlanta: Spirit & Life Publications[sm], 2019.

Matthews, Paula. *Seeking And Enjoying The True Treasure Of This Life*. Shaker Heights: Spirit & Life Publications[sm], 2013.

Josephus, Flavius. *The Complete Works Of Flavius Josephus (Illustrated) Translated By William Whiston,* 1600.

The Holy Bible: Authorized King James Version. Nashville: Thomas Nelson, 2003.

Matthews, Paula. *The War Journal (1999-2010) Volume I*. Los Angeles: Spirit & Life Publications, 2010.

Matthews, Paula. *The War Journal (1999-2010) Volume II*. Los Angeles: Spirit & Life Publications, 2011.

Paula Matthews, Author of *The War Journal (1999-2010) Volume I &II*, graces readers with yet another volume of prophetic insight concerning America, the Church, and their future. This book explores God's plan to heal and restore America in the midst of political strife and corruption, while unveiling a more powerful and prosperous people united as "One Nation Under God."

Ms. Matthews is a noted Apostle, Prophet and Teacher who has been called to train and lead God's end-time ministry leaders. Since 1997 God has been sending her to His prophetic leaders, ministering healing and deliverance and guidance in fulfilling their Kingdom destiny.

She is also a businesswoman with a background in Broadcasting, Advertising and Finance, having worked for the Bell System under AT&T, Gannett Broadcasting, and United Way of America.

In 1995, Ms. Matthews became an entrepreneur in film and broadcast production. In 2012 her corporation Eternal Purpose In Christ (E.P.I.C.) Ventures, Incorporated was formed, along with her nonprofit, Kingdom Benefit Charities, (K.B.C.), Incorporated. Since that time She has also launched EPIC Visionary Association partnership program and EPIC Film Ventures, an independent film production company.

The War Journal book was first published in Los Angeles under her publishing company, Spirit & Life Publications, in 2010. Since that time, Ms. Matthews has published almost two dozen books.

Her latest releases include:

Becoming People Of Integrity

I Sought God And Met Him Face To Face

Made in the USA
Middletown, DE
06 May 2022

65398846R00130